REFERENCE

D0301744

SHERLOCK'S SISTERS

For Sandra L. Vice

Sherlock's Sisters

The British Female Detective, 1864-1913

JOSEPH A. KESTNER
University of Tulsa, USA

ASHGATE

Published by
Ashgate Publishing Limited
Wey Court East
Union Road
Farnham
Surrey, GU9 7PT
England

Ashgate Publishing Company
110 Cherry Street
Suite 3-1
Burlington
VT 05401-3818
USA

Ashgate website: http://www.ashgate.com

British Library Cataloguing in Publication Data
Kestner, Joseph A.
   Sherlock's sisters : the British female dectective,
   1864-1913. – (The nineteenth century series)
   1. Detective and mystery stories, English – History and
   criticism 2. Women detectives in literature 3. Great Britain
   – History – Victoria, 1837-1901 4. Great Britain – History –
   Edward VII, 1901-1910
   I. Title
   823'.0872'0908

Library of Congress Cataloging-in-Publication Data
Kestner, Joseph A.
   Sherlock's sisters : the British female detective, 1864-1913 / Joseph A.
   Kestner.
      p. cm – (The nineteenth century series)
   Includes bibliographical references and index.
      1. Detective and mystery stories, English – History and criticism. 2. Women
   and literature – Great Britain – History – 19th century. 3. Women and literature – Great
   Britain – History – 20th century. 4. English fiction – 19th century – History and criticism.
   5. English fiction – 20th century – History and criticism. 6. Women detectives in
   literature. I. Title. II. Nineteenth century (Aldershot, England)

PR878.D4K457 2003
823'.087209352042–dc21

2003042185

ISBN 978-0-7546-0481-5

MIX
Paper from
responsible sources
FSC
www.fsc.org   FSC® C004959

Printed and bound in Great Britain
by Printondemand-worldwide.com

Contents

The Nineteenth Century Series
General Editors' Preface

The aim of the series is to reflect, develop and extend the great burgeoning of interest in the nineteenth century that has been an inevitable feature of recent years, as that former epoch has come more sharply into focus as a locus for our understanding not only of the past but of the contours of our modernity. It centres primarily upon major authors and subjects within Romantic and Victorian literature. It also includes studies of other British writers and issues, where these are matters of current debate: for example, biography and autobiography, journalism, periodical literature, travel writing, book production, gender, non-canonical writing. We are dedicated principally to publishing original monographs and symposia; our policy is to embrace a broad scope in chronology, approach and range of concern, and both to recognize and cut innovatively across such parameters as those suggested by the designations 'Romantic' and 'Victorian'. We welcome new ideas and theories, while valuing traditional scholarship. It is hoped that the world which predates yet so forcibly predicts and engages our own will emerge in parts, in the wider sweep, and in the lively streams of disputation and change that are so manifest an aspect of its intellectual, artistic and social landscape.

Vincent Newey
Joanne Shattock

University of Leicester

Acknowledgements

This book could not have been written without the cooperation of many individuals, libraries and institutions. The author wishes to express his gratitude for the assistance rendered by these individuals and institutions.

The author is grateful to Austin J. McLean, former Curator of Special Collections at the Wilson Library of the University of Minnesota, for providing access to The Mary Kahler and Philip S. Hench Arthur Conan Doyle Collection at the University. The resources of the Tage la Cour Collection and the Stafford Davis Collection in the Special Collections division of McFarlin Library of the University of Tulsa have been important. At McFarlin Library, the author wishes to thank Ann Blakely, Charles Brooks, Lori Curtis and Marc Carlson. For their advice and support, the author wishes to thank Garrick Bailey, Thomas A. Horne, Joseph J. Wiesenfarth, John Halperin, Gordon O. Taylor, Robert E. Spoo, Carl R. Woodring, Sandra L. Vice, Joseph A. Kestner Jr, Lillian B. Norberg, Blake Westerlund, Russell Renfrow, Caroline Cornish, Ira Nadel, Lynn M. Alexander and Bernard Duyfhuizen.

At Ashgate Publishing, the author is most grateful to Joanne Shattock, Sarah Charters, Vincent Newey and Erika Gaffney for their generous support.

The author is very grateful to Galla Cassettari, Assistant Librarian of the Metropolitan Police Service, London, for decisive information about policewomen in Great Britain.

The author thanks Pamela R. Matthews and Mary Ann O'Farrell, guest editors, for including a section of this book in another form in the special issue 'Recognizing Feminist Mystery and Detective Fiction' in the *South Central Review*.

The author is most grateful to William Baker for information about Leonard Merrick; to Susannah Fullerton for particulars about detective fiction in Australia; and to Winifred Hughes for details about sensation fiction.

For her outstanding fidelity, undying love to Topaz.

The author is most grateful to Allen H. Bauman for his precision, advice and assistance during the preparation of the final manuscript.

Anna H. Norberg has been a strong and loving source of support during the writing of this book.

1 The Female Detective in Britain

The appearance of the female detective in English fiction during the nineteenth century was a result of a complex intersection of legal, social, moral, institutional and gendered practises. This study, *Sherlock's Sisters*, concentrates on the emergence of the woman detective during the period from 1888 to 1913, but the origins of the female detective in fiction are actually in the 1860s. In 2000, Birgitta Berglund observed:

> The traditional pattern of representing women in fiction as objects and men as subjects has in general posed great difficulties for those (presumably female) writers who have wished to create strong and positive women protagonists. Because of the specific demands of the genre, this is even more true of detective fiction. Thus, in spite of the great number of women writers in this genre, it is a fact that the overwhelming majority of detectives in fiction have until quite recently been men. (138)

While in the aggregate it is certainly true that there are more male than female detectives, this project explores the manifestation of a number of fictional female detectives in the late nineteenth and early twentieth centuries, although one woman from 1856 and two from the early 1860s indicate that even then detection was becoming part of the activity of female protagonists.

In the tradition examined in this book, these female detectives may be private or official. Some, contrary to all historical actuality during this era, are detectives at Scotland Yard. Others are employed by private enquiry agencies, while some work independently of either an official or private institution, being self-employed. Berglund continues in her appraisal:

> Women in detective stories have been victims, or they have been perpetrators, but they have not, on the whole, been detectives — that is, they have not been given the most important part to play. In novels written by men, women detectives are very few indeed (although they do exist) but even in books written by women, male detectives dominate. (138)

Yet, in the period under consideration here, both male and female writers dared to create female detectives. It *was* daring, as Berglund remarks about the proclivities of readers: 'Writers who want to reach large groups of readers tend to choose a male protagonist rather than a female one, as women are on the whole much more willing to read about men than the other way round' (138).

Still, it is the case that some writers, for example Grant Allen, presented their women detectives in periodicals such as the *Strand Magazine*, which had a predominantly male readership, as Stephen Knight (1994) notes: 'The audience of the *Strand* was predominantly male; they bought the magazine, in shops, at bookstalls, especially on stations. They did take it home — there were sections for women and children, but they are just sections' (374). Nevertheless, the *Strand* published the serial short story exploits of Lois Cayley and of Hilda Wade in, respectively, 1898 and 1899. From 1911 to 1912, Richard Marsh created his unusual female detective Judith Lee in the pages of the *Strand*.

This interest in the female detective was evident in other periodicals as well. Catherine Louisa Pirkis's Loveday Brooke appeared in 1893 in the *Ludgate Monthly* before the book version in 1894. Beatrice Heron-Maxwell created her protagonist Mollie Delamere of *The Adventures of a Lady Pearl-Broker* in the pages of the *Harmsworth Magazine* in 1899, a magazine which had already published at least one famous tale involving a female detective, *The Stir Outside the Café Royal* by Clarence Rook, in September 1898.

The challenge facing creators of the female detective is summarized by Berglund:

> The real difficulty in creating a woman detective has more to do with literary patterns and expectations than it has to do with real life. The problem is the fact that the detective in the classic detective story is the typical hero: strong, intelligent, resourceful, a latter-day knight who fights and defeats evil. According to the pattern established by Conan Doyle with Sherlock Holmes, he is also an almost superhuman mastermind who is allowed a great degree of eccentricity and egocentricity because of his extraordinary powers. With such forefathers, what can a woman writer do? Or, to put it more precisely, what could the early women writers of detective fiction do? How could they unite this ideal with a traditional feminine ideal and come up with a credible woman detective? (139)

This is the dilemma faced by those creating 'Sherlock's sisters' at the end of the nineteenth century.

The central point, however, is that there were models of female independence and daring in numerous texts, even if these were not detectival, which could serve writers, both male and female, in creating their intrepid female investigators. One can think of a range of proto-models, women both good and bad, such as the protagonists of George Eliot's *The Mill on the Floss* (1860), Mary Elizabeth Braddon's *Lady Audley's Secret* (1862) and *Aurora Floyd* (1863), Rhoda Broughton's *Not Wisely, But Too Well* (1867), or Thomas Hardy's *Far from the Madding Crowd* (1874) or *The Return of the Native* (1878). Critics such as Elaine Showalter and Winifred Hughes have demonstrated that the female protagonist in the sensation novel displayed a deft intelligence in confronting circumstances, provoking in readers fantasies of empowerment.

Novels such as those by Braddon or Hardy create protagonists who defy the patriarchal constraints imposed upon them. As Hughes stresses: 'Whatever their value as escapism, the higher forms of the sensation novel . . . are also in the business of propaganda, of crusading for social or political reform' (34). As will be discussed below, the female detectives of *Revelations of a Lady Detective* (c. 1864) attributed to W. S. Hayward and of *The Female Detective* (1864) by Andrew Forrester Jr manifest the intelligence, daring and resourcefulness which could be linked with traits drawn from protagonists of non-detectival fiction to establish the fictional female detective in the late 1880s after the appearance of Sherlock Holmes in 1887 in *A Study in Scarlet*.

Intelligence, self-assertion, daring and defiance marked a range of female protagonists in English fiction before the creation of Sherlock Holmes. These traits, by the way, distinguish Holmes's adversary Irene Adler in the first Holmes short story, *A Scandal in Bohemia*, published in the *Strand* in July 1891. The fact that Holmes is not 'superhuman' but is rather defeated by Irene Adler gave the opening to create the female detectives who became his 'sisters' in the detectival tradition.

A number of key facts deserve immediate assessment. The origin of modern policing can be dated to 1829, with the establishment of the civilian police in London by the Metropolitan Police Act, which was the result of the appointment of Sir Robert Peel as Home Secretary in 1822. Peel established the principle of uniformed patrols, that is constables, for the purpose of *visible* surveillance. Each man carried a 'bull's-eye' lantern and a rattle, the latter soon replaced by a truncheon. Peelers wore a top hat until it was replaced by the 'Roman' helmet in 1864. These men were the famous Peelers or Bobbies.

In 1835, the Municipal Corporations Act established Borough police officers in other parts of the country, for example in Wigan in 1836, Manchester in 1839, Salford in 1844 and Oldham in 1849. The

Metropolitan Police Act of 1839 declared that official police personnel could be hired by private firms or individuals. The institution of a civilian police service assumed national prominence in 1856 when legislation established the Home Office Inspector of Constabulary to improve uniform standards of police efficiency throughout the country.

The Detective Branch of the police was formed in 1842 in response to two specific crimes, as Peter Haining notes in his introduction to his anthology of Charles Dickens's detective narratives:

> It was in 1842, after two exceptionally brutal murders in London, that a Detective Branch of the police was formed at Scotland Yard. It consisted of two inspectors, six sergeants and the first chief, Nicholas Pearce, who was a former member of the Bow Street Runners. These men were detailed for exclusive plainclothes detective work and thereby created the embryo C.I.D. that would eventually be formalised in 1876. (13)

The O.E.D. records the first use of the word 'detective' in 1843. The first mention of 'the detective force' was in 1845 in the criminal case in Hampstead of the murderer Hocker. As Haining (*Hunted Down* 1996) notes, Dickens was 'the first writer to recognise the importance of this revolutionary step in law enforcement' (13).

Dickens used the existence of the detective police to great effect. His first officer, Sergeant Witchem of the Detectives, made his appearance in 'The Modern Science of Thief-Taking' in *Household Words* on 13 July 1850. Dickens went on to write narratives about the detective police for *Household Words*, including 'A Detective Police Party' (27 July and 10 August) and 'Three Detective Anecdotes' (14 September). In the latter, in particular, the three small narratives contain elements which will be key for subsequent detective literature: the significant object, the patience of the detective, the use of disguise and impersonation, the emphasis on surveillance and observation, hiding and concealment, and knowledge of criminal signals.

Dickens based these anecdotes on the experience of actual Inspector Charles Frederick Field, who becomes Inspector Wield in the first anecdote, 'The Pair of Gloves.' Field appeared in 'On Duty with Inspector Field' in the issue of 14 June 1851, and Field served as the model for Inspector Bucket in *Bleak House* of 1853. Dickens's important amateur detective, Meltham, appears in his brilliant tale *Hunted Down* of 1859, in which an evil uncle tries to destroy his nieces, a clear anticipation of Conan Doyle's *The Speckled Band* in 1892.

Dickens had used details of actual murders in his fiction. For *Bleak House*, he drew on the case of Frederick and Maria Manning, who had murdered a money-lender, Patrick O'Connor. Dickens watched their execution in 1849. For *Hunted Down*, Dickens drew on the case of Thomas Griffiths Wainewright 'who in 1830 had poisoned his sister-in-law for her £18,000 insurance money' (Haining 18). In the tradition of the woman investigator in fiction, female detectives, such as Orczy's Lady Molly of Scotland Yard in 1910, do pursue killers, often female killers. It is likely that the depiction of female killers owed some elements to the notorious cases of Victorian murderesses (studied by Altick and Hartman) such as Constance Kent (1860), Florence Bravo (1876), Adelaide Bartlett (1886), and Florence Maybrick (1889).

As Michelle Slung observes in her introduction to her anthology *Crime on Her Mind*, 'there were no women actually attached to the Metropolitan Police in London until 1883, when two women were appointed to oversee female prisoners' (15). In her introduction to *Twelve Women Detective Stories*, Laura Marcus notes that 'in the 1880s women began to be employed as guards to female prisoners, but they were not given full police status by the Metropolitan Police until 1918' (viii). 'In 1916 an Act of Parliament expressly allowed Government grants for police purposes to include money spent on women police' (Ivimey 154). The uniformed Women's Police Service was founded in 1914. Metropolitan Women Police Patrols were approved in 1918 under the supervision of Mrs Sofia Stanley when Sir Nevil Macready was Commissioner. Joan Lock (1979) notes that 'the first public appearance of the uniformed women police patrols was in May 1919 at a memorial service in Westminster Abbey for Metropolitan Police officers who had fallen in the war' (94). 'Twenty-five women [were] recruited early in 1919 and a further 50 later in the year' as Martin Fido and Keith Skinner observe (289).

As early as 1905, Miss Eilidh MacDougall was appointed to the Criminal Investigation Department to take statements involving sex cases, but she was not a police officer. Potter comments: 'She had no police powers but took statements for the London C.I.D. from girls who had been the victims of assaults' (35). Rawlings specifies: 'A uniformed sergeant was transferred to the C.I.D. in December 1922 and became the first detective sergeant. This was Lilian Wyles, who was later to be the first woman detective inspector' (151). However, as William Rawlings continues:

> No detective work was allotted to [Lilian Wyles]; it was to a woman police constable, Louisa Pelling, who was appointed to Special Branch at about the same time, that the honour of being the first woman detective went. (151)

Rawlings comments about their reception:

> By the end of 1922, . . . there were rumours that women might
> be brought in. As can be imagined, there was a good deal of
> debate on the subject, most of us men ranging ourselves pretty
> solidly against the invasion of what we thought of as a purely
> masculine preserve . . . It didn't make any difference, naturally.
> The women of those days, full of the pioneering spirit, were
> determined and to oppose them at all was merely to fight a
> rearguard action. (150)

Clara Walkden became the first policewoman for Oldham Borough in 1921.
No other women were appointed to the C.I.D. until 1932. 'There was no
direct entry into the C.I.D. All were recruited from the uniformed
constables in the force' as Rawlings discusses (151). Writing in 1965, Ronald
Howe observed: 'During the last twenty years policewomen have acted in a
detective capacity, and brought many notorious criminals to justice. They
have proved that their work calls for as much quick wittedness and courage
as does that of a policeman' (143). In her introduction to Catherine Louisa
Pirkis's *Loveday Brooke*, Michelle Slung notes that 'in the early 1860s [in the
United States] a woman named Kate Warne was a celebrated operative of
the detective bureau founded by Allan Pinkerton' (x). The first female
detective in the United States was Isabella Goodwin, appointed Acting
Detective Sergeant in 1912; she had been a police matron since 1896.

The fact that women did not become involved in the Metropolitan
Police until 1883 is especially startling considering the advent of the first
female detectives in fiction. In the 1860s, two works appeared featuring
female detectives, the first attributed to W. S. Hayward, *Revelations of a Lady
Detective*, and the second by Andrew Forrester Jr, *The Female Detective*,
published in May 1864 (see Bleiler, ed. 1978, x). The dating of *Revelations of a
Lady Detective* is variously put at 1861 or 1864 (see Craig/Cadogan 15,
Marcus 230, Slung, ed. [1977] 14-15, Bleiler [1975]). Craig/Cadogan
summarize the significance of these two creations:

> It would . . . be wrong to suggest that their creation represented
> a serious expression of feminism; the stories that featured these
> two women were firmly escapist . . . As well as forming the basis
> of a genre, however, they anticipated historical fact by having
> professional associations with the police some twenty years
> before the force actually began to employ women in any capacity
> . . . Both these female sleuths possessed sufficient histrionic
> ability to pose when necessary as tradeswomen in order to gain
> access to evidence that might be concealed in the digs or salons
> of their suspects. These were untrained amateurs at the acting
> business; but the theatre soon proved a fertile breeding ground
> for the female sleuths and spies of English fiction, and the ability

to assume different roles was to become an even more important tool of the trade for women detectives than for men. (15-16)

Both Mrs Paschal, the detective in *Revelations*, and Mrs G in *The Female Detective* demonstrate qualities which become important to the flourishing of the female detective beginning in the 1880s.

W. S. Hayward (fl. 1861-80): *Revelations of a Lady Detective* (1861/1864)

The *Revelations of a Lady Detective* consists of ten episodes, the first of which, *The Mysterious Countess*, presents a fairly accurate summation of dimensions of the female detectives to follow subsequently. Mrs Paschal begins with a description of Colonel Warner, 'at the time of which I am writing, head of the Detective Department of the Metropolitan Police. It was through his instigation that women were first of all employed as detectives' (2). Mrs Paschal then details the circumstances which brought her to her profession:

> I was particularly desirous at all times of conciliating Colonel Warner, because I had not long been employed as a female detective, and now having given up my time and attention to what I may call a new profession, I was anxious to acquit myself as well and favourably as I could . . . It is hardly necessary to refer to the circumstances which led me to embark in a career at once strange, exciting and mysterious, but I may say that my husband died suddenly, leaving me badly off. An offer was made me through a peculiar channel. I accepted it without hesitation, and became one of the much-dreaded, but little-known people called Female Detectives, at the time I was verging upon forty. (2-3)

The returning of the male gaze is startlingly stressed in this first episode:

> I met the glance of Colonel Warner and returned it unflinchingly; he liked people to stare back again at him, because it betokened confidence in themselves, and evidence that they would not shrink in the hour of peril. (3)

It would appear that Hayward, the attributed author, grasps the parameters of the dynamics of the gaze well over a century before its enunciation by Laura Mulvey. It is vital for women to return the male gaze to establish their own subjectivity and to re-balance the power relations of surveillance which the gaze establishes.

Mrs Paschal is candid about the link between her accomplishments and acting:

> My brain was vigorous and subtle, and I concentrated all my energies upon the fulfilment and execution of those duties which devolved upon me . . . I was well born and well educated, so that, like an accomplished actress, I could play my part in any drama in which I was instructed to take a part. My dramas, however, were dramas of real life, not the mimetic representations which obtain on the stage. For the parts I had to play, it was necessary to have nerve and strength, cunning and confidence, resources unlimited, confidence and numerous other qualities of which actors are totally ignorant. They strut, and talk, and give expression to the thoughts of others, but it is such as I who really create the incidents upon which their dialogue is based and grounded. (3-4)

Colonel Warner tells Paschal: 'I do not know a woman more fitted for the task than yourself. Your services, if successful, will be handsomely rewarded' (4). Warner is willing to pay her daily expenses, but there is an ample reward should she succeed. He has confidence in her, as he notes 'you possess an unusual amount of common sense' (4). This remark contains the germ of the debate about female epistemology, whether women are persons of reason or intuition. 'Common sense' is strong praise in this instance. As Slung (1986) observes:

> It is difficult to comprehend how their creators came to decide on such an anomalous career for their heroines when there were no real-life models to work from, or to understand how they could make those heroines' decisions convincing even within the context of their stories . . . The very essence of criminal investigation is antithetical to what was considered proper feminine breeding, involving as it does eavesdropping, snooping and spying, dissimulation, immodest and aggressive pursuit and physical danger. (xi)

Warner asks Mrs Paschal to discover the origin of the widowed Countess of Vervaine's income, since she is appearing in London resplendent with diamonds. After mourning the dead earl for six months, Fanny, Countess of Vervaine had 'launched into all the gaiety and dissipation that the Babylon of the moderns could supply her with' (8). Fanny, the former actress, however, is about to meet her match.

Mrs Paschal is well prepared for her duties, having a wardrobe 'which was as extensive and as full of disguises as that of a costumier's shop. I wished to appear like a servant out of place' (9). The female detective fleetingly envies this famous woman, but then does not: 'I congratulated myself that I was not, like her, an object of suspicion and mistrust to the police, and that a female detective, like Nemesis, was not already upon my track' (9-10). As with many of the narratives involving female detectives from the 1880s and after, it is a woman who engages in acts of surveillance over another – and criminal – woman. Mrs Paschal is taken in as a servant, and she is soon convinced that the Countess 'had a secret' (12). Equally, 'the countess had not the remotest idea that I was in any way inimical to her' (13); at one point, the Countess hits Paschal with her hairbrush. She has an 'intuition' (14) that events will soon yield information.

Mrs Paschal discovers that the Countess disguises herself as a man and passes through a tunnel to a vault in a bank and steals gold. This transvestism will be central to Conan Doyle's first short story about Sherlock Holmes, *A Scandal in Bohemia* in 1891, and the tunnelling to the bank anticipates a similar component of *The Red-Headed League*. Paschal stresses that any element mysterious is 'eliminated by the calm light of reason and dissected by the keen knife of judgment' (16). She valiantly goes down a hole in a locked room:

> I with as much rapidity as possible took off the small crinoline I wore, for I considered that it would very much impede my movements. When I had divested myself of the obnoxious garment, and thrown it on the floor, I lowered myself into the hole and went down the ladder. (20)

Paschal wishes she had her 'Colt's revolver' (26) with her. Eventually, Mrs Paschal and the police track the Countess to Blinton Abbey in Yorkshire, where she is apprehended while burying some of the gold. 'She knew me, and the act of recognition informed her that she was hunted down' (38). However, she eludes punishment by taking a poison concealed in her ring.

Mrs Paschal, an individual of reason, of courage and of brave impersonations, establishes a pattern for the female detective who will appear in the 1880s after the appearance of Sherlock Holmes. For example, she does not feel compelled to have only one idea about a case: 'I was not a woman of one idea, and if one dart did not hit the mark I always had another feathered shaft ready for action in my well-stocked quiver' (27). In addition, she genuinely embraces her work: 'I was always happier in harness than out of it' (116). She also is not afraid of success: 'If I ever achieved a triumph, which I sometimes did, I did not like my laurels shared by any one else' (98). When an old woman, Dorothy, in *The Secret Band*, dies, the female detective reflects:

> I could not help feeling grieved that the old woman had met her fate through her efforts to befriend me; but I, too, was somewhat callous, through experience and contact with a hard world, so I dashed away the tear which was the apotheosis of the deceased woman, and applied myself with renewed ardour to the task before me. (71)

Mrs Paschal is tough, in ways not totally acceptable according to the patriarchy. In one episode, Mrs Paschal pretends to be interested in converting to Roman Catholicism to gain admission to a convent:

> In order to carry out my design, I made the acquaintance of a Catholic priest, and went through a hypocritical farce which I hope was not wrong; because I firmly believe the end justified the means, and detectives, whether male or female, must not be too nice. (155-6)

For the 1860s, her pragmatic professionalism is bold.

Andrew Forrester Jr (fl. 1863-4): *The Female Detective* (1864)

By the time he published *The Female Detective* in May 1864, Andrew Forrester Jr had already produced engrossing investigative narratives in *Revelations of a Private Detective* (1863) and *Secret Service* (1864). Forrester's *The Female Detective* consists of seven tales involving the exploits of the female detective, Mrs G, of the Metropolitan Police. Of particular interest in the volume is its introduction, which is an important statement about the ambiguity of the detectival profession with which the detective was confronted. The narrator begins with discussing a range of possible reasons for entering the profession:

> Who am I? . . . It can matter little who I am . . . It may be that I took to the trade sufficiently comprehended in the title of this work without a word of it being read, because I had no other means of making a living; or it may be that for the work of detection I had a longing which I could not overcome . . . It may be that I am a widow working for my children – or I may be an unmarried woman, whose only care is herself. (1)

The narrator states, however, that she has not completely departed from the accepted norm of her sex:

> But whether I work willingly or unwillingly, for myself or for others – whether I am married or single, old or young, I would have my readers at once accept my declaration that whatever may be the results of the practice of my profession in others, in me that profession has not led me towards hardheartedness. (1)

The reason for writing is to defend the detective police:

> I may as well at once say I write in order to show, in a small way, that the profession to which I belong is so useful that it should not be despised . . . I know well that my trade is despised . . . My friends suppose I am a dressmaker . . . My trade is a necessary one, but the world holds aloof my order. Nor do I blame the world over much for its determination. I am quite aware that there is something peculiarly objectionable in the spy, but nevertheless it will be admitted that the spy is as peculiarly necessary as he or she is peculiarly objectionable. We detectives are necessary . . . I therefore write this book to help to show, by my experience, that the detective has some demand upon the gratitude of society. (2-3)

It would appear in these statements that Forrester is echoing the purposes of the essays written by Charles Dickens defending the detective police.

Mrs G then defends the concept of the *female* detective:

> I am aware that the female detective may be regarded with even more aversion than her brother in profession . . . Criminals are both masculine and feminine – indeed, my experience tells me that when a woman becomes a criminal she is far worse than the average of her male companions, and therefore it follows that the necessary detective should be of both sexes . . . Being a necessary calling I am not ashamed of it. I know I have done good during my career. (3)

Mrs G also notes that 'the woman detective has far greater opportunities than a man of intimate watching, and of keeping her eyes upon matters near which a man could not conveniently play the eavesdropper . . . Man and woman detectives are necessities of daily English life' (4). Finally, she notes that she will tell her stories as much as possible in the third person, 'to avoid mentioning myself as much as possible' (3). This female detective has no hesitation in stating: 'Both men and women operatives . . . are the first movers in matters of great ultimate importance to individuals in particular, and the public at large' (6).

In the penultimate story *The Unknown Weapon* from Forrester's text, Mrs G investigates the murder of Graham Petleigh, the wastrel and neglected son of the miserly and avaricious Squire Petleigh. Graham Petleigh has himself smuggled into the family mansion in a box so he can steal the plate to aid his woman friend Frederica. The murderer turns out to be Margaret Quinion, the housekeeper, who suspected she would be murdered and took a rough iron barb and killed Petleigh, not knowing who he was. At the end of the episode, Mrs Quinion burns down the mansion to conceal evidence. Mrs G and another female detective, Martha, manage to escape from the burning mansion, where they had discovered the box which concealed Graham Petleigh. The female detective never finds Mrs Quinion.

Key conventions of detective literature include the scene of the inquest, the presence of the servant Dinah Yarton, the physician Dr Pitcherley and the useless local constable Joseph Higgins. Mrs G observes about the 'police-constable of Tram': '[He was] a stupid, hopeless dolt, . . . who was good at a rustic public-house row, but who as a detective was not worth my dog Dart' (227).

Mrs G emphasizes she is recounting an incident which came under 'my actual observation' when she details 'the exact preliminary facts of the case' (205). Mrs G is a detective addicted to precision. At one point, she enumerates the 'peculiar circumstance' (238) of the case and at another determines to 'recapitulate these inferences' (273) which she has drawn, specifically twelve of them. In sifting the issue of the removal of Petleigh's body, Mrs G debates:

> The only rational way of accounting for the deposition of the body where it was found, lay in the supposition that those who were mixed up with his death were just enough to carry the body to a spot where it would at once be recognised and cared for . . . But against this argument it might be held, the risk was so great that the ordinary instinct of self-preservation natural to man would prevent such a risk being encountered . . . Then, when it is remembered that it must have been quite dawn at the time of the assumed conveyance, the improbability becomes the greater that the body was brought any great distance. (277-8)

Forrester wishes to stress the processes of Mrs G's evolution of her position to reinforce her authority for the reader. And her authority is different. Kathleen Klein notes that 'unlike the later ratiocinative style of Holmes', Forrester's female detective 'does not seize upon a single interpretation and follow it to the conclusion, but deliberates among many possibilities' (22).

The conclusion of the narrative retains some suspension of finality. For example, it is difficult to determine whether the burning of the house, Petleighcote, constitutes a commentary about the oppressive nature of the squirearchy. It is certainly true that the housekeeper undoubtedly wished to save the family honour. Since Mrs Quinion is never apprehended, it can be argued that Mrs G fails; still, the case is solved. Kathleen Klein is correct, however, that Forrester 'develops a character who seldom identifies herself as a woman' (23). Yet, Forrester's point, underscored in the introduction to the volume, is that female detectives are as appropriate as male detectives, since both men and women commit crimes.

In his book, Forrester includes one of the earliest statements about the nature of a female or a male detective's character:

> Indeed it is the great pain and drawback to our profession that we have to doubt so imperiously. To believe every man to be honest till he is found out to be a thief, is a motto most self-respecting men cling to; but we detectives on the contrary would not gain salt to our bread, much less the bread itself, if we adopted such a belief. We have to believe every man a rogue till, after turning all sorts of evidence inside out, we can only discover that he is an honest man. And even then I am much afraid we are not quite sure of him. (268-9)

This ambiguity about the essential moral nature of the human race is striking for 1864. It may well reflect the disillusionment felt by the culture after such events as the war over the 'Indian Mutiny' in 1857-58, the publication of Charles Darwin's *Origin of Species* in 1859, and the concern about individual liberties generated by John Stuart Mill's *On Liberty* of the same year. In addition, Barbara Lee Smith's treatise *A Brief Summary in Plain Language of the Most Important Laws Concerning Women* of 1854 and Caroline Norton's *Open Letter to the Queen* of 1855 raised the question of the status of women in legal enforcement institutions. Since women had no vote, to what extent were they subject to the laws generated by the patriarchy?

Were women subjects protected by the law or were they its victims? In *Revelations of a Lady Detective* and in *The Female Detective*, the former attributed to a male and the latter by a male, it is possible to construe an answer to this question. These texts argue that women do have a place in law enforcement and therefore presumably in the protections it provides. Yet, since women had no place at all in the police, detective or otherwise, the texts are engaging in a fantasy of female empowerment completely at odds with actuality. Kathleen Klein thinks that both Hayward and Forrester made a 'provocative decision to use female protagonists' but that this feat 'is qualified by treating them more as neuter than female; they are honorary men' (29). However, both writers do not conceal that the protagonists are women. It is emphatically true, however, as Klein argues, that 'nothing of the historical realities for women in 1864 anticipates the portraits of these two characters' (29).

The legacy of legislation involving women in the 1840s and 1850s is evident in both of these early fictional works about the female detective. For example, the 1844 Matrimonial Causes Act mandated that a man could not force his wife to return home. The 1857 Divorce and Matrimonial Causes Act established civil courts to grant separation and divorce. Also, it stated that a divorced woman need not give income to a former husband. However, the grounds for divorce were not equal for men and women. Proof of adultery alone was sufficient for a man to obtain a divorce; a woman had to establish additional grounds beyond adultery. The 1858 Amendment Act made divorce less expensive and thus more accessible to the middle class; in addition, it mandated that a divorced woman could recover income she had obtained by lawful industry. Both *Revelations of a Lady Detective* and *The Female Detective* show women in an official capacity supporting state institutions of enforcement. One could construe them as arguments that women merited even greater engagement in enforcement after the passage of the Acts of 1857 and 1858.

Wilkie Collins (1824-89): *The Diary of Anne Rodway* (1856)

The journal *Household Words*, which in the early years of the 1850s had published Dickens's articles about the detective police, is also important for the appearance of the narrative *The Diary of Anne Rodway* in two instalments (19 and 26 July) in 1856, written by Dickens's close friend and associate Wilkie Collins. In the tradition of the female detective, the story is of great importance, for it is the most significant example of the amateur, unofficial female detective before the 1880s.

Anne Rodway is a seamstress who records in her diary of 1840 a series of events involving her friend Mary Mallinson. Mallinson is brought home with her head bashed in from a blow on her left temple. Mary had been taking laudanum to forget her dreadful life, in her words because it 'makes me forget myself' (131). She tells Anne in their last interview: 'I wish I was at the end of [my life] . . . I began my life wretchedly, and wretchedly I am sentenced to end it' (131-32). Confronted with her friend's corpse, Rodway gathers evidence: 'Something dark fell out of the palm of her hand as I straightened it. I picked the thing up, and smoothed it out, and saw that it was an end of a man's cravat' (137).

At the inquest, a verdict of Accidental Death is returned, even though the end of the cravat is produced. The opinion of the doctor is followed by the all-male jury. Anne Rodway assumes control: 'The cravat-end was given back to me, by my own desire; the police saying that they could make no investigations with such a slight clue to guide them' (143). She affirms that 'nothing should have induced me to consent to such a verdict as Accidental Death' (144) if she had been on the jury. Clearly, there is a marked difference between juries involving men only and the alternative if women were to serve. This point is reinforced when the landlord harasses Anne to pay her deceased friend's rent, threatening her: 'I'll teach you what the law is!' (144). A month later, Anne has found the cravat: 'I have found it! . . . I have found the cravat from which the end in Mary's hand was torn!'(148):

> It matched the torn side of the cravat exactly. I put them together, and satisfied myself that there was not a doubt of it . . . A kind of fever got possession of me – a vehement yearning to go on from this first discovery and find out more, no matter what the risk might be. The cravat now really became, to my mind, the clue that I thought I saw in my dream. (151)

With the assistance of her fiancé Robert, just returned from America, Anne Rodway discovers that the killer is Noah Truscott, the man who had ruined Mary Mallinson's father. He had killed Mary in a drunken rage. Anne gives evidence at the police office which gets Truscott 'committed for trial on a charge of manslaughter' (158).

The proto-feminist element of the tale is clear from Anne Rodway's next entry:

> Why not on a charge of murder? Robert explained the law to me when I asked that question. I accepted the explanation, but it did not satisfy me. Mary Mallinson was killed by a blow from the hand of Noah Truscott. That is murder in the sight of God. Why not murder in the sight of the law also? (158)

Truscott is convicted of manslaughter and condemned to transportation for life. Since he was old and a drunkard, the law did not convict him of murder. Although Anne marries Robert, she records in her final entry: 'I can't forget Mary, even on my wedding-day' (164). Collins's brilliant narrative is stark in its presentation of the plight of women under the law: all-male juries will, even in a case of murder, give the male killer the benefit of the doubt. The entire legal system encourages the lesser charge of manslaughter rather than of murder.

Anne Rodway, although as a seamstress one of a long oppressed group, perceives the inequities in the judicial system, especially in its deviation from the law of God. This realization of inequities anticipates John Stuart Mill's memorable essay *The Subjection of Women* completed in 1869, the century's strongest argument against the artificial construction of femininity by patriarchy. On the other hand, the Contagious Diseases Acts of 1864, 1866 and 1869 mandated that a woman suspected of prostitution could be subject to a pelvic examination – a major example of the sexual double standard in Victorian culture.

Legislation and events during the 1870s and early 1880s paved the way for the female detective who emerged at the end of the 1880s. The opening of Girton College, Cambridge, in 1869 and Newnham College, Cambridge, in 1871 provided significant progress for women in higher education. Similarly, Lady Margaret Hall in 1878 and Somerville in 1879 became colleges for women at Oxford. The Married Women's Property Act of 1870 transformed the economic situation of married women by granting them equitable property rights and permission to retain earnings after marriage. A married woman could make out life insurance policies on her own account. By 1877, the year of the Bradlaugh-Besant trial for disseminating information about birth control, the middle classes were definitely employing birth control for limitation of family size. In 1878, the Matrimonial Causes Act allowed separate maintenance for the wife of a husband convicted of aggravated assault. By 1878, as well, women were admitted to all degrees at the University of London.

The 1882 Married Women's Property Act gave married women the right to independent ownership of property, that is, the same property rights as unmarried women. The Act established that common law and equity must be fused. A married woman could sue and be sued, enter into contracts and be subject to bankruptcy laws. Such legislative intervention in the marital relationship began to rectify the imbalance of power within marriage. How symbolic as well as real such legislation could be is indicated by the 1884 action of Parliament which abolished imprisonment as a penalty for denying a spouse conjugal rights. By the Married Women's Property Act of 1884, a woman's will did not require re-execution after her husband's death. By the Matrimonial Causes Act of 1886, a woman could sue her husband for maintenance. A particular victory for women was the repeal of the Contagious Diseases Acts (suspended in 1883) in 1886.

As Kathleen Klein notes about Hayward's *Revelations of a Lady Detective* and Forrester's *The Female Detective*, however, their protagonists 'are anomalies; the novels apparently led to neither imitators nor followers. Even Forrester and Hayward abandoned their innovations after the first attempt' (29). However, these two works for their readers constituted a strong fantasy of female empowerment. If such narratives did not correspond with actuality, they accorded with cultural aspirations. Inherently, their nature is transgressive.

Albeit the historical reality was that no women were employed at Scotland Yard during the 1860s, the processes of legislation during the 1870s and 1880s suggest that these detective narratives were fictional records of women leading professional independent lives, an expectation which legal, marital and educational processes began to address in the 1870s and 1880s.

To assess the achievement of the female detective narrative from 1864 through 1913, two theoretical concepts are particularly applicable: first, the idea of the gaze and female surveillance; and second, the narratological strategies adopted in these texts. These two theoretical issues are interlinked. The specific nature of the female detective narrative is to address the practise of the woman having the power of the gaze as she executes her professional – private or official – responsibility of surveillance.

In turn, this presentation of surveillance by women is inflected by the narratological strategy. For example, if a specific text is narrated by the protagonist herself (autodiegesis), then there is no mediating of her subjectivity. If her record is written by an associate or observer (homodiegesis), then the protagonists's access to language is mediated, especially if the narrator is a male associate. If the narration is heterodiegetic, by a narrator not dramatized in the text, then additional differences are introduced in terms of the issue of surveillance.

In her landmark essay, first published in 1975, 'Visual Pleasure and Narrative Cinema', Laura Mulvey argues that the male gaze serves two ends: first, scopophilic, that is, 'pleasure in looking at another person as an erotic object', containing a strong element of male voyeurism which emphasizes a 'woman's to-be-looked-at-ness'; and second, narcissistic, serving 'ego libido . . . identification processes' (815). The 'determining male gaze' means that 'pleasure in looking has been split between active/male and passive/female' in Mulvey's terms (808); art is 'coded into the language of the dominant patriarchal order' (805). The gaze is both 'controlling and curious' (806). In Mulvey's conception, the male gaze establishes a hierarchy of gendered power, with the male empowered in the subject position and the woman lacking power in the object position, that is, the man looks, the woman is the object of that male look.

Yet, from the earliest narratives in the tradition of the female detective examined in this book, texts about the woman detective inherently challenge the supremacy of the male gaze, for it is the female who possesses the hierarchical power of the gaze when the subject is a female detective, exercising surveillance in the pursuit of her detection, whether unofficial or official. As an instance of the complexity of this issue of the gaze in female detective fiction, one might cite the example of Fergus Hume's *Madame Midas* from 1888. The play of gazes appears almost immediately when Madame Midas meets Gaston Vandeloup for the first time. She is first 'doubtfully eyeing the slender figure of the young man' (29). Although she hires him as a clerk in her business, Madame Midas is even at this initial moment uneasy:

> This young man pleased her. She was essentially a woman with social instincts, and the appearance of this young and polished stranger in the wilds of the Pactolus claim promised her a little excitement. It was true that every now and then, when she caught a glimpse from his scintillating eyes, she was conscious of a rather unpleasant sensation, but this she put down to fancy, as the young man's manners were really charming. (32)

Even Vandeloup, who will prove so villainous in the tale, is aware of the power of this businesswoman's gaze:

> She was too clever a woman to let him manage things himself, or even know how much she trusted him; and Vandeloup knew that whatever he did those calm dark eyes were on him, and that the least slip or neglect on his part would bring Madame Midas to his side with her quiet voice and inflexible will to put him right again. (46)

When Vandeloup meets Kitty Marchurst, the woman he will ruin, Madame Midas throws 'a keen glance at her clerk' (51) to warn him against preying on her protégée.

While Gaston Vandeloup succeeds in his enterprise of seducing Kitty Marchurst, he will not triumph over Madame Midas. In addition, the murder victim in *Madame Midas*, the protagonist's maid Selina Sprotts, is never deceived by Vandeloup, as she candidly informs her mistress: 'I don't like him . . . He's too smooth and handsome, his eyes ain't true, and his tongue's too smart. I hate him' (34). In terms of the structure of the plot of his novel, Hume constructs the tale via his focus on gazes and empowerment, in the contestation of gazes between men and women.

This concentration marks all the texts involving the woman who undertakes detection, for her surveillance becomes an act of challenging patriarchy and its hierarchy of genders. If in Mulvey's terms the woman as object of the male gaze is the one castrated, a different cultural situation arises when the woman returns the look or exercises surveillance. Any woman undertaking detection, whether amateur or professional, becomes transgressive.

Writing about Emily Brontë's 1847 novel *Wuthering Heights*, Beth Newman discusses the case of Brontë's intrusive male Lockwood and his 'fear of the returning female gaze' (1031). Stephen Heath observes that if the woman looks, which is the situation in all of these texts involving the female detective, then it is the male as object who is castrated, as the observing woman seizes and occupies the subject position:

> What then of the look for the woman, of woman subjects in seeing? The reply given by psychoanalysis is from the phallus. If the woman looks, the spectacle provokes, castration is in the air, the Medusa's head is not far off. (92)

Even beyond the shifting of castrated object from woman to man catalyzed by the female gaze, there is an additional consequence of the woman looking, as Newman concludes:

> [There is] a defusing of the gaze: not a simple inversion in which the woman is permitted to turn the tables with an appropriating look back but a destruction of the hierarchical positioning of male and female that the gendered gaze entails. (1037)

Thus, in the female detective novel, the protagonist/detective not merely grasps the empowering gaze from the male but may, even more subversively, implode all gendered hierarchies.

In speculating 'Is the Gaze Male?', Ann Kaplan notes about the culture where the male gaze is controlling:

> Dominance-submission patterns are apparently a crucial part of both male and female sexuality as constructed in western civilization . . . Men have a far wider range of positions available: more readily both dominant and submissive, they vacillate between supreme control and supreme abandonment. Women, meanwhile, are more consistently submissive, but not excessively abandoned. (27-8)

In narratives involving the female detective, however, surveillance is a component of the woman seizing the gaze and exercising professional if not institutional control.

In his important study *Detective Fiction and the Rise of Forensic Science*, Ronald Thomas advances several key arguments to reinforce the necessity of female surveillance through the power of the gaze of the woman detective. To begin with, surveillance and investigation by the professional detective – female or male – was becoming key during the latter decades of the nineteenth century, when the female detective in fiction began to flourish. A cultural change was occurring in criminal prosecutions

> with the diminished value placed on the testimony of [eye-] witnesses in Anglo-American courtroom practice in the latter half of the century and the rising authority of forensic science that was being accorded to material evidence and expert advice in the process. (78)

Thomas contends 'that the history of detective fiction and the history of forensic science are finally inseparable' (77). Thomas's book demonstrates that the rise of forensic science prevented sensation fiction from permeating detective fiction and led to the former's demise. The preference for scientific analysis, objective proof, rational discourse and professional observation rather than for eyewitnesses' accounts consigned sensation fiction to the margins by the 1870s. Sensational *elements* (the endangered woman, the woman as transgressor) are incorporated into detective fiction involving female detectives, but the detective genre attains supremacy.

Surveillance by the female gaze, however, becomes a necessity in the culture, for, as Thomas observes, the 'conception of persons as authentic characters has a gendered component' (87). In undertaking professional observation male detectives, even one so acute as Sherlock Holmes, can nevertheless be blinded by their masculine gender:

> The Victorian ideology of the female gender as a class blinded even the most observing machine [Holmes] in the world. It was capable of producing limitations on vision . . . The English [male] detectives not only represent privileged figures of authority as clients (kings and noblemen), they secure and safeguard those clients. (175)

As Kestner (1997 and 2000 *passim*) and Thomas reveal, male detectives often acted to secure male privileging in Victorian culture, even when the male was transgressive or criminal. Women detectives in the fiction of the last two decades of the nineteenth century become adroit at reading the legible body, male or female, 'locating the primary truth about the text in the body of the perpetrator' (Thomas 222). Furthermore, their expertise in understanding clothing as costume or disguise enables women detectives to garb their own bodies to enable professional surveillance or to detect the use of clothing as disguise by the suspect objects of their gaze.

As Thomas asserts, the 'investigative gaze' enables the detective's 'disciplinary powers' (79). Still, as Kestner and Thomas demonstrate, the male detective can ignore a woman's subjectivity, as in the notorious *A Case of Identity* involving Holmes (*Strand* September 1891). Thomas notes: 'The detective takes the part of the fathers by assuming the privilege of preserving the culture's story of itself' (89). Female detectives, on the other hand, having themselves endured objectification by the culture, more readily acknowledge female subjectivity, either in aiding a wronged woman or in exposing the malevolence of a female criminal.

In the texts examined in this study, female control through the gaze is evident in the desire of the woman to read her culture as a text and transform it by rectifying some particular abuse of power, whether that abuse originates from the transgressive behaviour of either a man or a woman. Obviously, when a woman subjects a transgressive male to her gaze and exposes his transgression, as in a work like Grant Allen's *Hilda Wade*, the woman's gaze facilitates the exposure of a criminal male and thereby indictment of the patriarchal institutions which unjustly participated in blaming another person (in this case another male) for the transgression.

In other instances, when the criminal is a woman, as in many of the cases solved in Orczy's *Lady Molly of Scotland Yard*, women occupy both the subject and the object positions. Both men and women may objectify a woman. When a woman is under investigation, she is indeed the object of the female detective's professional surveillance. The intention, however, is to grasp the subjectivity of the female transgressor. In many of these texts, female detectives seem more willing than their male counterparts to accept the potential transgressive behaviour of women, a result of their willingness to grant subjectivity (including power, motive and purpose) to other women. This complexity serves not to subvert gendered hierarchies but to consign them to irrelevance. Equally, as with the lower middle class Ellen Bunting of Lowndes's *The Lodger*, surveillance through the gaze enables a woman to transgress not only gendered but also classist borders.

In addition to the issues involving the gaze and surveillance by women detectives, one of the most crucial elements of determining the degree of empowerment through the gaze in these texts is the mode of narrative transmission adopted. In the case of Grant Allen, one text, *Miss Cayley*, is in the first person; the other, *Hilda Wade*, has a male Watsonian narrator. All these texts exhibit an array of narrative strategies, with individual inflections within the three narrational categories of autodiegetic, homodiegetic and heterodiegetic. The variations within these categories inflect the empowerment of the female detective via her probing professional gaze and surveillance.

In several of these texts, the narrator of the female detective's experiences is a male. The narrative strategy is homodiegetic, that is, the tales are recounted by an individual who is not the protagonist of the text. Such is the case, for instance, with Mr Saxon in Sims's *Dorcas Dene*, Dr Lonsdale in Meade/Eustace's *The Detections of Miss Cusack*, or Hubert Cumberledge in Allen's *Hilda Wade*. In such instances, one may argue that while the female detective has the power of the gaze, the narrating instance, that is, that her exploits are recounted by a male, does not free the female detective herself from male surveillance. But even in these examples, there are varying degrees of control by the male.

In the texts by Sims and Meade/Eustace, the male narrator does not have an amorous connection with the female detective. Sims's Dorcas Dene is married to the blind artist Paul Dene, a circumstance which compels her to seek a profession. In Allen's text, Cumberledge does marry Hilda Wade, but only after she has exposed the criminality of his mentor and saved the reputation of her father. While he ardently pursues her throughout the text, she refuses to marry him until she has freed her father from a nefarious condemnation. Thus, even in such instances of homodiegesis, the degree of male control via the gaze is limited and circumscribed. In the striking instance of Orczy's *Lady Molly of Scotland Yard*, the woman detective's activities are narrated by a devoted female associate, Mary Granard, who remains loyal to her friend Lady Molly, who is already married and desires to vindicate her husband.

In other texts, the female detective narrates her own exploits, that is, narration in an autodiegetic mode, where the protagonist is the narrator, as with Miriam Lea in Merrick's *Mr Bazalgette's Agent*, Lois Cayley in Allen's *Miss Cayley's Adventures*, Mollie Delamere in Heron-Maxwell's *Adventures of a Lady Pearl-Broker* and Judith Lee in Marsh's *Judith Lee, Some Pages from Her Life*. In each of these texts, the narrator demonstrates not only the female protagonist's expertise as detective but also her seizure of the language to record her own experiences. Unquestionably, the empowerment by the female gaze is doubled in these texts, as the protagonist has the gaze in a professional sense but also reinforces that gaze by gazing at herself to chronicle her adventures.

Some of these texts, such as those by Heron-Maxwell and Merrick, end with the marriage plot: Mollie Delamere marries the Australian millionaire Anderson; Miriam Lea acknowledges her love for James Vane, whom she had intensely subjected to her detectival gaze; and Lois Cayley espouses Harold Tillington, whom she had exonerated from charges of forgery. In the examples of Miriam Lea and Lois Cayley, the woman rescues the male from disaster, which allows her to signify power in spite of the resolution of the plot via marriage. Judith Lee never needs either a Watson to chronicle her exploits or a lover with whom to dwell. Even when a male narrator/observer is not present, therefore, some of these texts conclude with marriage. On the other hand, when a female detective's adventures are chronicled by a male, not all end in marriage, as demonstrated by the example of Meade/Eustace's Miss Cusack.

Both male and female writers appear equally drawn to a variety of narrative strategies in presenting their female detectives. Male and female writers, such as Marsh and Pirkis, reject the marriage plot; others, such as Heron-Maxwell and Merrick, deploy it. Others, such as Sims and Orczy, have the protagonist already married. A writer like Grant Allen uses the marriage plot in his two narratives but differentiates them by employing different narrational modes.

The third type of narration, the heterodiegetic, involves narration by a 'third-person' narrator not dramatized in the text, as with Braddon's *Thou Art the Man*, Pirkis's *Loveday Brooke*, or Hume's *Madame Midas* and *Hagar of the Pawn-shop*. Heterodiegesis accesses the widest range of presentation of attitudes about the female detective and her profession. The narrative can accommodate the consciousness of secondary but key characters, as does Hume with the evil solicitor Vark in *Hagar of the Pawn-shop* or with the antagonist Gaston Vandeloup in *Madame Midas*. In *Thou Art the Man*, Braddon is able to have two central female characters, Sibyl Penrith and Coralie Urquhart, on whom to focus. Just as significantly, however, heterodiegesis allows Braddon to depict the tormented consciousness of the epileptic Brandon Mountford, which is the fulcrum of the very tale narrated.

Furthermore, these heterodiegetic texts in particular display a range of attitudes about the marriage plot. In Pirkis's text, Loveday Brooke remains unattached and single. In Braddon, Sibyl Penrith, having had a loveless first marriage, is enabled to marry the activist priest Coverdale, who assisted her detections. In the same novel, Coralie Urquhart marries Nicholas Hildrop. In both instances, however, Braddon disposes of the marriages in a Postscript, demonstrating that the exigencies of the publishing market have compelled her to such resolutions. Hume's Madame Midas will never remarry, having had so disastrous a first marriage. Hume's gypsy detective Hagar Stanley does marry Eustace Lorn, but the force she exhibited in her detection at the pawn-shop endures, as Lorn adopts her roving way of life instead of Hagar accepting a stationary middle class existence. Annie Cory, the amateur detective of Elizabeth Corbett's *When the Sea Gives Up Its Dead*, marries Harley Riddell, a lover unjustly convicted whose innocence she establishes through her detection.

A study of the fictional female detective in Britain from 1864 to 1913 provides a new basis for assessing the construction of feminine gender during the period. Elements of this construction include several important dimensions. For example, the relationship of the female detective to legal and social reforms of the period, such as the various Married Women's Property Acts and suffragism, illuminates the practises of late-Victorian cultural institutions. The representation of women as empowered through the exercise of rationalism in detection is elucidated, as is the idea of the female detective as a New Woman construction.

The insertion of women in heretofore patriarchal institutions like the courts, law and criminal investigation is limned in these texts, as is the exercise of surveillance by women over transgressive behaviours of men and women. In these narratives the female detective is not so much under the law as through her ingress inflecting it to justice. Not infrequently she forms an alliance with a victimized woman to oppose evil men or criminal women. Each of these texts exposes complex constituents of the processes of gender-modelling during the decades examined in this analysis. Contexts legal, marital, gendered, political, historical, literary and social are disclosed through these texts.

Whether by men or women, all narratives about female detectives investigated in this book constitute documents, transgressive in varying degrees, of female empowerment through engagement with legal and judicial institutions and moral prerogatives. Events conspired that the 1880s were to see the renascence of the fictional female detective with the appearance in 1888 of Leonard Merrick's *Mr Bazalgette's Agent*. It is those events and narratives one must examine to find the next important female detectives in British literature.

2 The Victorian Female Detective, 1888-1894

After the appearance of W. S. Hayward's *Revelations of a Lady Detective* and Andrew Forrester's *The Female Detective* in the 1860s, it was over two decades later that the female fictional detective made a reappearance in 1888 with Leonard Merrick's *Mr Bazalgette's Agent*. A number of historical events lay behind this renascence of the female detective which have specifically to do with the character of the final years of the decade of the 1880s. After that, events in the 1890s propelled the number of texts involving the female detective.

Some of these events specifically involved law enforcement and the police. In 1877, the Turf Fraud Scandal had implicated detectives from Scotland Yard, to the extent that there was in 1878 a reorganization of the Yard. The roles of Detective and Constable were separated. The detectives were placed in the newly-formed Criminal Investigation Department (C.I.D.). In the scandal, three of four chief inspectors in Detective Branch had been found guilty of corruption. Since all these individuals were male, the result was that cultural observers may well have speculated about the department and its honesty if women had been part of the official order.

Soon there were greater reasons for wondering about the integrity of the Yard and its detectives. Beginning in 1883, there had been a number of terrorist incidents which raised concern about the country. In 1883 alone, there were at least three. In March, Local Government Board offices were blown up; there was also an unsuccessful attempt to blow up the offices of the *Times*; in October, two underground railway stations were dynamited. As a result, in 1886, a Special Branch of the C.I.D. was formed to deal with dynamite outrages by Irish nationalists, which did not prevent the same year the storming of Pall Mall private clubs.

The Trafalgar Square Riots, 'Bloody Sunday', occurred on 13 November 1887, a month before the appearance of Conan Doyle's *A Study in Scarlet*. These riots involved about 100,000 persons at Trafalgar Square, a location which had already been banned for public meetings by Sir Charles Warren, the Chief Commissioner. One hundred and fifty persons were injured in the confrontation which ensued between the demonstrators and a phalanx composed of three hundred Life Guards, an equal number of

Grenadier Guards and 4,000 policemen. The London Dock Strike of 1889 revealed extensive labour unrest. This event ultimately led to the formation of the Labour Party in 1900. In the 1890s, the population of London was around 6 million. It had been revealed in 1881 that only about 12% of the population was working on the land.

Above all were the momentous killings of five prostitutes in the Whitechapel district of East London by Jack the Ripper between 31 August and 9 November 1888, including the 'double event' of the slayings of Catherine Eddowes and Elizabeth Stride on 30 September. William T. Stead of the *Pall Mall Gazette* began a series of essays which brought the killings to the national consciousness, 'backtracking and retrospectively establishing a pattern of significance for preceding murders' (Walkowitz 191). As Walkowitz (1992) has explained in detail, the killings became 'a national scandal' (201) because of the inability of either the Metropolitan or the City police forces to solve the crimes. The East End was a 'city' in itself of one million people, with about one third of those living in poverty.

The killings terrorized the capital, with Stead arguing that the killer was a sadist and an evolutionary atavist, throwing into doubt notions of Victorian 'progress' and amelioration. The 'expert discourses' of law and medicine offered myriad explanations of motive and perpetrator – religious maniac, aristocrat, physician, rejected suitor, monomaniac, escaped lunatic, Jew or split personality (evoking the model of Jekyll and Hyde).

However, the failure of the official agents of surveillance and security to solve the crimes exposed ethnic, classist and sexual prejudices in the population. England had become as frightening as one of its colonies, as William Booth, founder of the Salvation Army in 1878, indicated in 1890 when he published his study of urban malaise, *In Darkest England and the Way Out*. In fiction, Arthur Morrison published his studies of East End crime, in 1894 *Tales of Mean Streets* and in 1896 *A Child of the Jago*. Morrison in 1894 created his detective Martin Hewitt in the pages of the *Strand Magazine*.

It was clear to everyone that the males involved in enforcement and investigation had failed. Marie Belloc Lowndes in *The Lodger* (short story 1911, novel 1913) was to depict a female amateur detective in her landlady sleuth Ellen Bunting to demonstrate that a 'woman on the case' may well have solved the murders. Hence, there is a certain suitability to the appearance of Miriam Lea as female detective in Merrick's *Mr Bazalgette's Agent* published the same year as the occurrence of the unsolved Ripper murders.

The 1890s saw considerable advances in investigative techniques. In 1890, the Metropolitan Police moved from Great Scotland Yard to New Scotland Yard, the same year which saw the Police Strike for higher wages and pensions. This new location was to be the site of improvements in investigation. For example, the first actual conviction by the identification of typewriters occurred in 1894. In that same year, Scotland Yard established the anthropomorphic measurement system of Alphonse Bertillon. Francis Galton in 1895 published *Fingerprint Directories*, the first statement in print of digital classification; two years later, a criminal was convicted in India based on fingerprint analysis.

It was in this culture of the late 1880s and 1890s – marked by poverty, secret societies, labour unrest, urbanism, Germanophobia, serial killings, scares of invasion and the economic threat of the United States – that the female detective reappeared. But this renascence in 1888 was propelled specifically by two books. One of these was by a man living in Australia, Fergus Hume, who in 1886 published *The Mystery of a Hansom Cab*. Hume sold the copyright of the novel and in 1887 it was published in Britain, where it sold 400,000 copies (Murch 141). The reasons for its success are summarized by Murch: 'Wealthy Australian settlers were much in the news at the time, which gave the story a topical interest, and Melbourne's dockland slums provided a background that was new in detective fiction' (141). In 1888, Hume was to deploy detectival elements involving two women in *Madame Midas*, in some details a sequel to *The Mystery of a Hansom Cab*.

The other key work appearing in 1887 was Arthur Conan Doyle's *A Study in Scarlet* in December in *Beeton's Christmas Annual*. While Doyle's famous tale of Sherlock Holmes, John H. Watson and renegade Mormons did not create the sensation of Hume's *The Mystery of a Hansom Cab*, the novel was strangely coincident with current fears of the culture about secret societies, the importation of criminality from abroad (in this instance from the United States) and the hazards of urbanism. Particularly eerie was that the novel included an incident of a killer writing on a wall, a practise replicated by Jack the Ripper at one of the locations of his murders. Holmes was distinguished by his powers of ratiocination, his daring, his celibacy and his arrogant confidence. The convention of having a loyal friend record the detective's exploits would become a practise followed by writers creating female detectives.

Holmes was to reappear in 1890 with the publication of *The Sign of Four*, which showed a decadent Holmes fighting crime coming again from abroad, but now from the sub-Continental area. Holmes's antagonist is Jonathan Small, a man with one leg who has been destroyed by colonial experiences. Doyle deliberately evoked Robert Louis Stevenson's one-legged villain Long John Silver from *Treasure Island*, published in book form in 1883. The city of London is dreary and depressing in *The Sign of Four*, filled with urban malaise.

Finally and momentously, George Newnes began the *Strand Magazine* in January 1891, a publication addressed to the literate and educated middle-class reader. Newnes laid down a number of policies regarding the *Strand* which were to have a great effect on the next reincarnation of Sherlock Holmes. Newnes mandated that there be an illustration on every page spread if not every page; and, just as crucial, there were to be no serial narratives, as every tale was expected to be complete in itself. While Sherlock Holmes would reappear, his exploits had generally to be concluded in a single number. This rule was broken, of course, in Doyle's serialization of *The Hound of the Baskervilles* during 1901-02, but the preference was for tales complete in one issue.

The initial issue of the *Strand* in 1891 sold 300,000 copies, predominantly at railway news-stands and bookstalls. Newnes used the finest artists of the day to illustrate the magazine, including Sidney Paget, who attained immortality with his illustrations for the Holmes narratives, and the famous war illustrator William Barnes Wollen. The first Sherlock Holmes short story, *A Scandal in Bohemia*, appeared in the *Strand* in July 1891. At its peak, the *Strand* sold about 500,000 issues a month, circulation being about 450,000 by 1897, and escalating by 30,000 whenever a tale involving Sherlock Holmes appeared. L. T. Meade, who was to create the female detective Florence Cusack in 1899, published in the *Strand*. Grant Allen's two female detectives, Lois Cayley and Hilda Wade, made their serial appearance in the *Strand*, beginning in 1898 and in 1899 respectively. The important amateur sleuth Susie Beech, created by Florence Warden in *The House by the Vaults*, appeared in the June 1905 issue of the *Strand*.

In her introduction to the Oxford anthology *Twelve Women Detective Stories*, Laura Marcus summarizes the reasons why both female and male writers were attracted to the female detective as a subject for fiction:

> That so many male writers . . . created women sleuths may say something about their feminist sympathies, but it also suggests that female characters allowed for quite specific kinds of detective work and detective narrative. Such particularities arise from entrenched cultural images of femininity, which work both for and against women. Summarized, these would include adeptness at disguise, including the 'disguises' of an only seemingly bedimmed old age or of an appealing, helpless femininity which conceals a ruthless intelligence; an acute eye for those telling details, which appear to others as trivia; a driving curiosity in which the stereotype of women's 'nosiness' is turned to good advantage; and 'outsider' status which gives knowledge of the motives and means of social transgressors. (ix)

Writers after Holmes had to face the challenge of constructing detectives, whether male or female, who could be sufficiently differentiated from his model. The challenge for those aspiring to create 'Sherlock's sisters' was to differentiate their detectives, but not only from the masculine model: deciding to create a female detective was the easiest mode of differentiation. However, it then became necessary to distinguish one female detective from another, which could be accomplished by the primary occupation of the sleuth, such as Grant Allen's Hilda Wade being a nurse or Richard Marsh's Judith Lee (1912) being a teacher of the deaf-and-dumb or Meade/Eustace's Florence Cusack or Pirkis's Loveday Brooke (1894) electing to work in detection. Also, the motives for the woman undertaking detection, official or private as the case may be, might be varied: Miriam Lea is a former governess and actress in need of work in Merrick's *Mr Bazalgette's Agent*; Dorcas Dene, created by George Sims in 1897, must work to support her artist husband, who has become blind; Hagar Stanley, created by Fergus Hume in 1898, is a gypsy pawn-broker who has fled harassment by a brutal male; Orczy's Lady Molly of 1910 works at Scotland Yard to vindicate her husband, falsely accused of murder.

Laura Marcus offers an additional reason for the appearance of the female detective in the last decades of the nineteenth century, the focus on the New Woman:

> The end of the century saw the mythologizing of the 'New Woman', a term which entered the language in the 1890s to describe a generation of women who rebelled against restrictive Victorian norms of femininity and were often committed to women's suffrage and women's rights. The concept of the 'new' suggests an evolutionary model of womanhood, in which women are seen as standing at the dawn of a new century and of a new age in which 'the future is female.' In popular imagery, positive and negative, the 'New Woman' is often represented as college-educated, independent, and physically, if not sexually, liberated. (vii)

In the ranks of the fictional female detective, the strongest model of this New Woman is Lois Cayley of Grant Allen's *Miss Cayley's Adventures* of 1899. As will be discussed in the section devoted to Allen's novel, this New Woman faced considerable opposition, above all from Eliza Lynn Linton, who in 1891 published her essay 'The Wild Women as Social Insurgents' in the October issue of *The Nineteenth Century*. The following year, in March 1892, in the same periodical, Linton published 'The Partisans of the Wild Women', again denouncing this revolt against the norms of femininity constructed by patriarchy. Writers such as S. P. White, with the essay

'Modern Mannish Maidens' in the February 1890 issue of *Blackwood's*, clearly perceived the New Woman as a threat to the social order.

The term 'New Woman' appeared in 1894, as Sally Ledger (9) has noted in her very important study of the fictional New Woman. This was the same year as the appearance of Catherine Louisa Pirkis's female detective Loveday Brooke. It is important to remember, as Ledger contends (10), that the New Woman 'as a category was by no means stable.' The 1891 census had revealed that there were approximately 900,000 more women than men in Britain (Ledger 11), which meant that the patriarchal construction of femininity, that every woman would marry and become the Ruskin/Patmore Angel in the House, was not only false but impossible. A component of the female detective in fiction was her becoming a *flâneuse*, the female equivalent of the male urban stroller, the *flâneur*. As a walker and worker in the city, the female detective, working alone, had elements of this intrepid urban figure directly aligned with her profession.

The appearance of the fictional female detective in the 1880s and later must be perceived in an additional context, that of the practise of the law during the era. Virginia Morris discusses this important context:

> Men dominated the legal system throughout the century; all judges, lawyers, and jurors were men. So were all the members of Parliament . . . No women were admitted to the English bar until 1919; the first women sat on juries in the same year, having finally become eligible when they gained the right to vote [Fourth Reform Bill, 1918, women over thirty]. Even then there were no female High Court or circuit court judges . . . The theory and practice of Victorian criminal justice that linked legal and moral issues in judging the criminal offenses of both men and women and made conformity to the middle-class morality the basis of criminal law in fact imposed more stringent standards for women because it demanded sexual as well as social (or gender-role) conformity from them although it did not from men. (42-3)

There were specific legal elements which worked against women, such as this one cited by Morris:

> A venerable and uniquely English tradition, which persisted until passage of the Criminal Evidence Act in 1898, was that a defendant neither took the witness stand nor was cross-examined. It was a controversial practice which had originated to prevent self-incrimination but evolved, especially for women, into an impediment to justice. (46)

As Laura Marcus has noted, it is difficult to determine the specific feminism of the male and female writers who created female detectives.

However, the fact that these women participate in the exposure of crime, sometimes work with the police and with detectives from the Yard, track malefactors both male and female and record or have recorded their exploits establishes a degree of pro-feminist advocacy in these tales. Even when the female detective (Dorcas Dene, Lady Molly) is working to support or clear a husband, and even if she abandons the profession after her aims are realized, the female sleuth is still a professional pursuing a career. In some instances, as with Loveday Brooke, the female detective is an unattached professional woman with no romantic interest at all. Richard Marsh, for example, never resorts to the 'marriage plot' to conclude the adventures of his female sleuth Judith Lee in 1912. Bodkin's Dora Myrl of 1900, Cambridge wrangler and Doctor of Medicine, never operates out of any romantic self-interest, although Bodkin does have her marry in a 1909 later volume. Grant Allen's Hilda Wade is determined to vindicate her father, unjustly convicted of murder, before marrying the physician who has loved and pursued her around the globe. The disillusioned Mrs Villiers of Hume's *Madame Midas* never remarries after her disastrous first marriage. As Slung (1977) summarizes: 'Though these early female characters represented in varying degrees the then emerging "modern" woman, they were all alike in eschewing domesticity in favour of detection, if only for long enough to give them a recordable career' (13).

The female characters examined in this chapter represent a wide spectrum of female detection, most of it unofficial and independent (Madame Midas) or the result of employment by a private detective agency (Miriam Lea, Loveday Brooke). In these investigations, these female detectives may encounter members of the police or detective forces, but in general the males are proved incompetent, ignorant or obstructionist. In all instances, however, they are the result of a confluence of cultural circumstances, ranging from the inadequacies of the law and the influence of the New Woman to the specific intention of challenging the pre-eminence of Conan Doyle's Sherlock Holmes.

As such, these women are 'Sherlock's sisters', having his allegiance to pursuing justice and to analysing detail but exercising their unique talents, such as gaining entrance to private domestic spaces and facility at disguise. Appearing in 1888, Leonard Merrick's Miriam Lea of *Mr Bazalgette's Agent*, with her professional attitude, global travelling and enterprise inaugurates a new era for the fictional female detective.

Leonard [Miller] Merrick (1864-1939): *Mr Bazalgette's Agent* (1888)

In the history of detective fiction, two publications in 1887 heralded a new direction for the genre, the publication in England of Fergus Hume's *The Mystery of a Hansom Cab* (previously published in 1886 in Australia) and of Arthur Conan Doyle's first narrative about Sherlock Holmes, *A Study in Scarlet*. In his immortal novel, Hume chronicles a crime set in Victorian Melbourne involving bigamy, blackmail, murder, a powerful erotic attraction between Madge Frettlby and Brian Fitzgerald, and above all two detectives, Kilsip and Samuel Gorby, who are competitors. Hume's narrative does not end with confirmed happiness, as Madge and Fitzgerald leave Australia for England and Fitzgerald knows, but keeps concealed, the fact of his lover's illegitimacy. *A Study in Scarlet* introduced Holmes, the rational, scientific, bachelor unofficial detective who solves several gruesome murders committed by Mormons in London.

Key conventions of subsequent detective narratives – such as the observer/friend/narrator, the superiority of the unofficial over the official agency of detection, the exposure of criminality in the middle classes and the urban environment of detection – all become confirmed in Doyle's landmark tale. The fact that the conflict among the males in the novel arose from the contestation over a woman's body, that of Lucy Ferrier, introduced the woman as a disturbance in the social field, an Other element which males, official and unofficial, were compelled to confront. Few writers could resist the challenge posed by Hume and by Conan Doyle: the money and the popularity were too much to resist.

The challenge was, however, considerable. How was one to advance the detective genre and compete with Hume and Conan Doyle? How was a writer to demarcate his or her individuality in the genre? How much difference from Hume or Conan Doyle would be accepted by the public in a detective narrative? How much innovation would be tolerated by publishers? How could originality be achieved without eccentricity for the men and women who read detective narratives on the railway while commuting to the suburbs?

Two events conspired in 1888 to direct the attention of the audience to women. One was the strike at Bryant and May match factory by women workers, an action which stressed the increasing power of women in the labour force. Much more significant in terms of the public's awareness of crime, however, was the sensational series of killings of five prostitutes in the Whitechapel district of East London by Jack the Ripper between 31 August and 9 November 1888. In an eerie evocation of *A Study in Scarlet*, the killer actually wrote on the wall of the room of one of his victims. Fresh in the minds of citizens was the horrifying model delineated in Robert

Louis Stevenson's *Dr Jekyll and Mr Hyde* of 1886, with its powerful suggestion that the killer might be a perfectly respectable individual by day and a butcher by night. The incompetence of the police forces competing to solve the Ripper murders, the wild speculations about the killer and the terrorized reactions of women to the events were propitious for the creation of a female detective in the same year, 1888.

This detective did appear in the figure of Miriam Lea in Leonard Merrick's *Mr Bazalgette's Agent* of 1888, published by Routledge as part of its Railway Library. Born as Leonard Miller, Merrick studied at Brighton and Heidelberg before going to South Africa, where he apparently worked in the Kimberley Diamond Fields which figure in his first novel. He became a novelist and playwright of moderate success, but his importance to detective literature has scarcely been recognized. His value to the study of the female detective in British literature is decisive albeit stupefyingly neglected, for Merrick's *Mr Bazalgette's Agent* demonstrates all the demands facing a detective story writer following in the wake of Hume and Conan Doyle.

Merrick's strategy in *Mr Bazalgette's Agent* is a brilliant one. First, he makes his detective a woman, a former governess and actress, Miriam Lea. Second, instead of deploying the device of the homodiegetic narrator/companion or the heterodiegetic narrator, Merrick has Miriam Lea record in her autodiegetic diary her experiences as a detective and the evolution of her professional career. Like Holmes, she is unofficial, with Scotland Yard having been unable to solve the case. Unlike Holmes, however, Miriam Lea finds employment at the private agency of Alfred Bazalgette. Living in a dreary boarding house run by a Mrs Everett, and running out of money, Miriam is alerted to a position by a German gentleman in the boarding house, a Mr Claussen. He directs her attention to the Agony Column of the newspaper, where she reads the following notice:

> ALFRED BAZALGETTE, 7, Queen's Row, High Holborn. –
> Suspected persons watched for divorce, and private matters
> investigated with secrecy and despatch. Agents of both sexes.
> Consultations free. (10)

There is a peculiar inflection to this advert, since in the second sentence of the novel Miriam Lea uses the word 'procurable' (5) and wonders how to obtain a 'marketable price' (9) for her brains and education, admired by Claussen. There is a suggestion that Bazalgette's agents, male or female, might actually be used to entrap persons into compromising relations in order to facilitate divorce as much as there is the more overt suggestion that the agents spy on lovers. In fact, of course, Miriam Lea is 'procurable' to the extent of being twenty-eight years old and in need of employment. This proves only the first element of Merrick's remarkable querying of the detective profession, its suggestion of taintedness, lack of respectability, lying and spying. Before visiting Mr Bazalgette's agency, Miriam muses: 'I told myself even to have considered such a vocation was preposterous' (11).

This impression is confirmed when she meets not Mr Bazalgette but his offensive partner, Mendes, whose very name smacks of mendacity. She thinks of him as 'a negative sort of man' (13), an expression so compelling that Merrick begins to explain it by physical characteristic but then shifts to the psychological: '[When] you met his eyes, . . . you started, they were so bright and cunning. It seemed as if all the wickedness of the human race must be known to the owner of those eyes, and there could be no mortal depravity so uncommonly vile as to surprise him' (13). When Miriam Lea asks if he employs women, Mendes declares: 'It depends on the business!' (13), at which he asks her about her 'case.' Mendes puts her off, at which Lea asserts: 'I should have thought . . . a *lady* would have been valuable from the first; I have understood that Scotland Yard will pay any amount for ladies and gentlemen, they are so difficult to secure, and still more difficult to keep!' (16), admitting to herself she knows nothing of the kind.

As Michelle Slung comments, 'there were no women actually attached to the Metropolitan Police in London until 1883' (16). Here again Merrick gambles that his audience will know this fact, tying the novel to a recent alteration in enforcement. Mendes claims that female agents usually go out in divorce cases as ladies' maids. Although Mendes dismisses her, Miriam makes one more desperate attempt to get employment. On the second visit to the agency, she meets Bazalgette himself, who, finding she knows languages, has accomplishments and can travel, engages her to investigate a case.

This situation concerns the fact that a managing clerk, Jasper Vining, of a financial firm on Lombard Street, has been gambling at cards and the turf and has 'been systematically forging bills upon the firm's correspondents . . . in his capacity of manager, himself opening the letters containing the forged bills accepted, and subsequently discounting them on the Exchange' (22-23). Bazalgette gives Lea a cipher code in order to communicate, funds for a new wardrobe, travel monies and a photograph of her quarry, Jasper Vining. She is also given another female agent, Emma Dunstan, to accompany her as her maid.

Although Emma Dunstan addresses her as 'ma'am', Lea ponders: 'I had wondered whether she would [address me so] when we were off the stage, I mean when we were not acting; but she did it as a matter of course, and I suppose there are degrees even among policemen' (29). The fact that Lea has been an actress both qualifies her for her position but also raises suspicion about the integrity of her being a female detective. Boldly, however, she declares in her diary 'I am a detective!' (30).

Lea travels to Hamburg, Paris, San Sebastian, Lisbon and eventually to South Africa and the Kimberley Diamond Fields in pursuit of Jasper Vining. She notes female customs in Spain and the arrogance of English female travellers but mistakes a man for her quarry. However, in Lisbon she spots someone who does plausibly resemble the photograph of Vining:

> He was a stranger in the hotel, . . . but directly his countenance caught my eye, it possessed some unexplained familiarity . . . It was the bearded face of a man who had *lived* every hour of his possibly forty years, with a dissatisfied, cynical expression upon it augmented by the droop of his brown moustache . . . How did I know him? I had recourse to a patent method of procedure of mine under these circumstances which I usually find effectual; I, in fancy, attired him in every variety of masculine habiliment that occurred to me. (50)

Having talked to the stranger about Tennyson and having a handkerchief with the correct initials on it, Lea concludes that she and Dunstan are 'two female police-agents on the right track' (54). What she labels her 'prey' (58), however, eludes her, and she is forced to follow him to South Africa.

The scenes in South Africa allow Merrick to utilize his own experiences of the terrain during his travels in the same locales. Also, as Doyle had exploited the arid wastes of Utah in *A Study in Scarlet* and as Hume had set his murder tale *The Mystery of a Hansom Cab* in Australia, Merrick follows their example in expanding the detection to unusual if not exotic locales. (A later female detective, the protagonist of Grant Allen's *Hilda Wade* of 1899-1900, will spend some time in South Africa as well, perhaps in homage to Merrick's female tec predecessor.) After undertaking some observations at hotels and railway stations in the area, Lea pursues Vining to the Kimberley Diamond Fields. South Africa would be extremely topical for Merrick's readers, since gold had been discovered in the Transvaal in 1886. There she encounters the man she thinks is Vining, who informs her his name is James Vane. Vane admits to Miriam Lea: 'I am to a certain extent a fatalist, a big word which only means I am able to perceive destiny is stronger than human beings!' (91).

After an emotionally powerful moment during which Lea performs a Chopin nocturne, Vane confesses: 'I've made an awful mess of my life, that's a fact; to put it in its mildest form, I've been a fool. There are some things one can't speak of without glossing over to a woman, more especially a woman whose opinion one values; but a short while back I, in an unexpected fashion, came into a lot of money' (94-95), which Vane admits he lost in gambling. Lea comes to realize that she loves this man, who, she concludes, is the 'prey' she is professionally pursuing: 'I knew now . . . that I loved! that the man I was deceiving had become to me far dearer than my own existence . . . I could not dupe myself; I did not try' (100). When Vane asks her to marry him, she consents: 'He was supplicating for more than he divined; he was begging his escape of me, me who could save him!' (112). In the end, a cable from Bazalgette informs her that the real Vining has been arrested in New York. Vane, therefore, despite his squandering of his inheritance, is innocent of embezzlement. On their wedding day, she determines to send him a letter, confessing her suspicions, but he arrives before she can write the letter that in effect constitutes *her* confession about her real role. She remains silent.

The complexity of Merrick's novel, however, rests in the issues it engages as Miriam Lea pursues her investigation. Most important, throughout the novel, the moral quality of being a detective is questioned. In Hamburg, at the very beginning of her investigation, Miriam Lea records:

> The work is not so bad as I had feared; there is an excitement about it, and you live like a lady; the only objection is you feel such an impostor when a nice woman is friendly with you . . . Here I am in a profession (is it a profession, I wonder? – I daresay; it is called a profession to murder innocent men, why then should it not be one to detect the guilty!) Here I am on a mission which if they knew it would cause people to shrink away from me, and yet my offence is, that, after struggling to obtain a livelihood for the best part of a year in the greatest capital of modern civilization, I was absolutely forced to make myself an object of general abhorrence by the discreditable fact that circumstances were stronger than I! What a crime! Britannia rules the waves! She would be better occupied in finding food for the Britons! (32-3)

The economic circumstances of a woman alone in London, having ceased to be an actress and dismissed as governess for being an actress, are sharply focused by Merrick. The idea that Britain should care for its own, not its foreign others, is linked with the idea that women are themselves the Other in the greatest city in the world. There is an idea that only the desperate find employment as agents in a private inquiry office. Lea refers to her profession as playing a 'rôle' (38), but at Kimberley she recognizes that 'an inevitable part of the vocation I had entered was to lie' (85).

When Lea realizes that Vane does not suspect her of being an agent exercising surveillance over him, her doubts about the morality of her vocation only multiply. She concludes:

> There is another side to the picture: to take advantage of his good faith is hardly a lady's mode of action . . . He is a thief; he himself has betrayed confidence; more, he has broken the law! I want to remember it; I want to retain the knowledge in my memory, and not allow it to slip away from me for so much as a minute, because (it is an ignominious, puerile confession) I am beginning to regard myself as only one degree less vile! (88)

At this point in the text, Lea has not even admitted to herself that she loves Vane. Furthermore, she does not know he is innocent of the crime she is investigating. Yet, she recognizes that being a female detective involves a lady in behaviour which is dishonest and 'dishonourable' (89). Far from welcoming the power her profession confers, she despises it.

Again, even before she admits her love for Vane, these reactions to her profession continue to intensify:

> Oh, why did I not starve with my self-respect before I became a spy! What is it to me he is a scoundrel, does his criminality lessen my degradation? Who was the author of the precept, There can be no friendship without respect? False every word of it! For if it is not friendship I have for this man what is it? why am I trembling at that horrid thought which crossed my mind? Why do I feel I would gladly take his guilt upon my shoulders, work for him, suffer for him, so that he, my friend, should be innocent and free? (97)

These doubts become torments once Miriam acknowledges she loves James Vane:

> The notion crossed my mind that if he should, – should grow to like me before my errand had been completed, how much more vile he would hold me when the blow fell; the thought was wonderful, it was so full of mixed emotions. To be hated by him would be torture, but – to be *loved* by him first! It seemed to me there would be joy enough in that to live upon in recollection through my future of suffering; besides I could always die! (104)

It suffices to say that nothing of this kind could ever appear in the 1887 texts of Conan Doyle or of Hume. The conflict of the personal and the professional, which becomes part of the configuration of the female detective in the work of subsequent writers, is never given so distilled an expression as in Merrick's *Mr Bazalgette's Agent*. What Merrick produces in the narrative is bold, for in her career of detection the result is to lead

Miriam Lea to detect herself rather than the man she is tracking. His situation then hits her with all its force:

> But for him, I was only thinking of myself! Would not his punishment be greater if he were fond of the woman who had denounced him? If during those years of miserable atonement he should be deeming every sign of my affection false; be cursing that very utterance in one happy moment, when perhaps I had forgotten, as a trap to lead him to his ruin; greater? Yes, immeasurably more hard! (104)

When Vane proposes after finding a huge diamond in the tract he has purchased, she reacts: 'I loathed myself and my existence, everything but him I was sending from me' (110). In such passages, Merrick recalls the impassioned reflections of Charlotte Brontë's protagonists in *Jane Eyre* (1847) and *Villette* (1853).

A key element of Miriam Lea's situation in *Mr Bazalgette's Agent* is that after consenting to be Vane's wife, even still believing him guilty, she determines that she will rescue and save him, even if she is complicit in his guilt:

> I have no excuse to offer, I am committing an infamous action, and I am aware of it; I may even be amenable to the law; let them punish me, – they shall never have him! I have done with scruples and conscience, and I will shield him against them all; no information of mine—! (114-15)

As her marriage approaches, she thinks: 'In a week I shall have betrayed my trust [to the detective agency and her profession], and saved him who is dearer than my honour' (116). It is during this confrontation with herself that Merrick's decision to dispense with a narrator/companion and to deploy the device of the diary is vindicated. With few other detectives – male or female – does a reader come into such close affiliation with the investigator. Very significantly, she rereads her diary, acknowledging that 'my very diary is gritty' (117), an admission that her soiled self has been disclosed. It is indisputable that this detection has become a problem of self-knowledge: 'It is funny that renewing the acquaintance of one's old self, and yet it is melancholy' (117).

Given the predominance of the male rescue of women in Victorian literature and art, ranging from Robert Browning's *The Ring and the Book* (1868-69) to the innumerable inflections of this theme in Victorian painting, it is striking that at Cape Town Miriam Lea stays at the St George's Hotel. The St George legend is the quintessential narrative of rescue, painted by a range of artists (Kestner 1995) in either its classical version of Perseus and Andromeda or the 'medieval' one of St George and the dragon.

In *Mr Bazalgette's Agent*, it is given a startling twist by Merrick, as Lea determines to 'rescue' Vane even though she believes he is a criminal and such an action violates her professional identity. The supposedly moral female detective determines to rescue a criminal man in defiance of the law she serves. By evoking this rescue theme, Merrick demonstrates how othered woman actually is in the culture. Miriam Lea's action anticipates the silence of the landlady in Marie Belloc Lowndes's *The Lodger* in the early twentieth century. Being an outcast, a woman can ignore or go beyond the law, the privilege of the disenfranchised.

Merrick's decision to use the diary as a narrative format in the novel is given particular point in the passages which stress the present tense. In this respect, the novel evokes the similar practise in the seven or eight places in Brontë's *Jane Eyre* where the protagonist's recollections are recorded in a continuing present. Not only does this practise lend immediacy to Miriam Lea's recollections. It also permits the reader to engage her mind in the most intimate manner possible.

Although Lea is a detective who must perforce practise concealment, the record of her activities is paradoxically the most intimate form, other than a letter, which might be available as a narrative strategy. In recording her initial excursion to the Continent, Lea is travelling with the other agent, Dunstan, in the train: 'She occupies the second-class compartment behind me now, and I . . . am scribbling this in the train' (29). Thus the first foray in her detective enterprise is recorded in the immediate present. When she thinks of her 'prey' who has been identified, she records: 'Have I been wise, I speculate; will he leap at the conclusion I am an adventuress . . .? It has been a bold move' (60). In particular, Lea's record of the night before her marriage recalls passages in *Jane Eyre* before a similar event:

> He left me an hour ago, and I am alone. It is my wedding-eve; . . . There is nobody to congratulate me, not a voice to say a kind word, yet in twelve hours I shall be a wife . . . It is curious I should feel the loneliness of my position more acutely this evening, when it is nearly over, than I have done at any other period of my life; but I seem to be bestowing so worthless a gift in going to him as a woman whom no one will miss. (118-19)

At the conclusion of the narrative, this immediacy is present as one's final impression of Miriam Lea: 'I close my diary; he is outside; I shall not look at it again. It might have finished better, but I shall never pen another entry while I live. He is calling to me, – ' (125). This passage again evokes

Brontë's Jane Eyre when she examines the impression Edward Rochester makes on her.

In providing the record of his female detective, Merrick does not neglect to have her advance some proto-feminist insights about gender construction during the Victorian period. Miriam Lea alludes to an idea that over several generations a man's nature and disposition may alter. 'It has not taken three generations in this case, merely three months, perhaps because I am a woman' (44), Lea surmises. She then demonstrates that the diary format, involved as it is in presenting the undiluted self, is 'a monstrously egotistical production.' She follows this recognition with another: 'I wonder if I could have scribbled so much of any other kind of composition, – probably not' (44). For a narrator who wondered if she was procurable or marketable, this reflection adds another component to her transgressive behaviour. The very record of the diary, which obviously is published, flags its own transgression.

This is not to say that Merrick does not recognize the situation of women at the end of the nineteenth century. Thinking there is a certain element of 'bravery' in making the voyage to South Africa in connection with her duties, Lea ruminates:

> Bravery? – Well, say 'Endurance!' The qualities are near akin, though the latter unreverenced word has to slink through the language associated with so far less pretentious a meaning; – definition probably due to the fact that men write dictionaries, and women endure! (68-9)

One needs no evidence to grasp that Merrick, and his protagonist, understand that males own the language. No woman would be credited with 'bravery' by the male establishment. For women, this is labelled 'endurance' so men may arrogate to themselves the more heroic and public quality of bravery. Again, if men own language, then the use of a diary is transgressive in itself for a woman.

Likewise Merrick recognizes the peculiar nature of marriage in the construction of a woman's identity. Before her marriage, Miriam Lea acknowledges how strange is the institution itself:

> Ours will be a curious marriage, as it has been a strange betrothal; we shall leave the hotel together and unaccompanied. What do we want of friends when each of us can bring sufficience to the other? On the 21st, the anniversary of my birth, I commence a new existence dedicated to my husband; our hearts will hide their bitterness, but everything save two secrets that are pain we give and share. I do not dread the

prospect: dread! Were my deserts as infinite as the bounty of
Heaven it could vouchsafe no greater blessing than this which
crowns a crime! (118)

It is shocking enough that the narrator leaves for her marriage alone with
the bridegroom. But it is Miriam Lea's next statement which is quite
startling:

> I wish I had not said that; it sounds like a boast! It makes me
> tremble lest on the verge of fulfilment I should be reminded of
> it. What has Heaven to do with me, – with us? To beg its aid,
> would be a blasphemy; – I cannot see to write, I am crying. –
> Oh, how helpless is a woman deprived of the resource of prayer!
> (118)

Miriam Lea becomes almost completely transgressive at this point in the
narrative: she is a woman; she is a detective; she is sufficiently self-confident
to resort to a diary; she is betrothed to a man she believes is guilty and – she
does not believe in God. It can be seen that, in the course of *Mr Bazalgette's
Agent*, Miriam Lea abandons nearly every regulation males might enforce as
appropriate gender-specific behaviour.

Furthermore, she wonders about the entire idea of marrying at all:

> How incomprehensible it is a man should have the power of
> altering the whole current of my ideas as he has done; I am as
> pliable under his influence as if I were sixteen! The hardest
> attendant upon matureness, it strikes me, is to love deeply, and
> be conscious the while that the display of your subjection must
> always have the appearance of aping juvenility.
>
> It is a problem, also, what attributes, imperceptible to
> herself, a woman possesses to exert so subtle a dominion over
> the man. What does he see in *me?* perhaps – . (120-21)

Two issues are addressed in these paragraphs. In the first, there is,
particularly for women, the fact that their very subjection to their husbands
entails their being as children in relation to their husbands, accepting their
rule and control. Merrick perceives the long legacy of John Ruskin's *Of
Queens' Gardens* (1864) even as he creates a protagonist more attuned to the
nuances of John Stuart Mill's *The Subjection of Women* (1869).

In the second paragraph, Merrick returns to the issue of power. Not
only does Miriam Lea have power over Vane so long as she suspects he is
Jasper Vining. The erotic situation is not only in conflict with the
professional circumstance. It is also in one way identical with it, for Lea as

woman and as detective equally can exercise a disturbing power and control over the man, whom earlier she has designated her 'prey.' Personally and professionally, she has power over a male, at the same time she questions the morality of that power and even despises it. It is crucial in *Mr Bazalgette's Agent* that Miriam Lea confronts issues and makes decisions before she learns that Vane is not Vining, that he is 'the wrong man' (122).

But Merrick does not leave the case there. In what sense, he forces the reader to wonder, is Vane 'wrong', if he is 'wrong'? Certainly, one construction of his surname is that he is a forecasting device of the future. Rather than the 'vining' expected of a wife, he will be a positive force in her future, permitting her to 'weather' the 'whether' of her existence. A 'vine' is what she does not have to become. To do so would constitute a betrayal of the self she has detected in the course of her detection. In this respect, she rejects Bazalgette as a guiding father figure: he brought her 'into the world', but he will not determine her insertion into it.

The final pages of the novel, however, render any total resolution of Miriam Lea's situation indeterminate. Miriam Lea wonders, now that she knows 'he is not Jasper Vining; he is a gentleman' (124), if she ought to confess to him that she has been a detective and has suspected him all along, even when she determined to marry him? Ought she to reveal this fact to her betrothed? She first thinks that to be silent about her role and suspicions would 'not be delicacy any more, it would be guilt':

> My exultance is transient; it ebbs from me, and is succeeded by a sensation of blank dismay. I have been 'staunch', – to whom? To Mr Jack Vane: what will that avail me? I feel suddenly as if I were betrothed to a stranger; I shall be more degraded in his sight by that very treachery than if I had been just. I have only been his equal while I imagined him a thief, and he will refuse to marry me. (124)

Lea recognizes that a confession about her true identity would destroy any possibility of marriage:

> Acknowledgment will deal the death-blow to my own future; confession is equivalent to telling the man I love I am no longer fit to be his wife; I will not do this thing, I cannot, no woman could!
>
> Why should I not keep silence still? It would be a safe course. (124)

Then, Lea decides she will tell him, but only by letter:

> I am no heroine, I am flesh and blood, and with all the
> capabilities of flesh and blood I am suffering now; to make the
> declaration with my own lips, and to watch the disgust upon his
> face would kill me. (125)

Just as she is about to pen the letter, Vane appears and it is 'too late' to do anything but embrace him.

This concluding episode of *Mr Bazalgette's Agent* places the work on an entirely different plane from that of a mere detective narrative. In debating the degree of frankness with which a woman should confront a lover, the novel anticipates the much more harsh but not essentially different dilemma of Thomas Hardy's protagonist in *Tess of the d'Urbervilles* (1891). If men have made the language, as Miriam Lea has determined earlier, then women have earned the right to strategic silence, if nothing else, as a mode of language and self-identity. Vane never will see the diary, but the legacy of the detection belongs to the reader of Miriam Lea's text.

Yet, the marriage will be established on a secret, known to the wife and the reader but not to the husband. It is left open whether this is always the case or whether such is possible. Is marriage always built on concealment? If so, it may be the human condition which most eludes detection. It is the state where, even if detection is possible, it is not desirable. In Grant Allen's *Hilda Wade* a decade later, the dramas of Henrik Ibsen are discussed, but already Merrick is perceiving the parameters of the debate unleashed in such drama.

In *Mr Bazalgette's Agent*, just before Miriam Lea acknowledges her love for James Vane, she has 'a frightful dream' (98), which she records. The dream describes how she is leading two men down 'a wide, strange road' (98). She guides them through long passages until they come to a door 'shaped like a coffin-lid.' Within the room, a human being is lying on the floor, extending its arms. 'It was the face of the man I had hunted' she records (99). As the two men with her fade into the distance, she embraces the dying man, and they begin to rise above the Earth. When her arms drop, 'the man I loved fell downward beyond my reach, beyond my sight, down – down – down through Space, only his scream re-echoed through the Universe' (100).

This dream represents Miriam Lea's emancipation from the detective agency fathers/partners Bazalgette and Mendes, but at the same time it establishes her transgression in loving a dying, that is, guilty/condemned, man. She relates that the dream stayed with her for forty-eight hours, after which she establishes she loves Vane, even if he is the criminal Vining. 'I could not dupe myself; I did not try' (100). She recognizes *she* must be a genuine agent, discovering herself, whatever the transgressive potential.

Writing *Mr Bazalgette's Agent* in 1888 was a brave achievement for Leonard Merrick. With his creation of Miriam Lea, he demarcated his detective from Conan Doyle's Sherlock Holmes. This achievement he realized in many crucial ways: by making his detective a woman, by giving her an independent life, by the abandonment of the narrator/companion, by the deployment of the diary form, by granting her an erotic involvement and by constructing her as a woman not afraid to challenge patriarchy in all its forms, be they legal, religious or moral. Only a year after the appearance of Holmes, an alternative to his model had appeared, one of 'Sherlock's sisters' – but from another world.

Fergus W. Hume (1859-1932): *Madame Midas* (1888)

In the history of detective literature, Fergus Hume retains a distinguished place as the author of the century's best-selling mystery novel, *The Mystery of a Hansom Cab*, which Hume published in 1886 in Australia. He sold the copyright for £50, and when the book was published in London in 1887 it became a stupendous bestseller, from which Hume made no money. Born in England, Hume had been raised in New Zealand. Educated at the University of Otago, he became a barrister's clerk and was called to the New Zealand bar in 1885. Hume moved to Melbourne and eventually in 1888 emigrated to England.

In the tradition of the female detective, Hume holds an important place for his series of stories which became *Hagar of the Pawn-shop* in 1898. However, while Hume was living in Australia before he emigrated, he published a novel in 1888, *Madame Midas*, which deserves inclusion in any appraisal of the woman detective in the nineteenth century. Appearing the year after the English publication of *The Mystery of a Hansom Cab*, *Madame Midas* is a challenging work to evaluate because some of the characters from the earlier novel reappear in its pages, especially the strange detective Kilsip. The question of the status of *Madame Midas* as a female detective novel rests on its relationship with the earlier novel, therefore.

The Mystery of a Hansom Cab involves the discovery of a body in a cab in Melbourne. The central characters include Mark Frettlby, who had come to Melbourne in the early days and had made a fortune in wool. He had married a dancer, Rosanna Moore, by whom he had a daughter, Sally Rawlins. When Rosanna left him and went to England, Frettlby, thinking Rosanna dead, remarried and had a second daughter, Madge.

At the conclusion of *The Mystery of a Hansom Cab*, it results that Oliver Whyte, who has Moore as his mistress, blackmails Frettlby in Melbourne, since he knows that technically Frettlby is a bigamist and that hence

Frettlby's daughter Madge is illegitimate. Whyte is murdered by his associate Roger Moreland, who had learned of the marriage certificate and continues blackmailing Frettlby. Brian Fitzgerald, accused of the murder of Whyte, half-way through the novel is acquitted, which allows Hume to re-start the mystery. Fitzgerald had come from Ireland to make his way, and in the end he and Madge Frettlby marry and leave Australia for England.

As Stephen Knight notes in his introduction to *The Mystery of a Hansom Cab*, the detective Kilsip is 'soft-footed' and 'malignant' (ii), although it is Kilsip who suspects Moreland and is proved correct. Throughout the novel, Kilsip is in competition with another detective, Samuel Gorby. Kilsip is malignant because he becomes part of a conspiracy of silence enacted by males against women in the novel at its conclusion. No one ever tells Sally Rawlins, Frettlby's daughter by Rosanna Moore, that she is legitimate and hence the heir to Frettlby's money. Kilsip gets money from Madge Frettlby's lover, Brian Fitzgerald, to silence him, since he knows the truth about Madge's illegitimacy. Hence, the novel is very much a text inflected by male power against women.

Throughout *The Mystery of a Hansom Cab*, Hume alludes to his detective writer predecessors, such as Émile Gaboriau, Fortuné du Boisgobey, and Poe, and he even alludes to Thomas De Quincey's famous essay *Murder Considered as One of the Fine Arts* of 1827. As recorded by Knight, Hume was explicit about the model he chose before writing *The Mystery of a Hansom Cab*:

> I inquired of a leading Melbourne bookseller what style of book he sold most of. He replied that the detective stories of Gaboriau had a large sale, and as I had never even heard of this author I bought all his works — eleven or thereabouts — and read them carefully. The style of these attracted me, and I determined to write a book of the same class, containing a mystery, a murder and a description of low life in Melbourne. (i)

In addition to Gaboriau, the influence of Dickens's *Great Expectations* (1861) is evident in the idea of the lovely woman with the criminal father (Madge/Mark Frettlby||Estella/Magwitch) and the sufferings of a young protagonist in achieving success (Brian Fitzgerald/Pip). The cityscape of Melbourne retains the same nightmarish quality as the London fabricated by Dickens.

As the title *Madame Midas* indicates, Hume's emphasis on this successor novel is on women, as if to correct the male bias and male conspiracy of silence revealed in *The Mystery of a Hansom Cab*. Yet, several of the male characters from that novel reappear in *Madame Midas*. For example, when

Madame Midas moves from Ballarat to Melbourne, 'she took a house at St Kilda, which had been formerly occupied by Mark Frettlby, the millionaire, who had been mixed up in the famous hansom cab murder nearly eighteen months before' (195-96). Thus, Madame Midas, originally Miss Curtis, the daughter of Robert Curtis, who had made a fortune in gold, is tainted with the criminality, bigamy and murder associated with Frettlby from the earlier novel.

The legacy of such dangerous men from *The Mystery of a Hansom Cab* extends to *Madame Midas*, which, as Stephen Knight asserts, is 'in some ways . . . a sequel' (i) to Hume's first famous detection text. In addition, Duncan Calton, the brilliant lawyer of the earlier novel, reappears here as Madame Midas's counsel. When Gaston Vandeloup, the consummate villain of *Madame Midas*, mentions he had heard of Calton having 'something to do with a former owner of this house', Madame Midas responds: 'Don't talk of that . . .; the first time I took the house, I heard all about the Hansom Cab murder' (209).

Also from the previous novel are the physician Robert Chinston and the man about town Felix Rolleston, whose testimony helps acquit Fitzgerald of murder charges. Most significantly, the detective Kilsip returns in *Madame Midas*, where on his first appearance at the inquest about another murder is described as 'curled up like a cat in the corner, . . . listening to every word of the evidence' (237). As he is in *The Mystery of a Hansom Cab*, Kilsip is also threatening in *Madame Midas*. When Kitty Marchurst, Madame Midas's protégée who has been ruined by Gaston Vandeloup, is called to testify at the inquest, Kilsip 'scenting a mystery, rubbed his lean hands together softly' (238). After Kitty gives her evidence, 'Kilsip bent forward and whispered something to the Coroner, whereupon Kitty was recalled' (239). In other words, behind the professional screen of pursuing an investigation, the detective shadows and torments women.

The fact that even fairly benevolent males like Rolleston, Calton and Chinston reappear in *Madame Midas*, not to mention the malign detective Kilsip, demonstrates that the detectival environment of the novel is threatening to women, who must try to survive by developing skills which entail their own kind of detection. In *Madame Midas*, the two central female characters, Madame Midas and Kitty Marchurst, must mount surveillance over men and suspect them to avoid being deceived and destroyed by renegade males. Hume appears to be reestablishing a balance between the power of men and of women in this novel, to augment and correct the power relations of men and women in *Hansom Cab*, where males mostly deceive women by their conspiracies of silence.

This necessity to maintain surveillance to survive is especially marked in the behaviour of Madame Midas, the former Miss Curtis, an heiress who, as

Knight points out in his introduction to the novel, is 'so deeply dehumanized that her Christian name is never mentioned' (iv). After her father's death, Miss Curtis is left alone and marries disastrously Randolph Villiers, 'a penniless young Englishman' who 'had a handsome face and figure, a varied and extensive wardrobe, and a bad character' (8). Robert Curtis 'had settled a large sum of money on his daughter absolutely, which no one, not even her future husband, could touch' (8). However, out of her love for Villiers, Miss Curtis 'gave him full control of all her property, excepting that which was settled on herself by her father, which was, of course, beyond marital control' (8).

Villiers proceeds over the next two years to lose all the money he could take from his wife. At last, she casts him off:

> When Villiers, after spending all her wealth in riotous living, actually proceeded to ill-treat her in order to force her to give up the money her father had settled on her, she rebelled. She tore off her wedding-ring, threw it at his feet, renounced his name, and went off to Ballarat with her old nurse and the remnants of her fortune. (9)

For 1888, Hume minces few words in underscoring the victimization of women, who endure physical abuse and financial ruin at the hands of their lovers. The result is that the former Mrs Villiers 'became a cold suspicious woman who disbelieved in everyone and in everything' (9-10).

However, in the course of two years of managing the Pactolus claim, a gold mine, she prospers so much that she is christened Madame Midas by the mining community in Ballarat. Villiers 'threatened to bring the law into force to make her live with him, but she laughed in his face' (11), but Hume, a lawyer himself, recognizes how inimical is the law to a woman, even if she leaves her husband. Villiers joins forces with an evil mining agent, Slivers, to try to discover the location of a specific vein, the Devil's Lead, in the mine, which is reputed to be worth a fortune.

If suspicion and surveillance mark a detective, then Madame Midas is compelled to become one to survive:

> She had hoped to cut herself off from all the bitterness and sorrow of her past life, but this husband [Villiers] of hers, like an unquiet spirit, came to trouble her and remind her of a time she would willingly have forgotten . . . She was always haunted by a secret dread of her husband breaking in on her . . . Experience of her husband had inspired her with an instinctive distrust of men. (26, 28, 33)

All her vigilance is required to combat male predators, especially with the advent of the handsome Gaston Vandeloup, actually Octave Braulard, a Frenchman who had escaped New Caledonia, to which he had been consigned for murdering his mistress, Adèle Blondet, by poison in France.

When Vandeloup applies to Madame Midas to be a clerk at her business, she is first 'doubtfully eyeing the slender figure of the young man' (29). Even after Madame Midas hires Vandeloup, she is fleetingly uneasy:

> This young man pleased her. She was essentially a woman with social instincts, and the appearance of this young and polished stranger in the wilds of the Pactolus claim promised her a little excitement. It was true that every now and then, when she caught a glimpse from his scintillating eyes, she was conscious of a rather unpleasant sensation, but this she put down to fancy, as the young man's manners were really charming. (32)

However, Madame Midas's maid and confidante, Selina Sprotts, is not deluded by Vandeloup: 'I don't like him . . . He's too smooth and handsome, his eyes ain't true, and his tongue's too smart. I hate him' (34).

Madame Midas exercises her gaze as if she were a professional detective rather than an amateur who must detect out of self-interest:

> She was too clever a woman to let him manage things himself, or even know how much she trusted him; and Vandeloup knew that whatever he did those calm dark eyes were on him, and that the least slip or neglect on his part would bring Madame Midas to his side with her quiet voice and inflexible will to put him right again. (46)

Vandeloup meets Kitty, the daughter of Presbyterian minister Mark Marchurst, through Madame Midas. Madame throws 'a keen glance at her clerk' (51) as a warning against his preying on her protégée.

As if to counteract the overwhelming power of the male gaze in the detection novel *The Mystery of a Hansom Cab*, Hume deploys the female gaze of Madame Midas in this detective text, since no formal detective appears until Kilsip does much later in the novel. By diminishing the role of the actual detective in *Madame Midas*, Hume stresses that a woman must be her own detective to survive in a world of predatory men like Slivers, Villiers and Vandeloup. Villiers tries to blackmail money from her by suggesting that Vandeloup is her lover: 'Mrs Villiers felt herself grow faint — the accusation was so horrible. This man, who had embittered her life from the time she married him, was still her evil genius, and was trying to ruin her in the eyes of the world' (59).

Not only does her exercise of the female gaze render Madame Midas a detective. In one of the most violent episodes to involve a woman in Victorian fiction, Madame Midas is the victim of a vicious robbery in the novel. When the mine yields a three hundred ounce nugget of gold, Madame Midas takes it to Ballarat. Knowing of her journey, no less than three men plot to steal the nugget when she returns at evening to the Pactolus claim. These are her dreadful husband, Villiers; Gaston Vandeloup, her supposedly loyal clerk; and Vandeloup's associate Pierre Lemaire, who had escaped with Vandeloup from New Caledonia.

The robbery of the gold nugget is violent:

> Villiers dropped suddenly from the bank on to the trap, and caught her [Madame Midas] by the throat . . . [He] tightened his grasp on her throat and shortened his stick to give her a blow on the head. Fortunately, Madame Midas saw his intention, and managed to wrench herself free, so the blow aimed at her only slightly touched her, otherwise it would have killed her . . . The unhappy woman recognised her husband, and uttered a cry. (97)

Finally, she manages to escape this fiendish husband's attack:

> Maddened with anger and disgust, his wife snatched up the stick he had dropped, and struck him on the head as he took a step forward. With a stifled cry he staggered and fell over the embankment, still clutching the box in his arms . . . Madame Midas lay in a dead faint for some time, and when she came to herself she was still in the trap, and Rory was calmly trotting along the road home. (98)

Madame Midas believes, wrongly, that she has killed her husband. 'Though she hated the man who had ruined her life, and who had tried to rob her, still she did not care about becoming his murderess, and the thought was madness to her' (108). Then, she reasons like a detective: 'Not that she was afraid of punishment, for she had only acted in self-defence, and Villiers, not she, was the aggressor' (108). In a conversation with Vandeloup which reads like an interrogation, she learns that her husband is not dead. Villiers disappears, and Slivers, the evil mining agent, believing Villiers was murdered by his wife, decides to 'track her down, and put her in gaol, and hang her' (118).

Meanwhile, Gaston Vandeloup manages to cajole Kitty Marchurst to leave Ballarat and go to Melbourne as his mistress. Although Kitty pleads for him to marry her, invoking God, Vandeloup remarks: '[God] speaks too indistinctly for us to guess what he means' (133). When Kitty disappears from Ballarat, Madame Midas suspects Vandeloup, exercising her detectival skills:

> Mrs Villiers felt uneasy; was it likely that Vandeloup could have any connection with Kitty's disappearance? Impossible! he had given her his word of honour, and yet – it was very strange. Mrs Villiers was not, by any means, a timid woman, so she determined to ask Gaston right out, and get a decided answer from him, so as to set her mind at rest. (139)

Confronting Vandeloup, who lies splendidly, Madame Midas is a failed detective as she 'withdrew her eyes quite satisfied' (141) with Vandeloup's response. This withdrawal of the female gaze proves disastrous. Vandeloup recognizes that 'Madame had intuitively guessed the whole situation, and Vandeloup could not help admiring her cleverness' (140).

During the ensuing year, the major characters – Madame Midas, Vandeloup and Kitty – move to Melbourne, for by this time the Devil's Lead, the rich vein of gold at the Pactolus claim, has been discovered and has yielded a fortune for Mrs Villiers. This second part of the novel concentrates immediately on the contrast between the attitudes of the unofficial detective Madame Midas, still profoundly disturbed by the disappearance of Villiers, and the incompetence of the official police:

> One thing astonished Madame Midas very much, and that was the continuous absence of her husband. She did not believe he was dead . . . The idea of his lurking round was a constant nightmare to her, and at last she placed the matter in the hands of the police, with instructions to try to ascertain what became of him.
> The police did everything in their power to discover Villiers' whereabouts, but without success . . . After trying for about three months to find some traces of Villiers, the police gave up the search in despair. (154)

Part 2 of the novel, set in the Melbourne familiar to readers from *The Mystery of a Hansom Cab*, becomes a duel of wits between Vandeloup and Madame Midas.

Vandeloup casts off Kitty, who is rescued by Theodore Wopples and his theatrical troupe, which Kitty eventually joins in order to have some chance of financial survival. Vandeloup encounters in Melbourne the millionaire Ebenezer Meddlechip, one of the city's leading citizens, who is in reality Kestrike, a man who had also been Adèle Blondet's lover and for whom she had left Vandeloup, in return for which Vandeloup/Octave

Braulard had poisoned her. Knowing of Meddlechip's past, Vandeloup blackmails him and uses the money obtained to make some quick deals on the stock exchange. Hume perceives Australia in the 1880s as pervaded by gambling:

> Young Australia has a wonderful love for the excitement of gambling – take him away from the betting ring and he goes straight to the share market to dabble in gold and silver shares . . . Young Australia sees a chance of making thousands in a week; buys one thousand shares at four shillings – only two hundred pounds; shares will rise and Young Australia hopefully looks forward to pocketing two or three thousand by his modest venture of two hundred . . . Vandeloup was of a speculative nature himself. (189)

Stephen Knight incisively notes the parallel between Vandeloup and some of the rogues in Conan Doyle's tales:

> Like the villains in Conan Doyle, bourgeois professionals gone desperately wrong, Vandeloup projects the wolfish aspect of nineteenth-century society, when new commercial values and increased social mobility made the fear of competitive others a compulsive force – and also made crime fiction the authentic genre of that new social structure. (iii)

Dealing with the stockbroker Polglaze, Vandeloup realizes considerable money from the funds he blackmails from Kestrike.

The circle of men from *The Mystery of a Hansom Cab* reappears in the second part of *Madame Midas*. The attorney Duncan Calton is deceived by Vandeloup: 'Calton put into force his cross-examination. He might as well have tried his artful questions on a rock as on Vandeloup, for that clever young gentleman saw through the barrister at once' (211). At a ball given by the Meddlechips, Felix Rolleston informs Kitty that he was a friend of Brian Fitzgerald, who had married Madge Frettlby, who had lived in the house now occupied by Madame Midas. She has taken Kitty into her home, not knowing of her involvement with Vandeloup. When Kitty Marchurst hears a rumour that Madame Midas might marry her former lover Vandeloup, she confronts him, vowing to poison Madame Midas herself rather than have Madame Midas ruin herself with Vandeloup. Kitty has in her possession a bottle of aconite she had obtained from Vandeloup, who had been moved to prepare poison out of scientific curiosity when he found some Australian hemlock. Vandeloup decides that he must kill his former mistress, Kitty Marchurst.

The night of the Meddlechip ball, however, Selina Sprotts, Madame Midas's maid and companion, sleeps beside her restless and frightened mistress:

> Ever since the disappearance of her husband she was a prey to a secret dread [the return of Villiers] which, reacting on her nerves, rendered her miserable. Had Mr Villiers only appeared, she would have known how to deal with him, and done so promptly, but it was his absence that made her afraid. Was he dead? . . . It was this unpleasant feeling of being watched that haunted her and made her uneasy. The constant strain began to tell on her . . . Mrs Villiers' life became a perfect hell upon earth. (228, 229)

Hume renders the moment of the murder in *Madame Midas* as one of contesting gazes, of a woman forced to be on the watch for fear of being gazed upon by a dreadful husband.

When Kitty returns to the house, she sits in Madame Midas's bedroom, through which she must pass to her own, staring at a photograph of Vandeloup before dozing off. Drowsy, Kitty perceives a hand pouring something into a glass beside the bed. She is awakened by the voice of Madame Midas, who has discovered that her companion Selina Sprotts is dead. Intending to kill her, someone has poisoned the companion sleeping alongside her.

At the inquest, Kilsip, the detective from *The Mystery of a Hansom Cab*, reappears, urging the coroner to discover that Kitty Marchurst, during her tenure as an actress with the Wopples company, had played in a melodrama, *The Hidden Hand*, which also involved someone administering poison through a window. It is decided to have the stomach contents analysed, for which a doctor, Gollipeck, comes to Melbourne. He has suspected, correctly, that Vandeloup is the poisoner Octave Braulard. When it is established that Sprotts died of poisoning, not apoplexy, Vandeloup testifies that Kitty Marchurst, his mistress, had stolen the poison from his desk when she was his mistress.

During this testimony, Kilsip 'stole a look at [Kitty Marchurst] and then rubbed his hands together' (253). Hume creates an environment where even detectives would rather hang a woman than find the genuine murderer. Kilsip testifies that he found a half bottle of aconite in Kitty Marchurst's room. Kitty is arrested on a charge of wilful murder.

It is precisely at this point in the novel that the two women become detectives to gain their own survival. When Vandeloup visits Kitty in Melbourne Prison, she informs him that she witnessed him killing Randolph Villiers during the robbery of Mrs Villiers when she left Ballarat with the gold nugget. She claims he used the knife he snatched from Pierre Lemaire's back. In fact, Vandeloup had killed Lemaire, to be free of a man who knew his past, and had made Villiers, full of insensate fury, believe he had done it, forcing him to impersonate Lemaire. Since he accompanied Vandeloup to the prison as Lemaire, Villiers now realizes his own innocence, but he is in turn accused of murdering Sprotts, believing she was his hated wife Madame Midas.

Meanwhile, Madame Midas discusses the murder of Sprotts with Calton. Here, she defends the female accused, Kitty Marchurst, doubting the males who have had her arrested:

> 'Do you know, . . . I cannot help thinking Kitty is innocent of this crime.'
> 'She may be . . . , but the evidence seems very strong against her.'
> 'Purely circumstantial . . . '
> 'Purely circumstantial, as you [Madame Midas] say . . . ; still, some new facts may be discovered before the trial which may prove her [Kitty Marchurst] to be innocent. After the mystery which enveloped the death of Oliver Whyte in the hansom cab murder I [Calton] hesitate giving a decided answer.' (271-2)

When the furious Villiers returns, Madame Midas claims he tried to kill her. The arrival of Kilsip brings the real murderer, the dandy man about town Bartholomew Jarper, who had forged cheques with Madame Midas's signature. Ironically, it is Villiers who, spying on his wife, had seen Jarper near the house when the murder was committed. Knowing Jarper was the murderer, he had informed Kilsip. Thus, the evil husband Villiers discovers the true killer.

Both Madame Midas and Kitty Marchurst in their separate ways exercise detectival surveillance. In contrast to his position in *The Mystery of a Hansom Cab*, where males discover the murderer but conceal actualities from women, in *Madame Midas* Hume states that every woman *must* be a detective to survive in a patriarchal world. Yet, Hume cannot believe that patriarchy can fully rectify itself, for both women are damaged if not destroyed by males.

Their fates, however, are different. Gaston Vandeloup trails Kitty Marchurst to the Yarra River, where she plans to commit suicide. Seeking to murder her, he accidentally slips into the stream and drowns, while Kitty vanishes into the night. Kitty's strongest detectival act is inadvertently to instigate the death of her betrayer. Throughout the novel, she has not avoided painful confrontations with Vandeloup. Stephen Knight astutely appraises Hume's construction of his character Kitty Marchurst:

> Mrs Villiers' [Madame Midas's] own innocence is gone by the
> start of the story, but her friend and protégée, Kitty Marchurst,
> is full of supple and natural responses. Hume probes her story
> with a sensitive and frank touch: she lights her lover's cigarette
> with sensual delight, but confronts the problems that follow with
> firm determination, developing a theatrical career and then, at
> the end of the novel, adopting some dramatically independent
> ideas. (ii)

In her daring to live with her lover and to undertake a career on the stage,
Kitty Marchurst evidences signs of the New Woman.

For Madame Midas, life continues, although she is forever altered:

> Madame Midas suffered severely from the shocks she had
> undergone with the discovery of everyone's baseness. She settled
> a certain income on her husband [Villiers], on condition she
> never was to see him again, which offer he readily accepted, and
> having arranged all her affairs in Australia, she left for England,
> hoping to find in travel some alleviation, if not forgetfulness, of
> the sorrow of the past. A good woman – a noble woman, yet
> one who went forth into the world broken-hearted and
> friendless, with no belief in anyone and no pleasure in life. (277)

Hume never has Madame Midas find any fulfilment in another sexual
relationship. Instead, she becomes a philanthropist:

> She, however, was of too fine a nature ever to sink into the base,
> cynical indifference of a misanthropic life, and the wealth which
> she possessed was nobly used by her to alleviate the horrors of
> poverty and to help those who needed help . . . Though it
> brought her no happiness, yet it was the cause of happiness to
> others; but she would give all her wealth could she but once
> more regain that trust in human nature which had been so
> cruelly betrayed. (277-8)

Fergus Hume demonstrates that survival represents for both women no
victory.

The relationship of *Madame Midas* to *The Mystery of a Hansom Cab*
provokes one of the most intriguing instances of female detection. By
resurrecting male characters from the earlier novel in *Madame Midas*, Hume
automatically re-creates an intimidating environment of murder and fear,
but now from the perspective of women. Both Madame Midas and Kitty
Marchurst experience crime. Both women are thought to be guilty of
murders: Slivers, the mining agent, thinks Mrs Villiers killed her husband;

the legal community believes Kitty Marchurst killed Selina Sprotts. Both women are required to give testimony at inquests. Both women, suffering under patriarchy, are compelled to investigate. Stephen Knight summarizes: 'Hume's sense of the roles forced on women in Australian society ranks with better-known voices of his period like Barbara Baynton and Mary Gilmore' (ii).

Both Madame Midas and Kitty Marchurst must exercise the power of the female gaze to oppose the male gaze. Kitty perceives enough of the gold robbery to unsettle her seducer Vandeloup. Madame Midas must interrogate males such as Vandeloup, confront blackmailing men such as her husband Villiers and suspect the motives and violence of most of the male community. Her authority is such that even a callous killer like Vandeloup can be brought momentarily to heel by her. She has sufficient conviction about her powers of observation to discuss with the lawyer Duncan Calton the validity of the evidence in the murder trial.

In *Madame Midas*, Hume brilliantly uses the existence of mining for gold as a trope for the need to mine for information as a detective. Just as Madame Midas owns the Pactolus claim and eventually uncovers the gold in the Devil's Lead, she is detective enough to uncover information sufficient for her to survive the murderous surveillance of men. That *Madame Midas* appeared the same year as the Ripper murders gives the novel a contemporary relevance – women must exercise surveillance in the manner of detectives. Having emigrated to England in 1888 after the publication of *Madame Midas*, Hume would reaffirm the role of the female sleuth when he created his amateur gypsy detective with *Hagar of the Pawn-shop* a decade later.

Mary Elizabeth Braddon (1835-1915): *Thou Art the Man* (1894)

The year 1894 was an important one in the evolution of the late Victorian female detective. It represented the passing of the torch from one of the century's most famous writers, Mary Elizabeth Braddon, to one of the earliest creators of post-Holmes female detectives, Catherine Louisa Pirkis, who wrote about Loveday Brooke that year. In 1894, Braddon, notorious writer of the great sensation novels *Lady Audley's Secret* (1862) and *Aurora Floyd* (1863), produced *Thou Art the Man*, a triple-decker which deployed devices of the sensation novel (the hidden murder, the return of the past, the fear of servants) along with an active engagement with detection by a woman.

Neither Craig/Cadogan nor Klein discusses Braddon in their critical studies, but Michelle Slung lists Coralie Urquhart of *Thou Art the Man* as a female sleuth. In the recent volume of critical essays about Braddon, *Beyond Sensation* (Tromp, ed.), Heidi Johnson discusses this novel with several others to argue that Braddon's texts are replete with detectival situations which involve the Electra complex. Like Slung, Johnson focuses on Coralie Urquhart as the female detective in *Thou Art the Man*. Kathleen Maio believes that 'two women – aunt [Sibyl Penrith] and niece [Coralie Urquhart] – try to unravel a murder/frameup mystery . . . Together the unhappy wife and the unhappy daughter solve the mystery' (94). The difficulty with Maio's position is that neither woman works in concert with the other, with Coralie more resenting than assisting Sibyl Penrith.

The surprising fact is, however, that it is not Coralie Urquhart who is the primary female detective in the novel at all. Instead, it is Sibyl Penrith, daughter of wealthy Cumberland mine-owner Joseph Higginson, who is the true female detective. To some degree, critical misapprehensions and neglect suggest that Braddon's place in detective literature remains ambiguous. The important studies of sensation literature by such scholars as Hughes (1980) and Showalter (1978) have demonstrated the central importance of Braddon's sensation novels in the literature of the 1860s. The question is, what is the influence of this literature to the female detection texts of the late Victorian period?

The narrative of *Thou Art the Man* has many indications that Braddon is evoking the tradition of detective fiction in the novel. The title, for example, coming from 2 Samuel 12.3, echoes that of Edgar Allan Poe's dazzling short story *Thou Art the Man* of 1844. Poe's tale is key for establishing elements central to the evolution of the detective genre: the detective/narrator, the least likely person as murderer, the planting of false clues, the use of ballistics and even the small-town setting. Hence, if Braddon's title evokes Poe, it is to place *Thou Art the Man* firmly in the detective genre, not in the sensation tradition. The plot, for instance, excludes such famous sensation elements as impersonation and bigamy. Instead of underscoring the marriage plot, Coralie Urquhart's marriage is disposed of in two paragraphs at the end in a Postscript, suggesting that Braddon is repudiating devices identified with her from the sensation tradition.

Is there the influence of Conan Doyle and Sherlock Holmes? It would appear that Braddon has read her Holmes and has re-formed that legacy to suit a more proto-feminist objective. Most conspicuous in the novel is the mode of narration itself, veering between an omniscient heterodiegetic third person narrator and, at intervals, the first person diary records of Coralie Urquhart. This strategy evokes that of Charles Dickens's *Bleak House* (1853) with its shifting third and first person narrators.

There is, however, an apparent Holmes influence. In the 1890 *The Sign of Four*, two chapters record first-person retrospective accounts, chapter 4 by Thaddeus Sholto and chapter 12 by Jonathan Small, about the Agra treasure. Albeit these are not diary entries, they are first-person records of past criminous events. In addition, in *The Sign of Four* the death of Thaddeus Sholto is reported in a newspaper article in chapter 8, similar to the account of the Earl of Penrith's death recorded in a newspaper in chapter 29 of *Thou Art the Man*. The advertisement for the lost launch in chapter 9 of Doyle's novel recalls the loss of the boat the *Mary Jane* in Braddon's text.

Even more significant to *Thou Art the Man* is the device of the retrospective narration. In Braddon's novel, chapters 4 through 17 inclusive contain the background of the crime, murder and escape that forms its main focus. This inclusion of a long retrospective narration in third person heterodiegetic record echoes that of Part 2 of *A Study in Scarlet*, titled by Doyle 'The Country of the Saints' about the Mormons and revenge in the state of Utah. Instead of dividing *Thou Art the Man* into two distinct parts, Braddon uses chapters 1-3 to lead into the retrospection, with chapters 18-32 to bracket its termination. This serves the detection plot satisfactorily, for the clue of the message delivered in chapter 1 is resumed in chapter 18, with the reader expected to retain concern for this strange missive.

Furthermore, in Braddon's novel there is the motif of being 'locked-up', but here she departs from Conan Doyle's practise. In the Holmes tales, such as *The Copper Beeches* or *The Speckled Band*, women are confined to rooms by tyrannical fathers or stepfathers, and the model of Brontë's Bertha Mason in *Jane Eyre* endures as an influence in both Conan Doyle and Braddon. However, in *Thou Art the Man*, it is a male who is locked up. Brandon Mountford, loved by Sibyl Higginson, is falsely accused of the murder of Marie Arnold, since he was found with bloody hands bending over her body. He is in effect locked up twice. First, he is incarcerated by the local police. Then, the real killer, Hubert Urquhart, the father of Coralie Urquhart, induces Sibyl Higginson to assist in the escape of Mountford from the gaol, after he convinces Sibyl her lover Mountford will swing for the murder. This flight confirms to the community that in fact the innocent Mountford is the guilty party. Throughout *Thou Art the Man*, Braddon includes references to Mountford's being locked up (126, 212, 232, 302) to differentiate her text from those in which a woman is confined.

By this stratagem of the flight, Urquhart deflects suspicion from himself, for in reality he had murdered Marie Arnold when she had repudiated his advances. Unknown to Sibyl, the boat puts into shore and Mountford is imprisoned for ten years in the vicarage of St Jude's by the corrupt Reverend Ebenezer Carpew, who as the killer's former tutor is in Urquhart's pay. Prompted by Sibyl Penrith, another Church of England priest, John Coverdale, discovers the truth and eventually rescues

Mountford, who nevertheless dies from the confinement. In this instance, Braddon subverts the practise of males incarcerating women from Conan Doyle and Brontë and instead has a man incarcerating another man.

Other elements from literary tradition appear in *Thou Art the Man* as well. The criminal father recalls Pip's criminal surrogate father Magwitch in Dickens's *Great Expectations* (1861). If one contends that there are two female detectives in *Thou Art the Man*, the parallel instance is Fergus Hume's famous *The Mystery of a Hansom Cab* (1886 Australia; 1887 London) with its two male detectives, Kilsip and Samuel Gorby.

When Coralie Urquhart comes to Killander Castle to stay with her aunt Sibyl Penrith, she discovers a book, *My African Apprenticeship*, written by Brandon Mountford in 1874, twelve years before the current events in 1886. There is also an inscription by Mountford to Sibyl dated May 6, 1876, the year in which the lovers met and the murder of Marie Arnold occurred. After believing Mountford dead, Sibyl marries Hubert Urquhart's half-brother, Archibald, the Earl of Penrith. Braddon clearly evokes the finding of Catherine Earnshaw's diary by Lockwood from Emily Brontë's *Wuthering Heights* (1847), as well as the unfortunate marriage of Catherine to Edgar Linton when she believes Heathcliff has vanished. Just as Heathcliff returns in Brontë's text, so too is the long-lost beloved Mountford recovered at the conclusion of *Thou Art the Man*.

Another important precedent for the lost lover who returns after an unfortunate marriage is Elizabeth Gaskell's *Sylvia's Lovers* of 1863. Philip Hepburn, in love with Sylvia Robson, never tells her that her lover Charley Kinraid, a harpooner, was seized by a press gang. Sylvia eventually marries Hepburn and has a child by him. The return of Charley Kinraid destroys Sylvia's life. Kinraid, however, is not locked up for ten years as is Mountford in *Thou Art the Man*: he lives to marry a Bristol heiress.

Other literary texts provide some precedent for details in *Thou Art the Man*. The dating of the dramatic events to 1886 (the discovery of the murderer, Hubert Urquhart, of Marie Arnold and the recovery of Brandon Mountford) evokes the year of publication of Stevenson's *Dr Jekyll and Mr Hyde*. Its dual personalities parallel the similar nature of Hubert Urquhart. He appears hard-living but genteel at one moment but can commit two murders in the course of the novel at two other moments. Mountford in the novel fears he is composed of two selves, again a deliberate evocation of the situation in Stevenson's text and also suggestive of the indeterminacy of the identity of Jack the Ripper, perhaps nobleman by day, killer by night. The discovery of the captive Mountford after ten years of imprisonment by the evil vicar Carpew and Urquhart suggests the influence of the recovery of Dr Manette in Dickens's *A Tale of Two Cities* (1859) after eighteen years of incarceration in the Bastille.

As is well known, Braddon had already been engaged in creating an amateur detective in the figure of Lucy, Lady Audley's nemesis, her husband's barrister nephew Robert Audley in *Lady Audley's Secret*. Robert Audley succeeds in uncovering his beautiful aunt's criminality when she tries to kill George Talboys, her first husband, when he returns from America, establishing that she is at the least a bigamist and at the worst an attempted murderess. Whether Lucy Audley is mad or not, she is confined to an asylum in Belgium and there dies.

As John Sutherland notes (33), *Aurora Floyd* also uses the device of the 'dead but not dead' in its plotting, as Aurora marries a groom, James Conyers, but believing him dead later marries the Yorkshire squire John Mellish. Needless to say, the first husband returns and, when he is murdered, Aurora Floyd is believed the killer. Braddon evokes these plots with the device of rediscovered Brandon Mountford in *Thou Art the Man*, but in a key strategic move from sensation to detection, the female lover, Sibyl Penrith, is not a bigamist and is not even suspected of being a murderess. By such a signal, Braddon indicates that her motives in *Thou Art the Man* are not in fact sensational but detectival.

Braddon also reinflects the motif of female madness from sensation fiction in *Thou Art the Man*. The fear of hereditary madness, passed from mother to daughter in *Lady Audley's Secret*, takes the form of Brandon Mountford's epilepsy, which he fears in its advanced stages can progress to sudden violent impulses which could lead to murder. Mountford inherits this malady from his mother. What is a female proclivity in sensation fiction is transformed in this detective narrative into a male susceptibility. In such ways, Braddon draws upon sensation conventions, but in the 1890s she now applies them in a proto-feminist manner, subverting the patriarchy by having the male be locked up, the male potentially mad, the male a killer and the female the detective.

The stress on detection in *Thou Art the Man* is indicated early in the novel. Coralie Urquhart, living with her aunt Sibyl Penrith at Killander Castle, writes a diary, an activity 'imposed' (15) upon her by her father Hubert, the killer of Marie Arnold ten years earlier. He instructs her:

> 'You will keep a diary in future, if you please, Cora; and you will keep it in such a manner as will admit of your allowing me to read it . . . I want you to observe [Sibyl Penrith] closely, and to write down everything that concerns her . . . I only want you to be an observer [not a spy]. My interest in Lady Penrith is founded on the purest motives. I want to put an end to the feud between us . . . Ten years ago I was her adoring lover. She refused me – her heart was buried in another man's [Brandon Mountford's] grave – and a few months afterwards she married

my elder brother. The match was of old Sir Joseph Higginson's making, I have no doubt . . . You will be with her in a confidential capacity; you are keen enough to scent either danger [of her being robbed or tempted to fall], and to pass the warning on to me. You can send me your diary weekly.' (13-14)

Braddon's startling strategy about this diary record, however, is to have Coralie decide to produce two diaries:

I have therefore commenced a system of diary-keeping by double entry. What I mean him to read I write in one volume; my own little reveries I keep to myself in another volume. (16)

Chapter 3 is entitled 'Cora's Diary: For Paternal Perusal' (17), and amid reflections about marriage, reading and other matters, Cora includes the detail of discovering Mountford's account of his experiences in Africa.

Then, with chapter 4, Braddon begins the long history of the situations which led to the murder of Marie Arnold and the disappearance of Brandon Mountford. Coralie's journal, again for 'paternal inspection', reappears in chapter 19. In chapter 21, the reader encounters her 'private journal.' Chapter 25 includes her 'private diary', and chapter 27 includes 'Cora Expatiates' as its title. She refers once to her duty as 'police work' (224) and records key elements of the plot, such as her father quarrelling with her uncle the Earl of Penrith, whom her father will murder but make appear to be a hunting accident.

The difficulty of this scattered appearance of Coralie's diary in the 32 chapters of the novel, however, is that Coralie basically does no detection at all. It is difficult to see how she is a detective in any genuine sense. She records events, but she never actively engages in their discovery, at best overhearing or observing or at one point confronting her father. At the end of the novel, however, she is the only character to know that her father Hubert Urquhart killed his brother the Earl, which she concludes after seeing him walking on the heath with a gun in a hunting outfit the day of her uncle's death.

Sibyl Higginson, now Lady Penrith, is the true female detective in the narrative. Braddon makes this evident in the first chapter, when Sibyl is handed a message scrawled in pencil, which turns out to be from her long disappeared captive lover Brandon Mountford:

There was only a few pencilled words in four straggling lines along the paper; and those few words were so difficult to decipher that Lady Penrith had to pore over them for a long

time in the waning light before she made them into the following
sentences: --
    'Out of the grave, the living grave, a long-forgotten voice
calls to you. Where their worm dieth not, and their fire is not
quenched.'
    No signature; no indication of from whom or whence the
message came. A madman's scrawl, no doubt, inspired by some
half-cloudy purpose in the troubled brain of lunacy. (3)

Braddon indicates that Sibyl's purpose is to 'decipher', and she begins by
comparing the handwriting to that in the letters sent her by her lost lover
Mountford. Braddon suggests there is a mystery to be detected when Sibyl
reflects about Coralie that 'the girl was the daughter of that man whom she
regarded as her worst enemy, the man who had turned the sweetest gift of
life to bitterness and despair. She believed the worst of Hubert Urquhart,
her husband's half-brother' (10).
    That the novel emphasizes detection, therefore, is signalled in the first
chapter by the message given to Lady Penrith and by the writing of the
diary commanded by Urquhart for his daughter Coralie. One woman must
read and decipher, the other must observe and record. Lady Penrith's
Christian name, Sibyl, properly marks her mission of disclosing the crime.
    Two individuals enter Sibyl's life as recounted in the long retrospective
narration of the persons involved in the case. The first is Marie Arnold,
introduced by her father Sir Joseph Higginson into the household as the
daughter of an engineer from his business in France who had been killed in
an accident (72). In fact, Marie Arnold is Higginson's illegitimate daughter
by his French mistress, as he reveals (179+) much later to the Earl of
Penrith when Penrith discusses marrying Sibyl Higginson after the
disappearance and presumed death of the man she loves, Brandon
Mountford. Marie Arnold differs from Sibyl: she is Roman Catholic and has
a rich contralto voice.
    Brandon Mountford is destined to be the man of Sibyl Higginson's
dreams: 'tall, well set up, with a fine, frank countenance, well cut features,
the Mountford nose, which inclined to the aquiline, bright blue eyes, light
brown hair, curling close to the well shaped head, and a complexion tanned
by a hotter sun [in Africa] than ever shone upon Cumbrian cliffs' (54). In
his refinement, he is distinctly different from Hubert Urquhart, who at 34 is
five years younger than his half-brother, the Earl. He 'had been in a cavalry
regiment . . . had married badly . . . had married in haste and repented with
equal celerity' (59). Two facts emerge which have key consequences for the
crime: first, that Brandon Mountford's mother 'went out of her mind soon
after his birth, and there was a strain of madness in his blood' (75); and

second, that Hubert Urquhart loves Marie Arnold but that she does not return his love, a fact which causes Sir Joseph to reject Urquhart as a suitor.

Perhaps as a legacy of the motif of 'inherited madness' in her most famous sensation novel, *Lady Audley's Secret*, Braddon again devotes many pages to Mountford's inherited tendency. In *Thou Art the Man*, however, the motif is given an entirely different inflection because the afflicted individual is a male. This strategy turns the novel from sensation to detection. The torments caused Mountford by this situation are recorded in detail:

> Over Brandon's life henceforth there brooded the shadow of a dark fate. He had talked to the doctor at Highgate [where his mother is kept], had pressed him closely upon the question of hereditary lunacy, had inquired into the nature of his mother's malady, and had discovered that the mental flaw had first showed itself in the form of epilepsy . . . Over him, too, hung that horror of possible epilepsy . . . He was nearly eighteen years of age when the first attack occurred . . . Henceforth he knew himself doomed. (77-8)

He takes a degree at Cambridge, and then he goes as an adventurer and explorer to Africa, which is clearly an attempt to perceive his own 'darkness' in the then-named Dark Continent, where he feels an intense affinity with the natives.

Brandon wonders when the 'dementia' (79) experienced by his mother will afflict him. From reading a treatise on epilepsy, he learns of a case where an epileptic became 'the victim of a murderous instinct' (95), which makes him wonder about his own Jekyll/Hyde propensity:

> Horror unutterable, to have won the woman he loved, to have promised to care for her and cherish her, to be trusted and loved by her; and after a year or so of bliss to wake one day a creature of demoniac impulses, transformed from man to devil, yet knowing himself man, fighting against his evil genius, conscious of his criminal instincts, yet unable to conquer them . . . Yes, in that homicidal fury he might murder [Sibyl] – her, the woman he loved. (95)

Brandon confesses his 'case' (102) to Sibyl, who does not fear the situation, but he leaves her after one passionate kiss. Falling into depression, Mountford suffers a ferocious attack of epilepsy, awakening to find himself at Marie Arnold's body, covered with her blood.

The situation of Brandon Mountford as an epileptic is of particular interest in *Thou Art the Man*. In having Mountford afflicted by epilepsy,

Braddon is bringing the text into a debate about the medical causes of criminality, including the role of epilepsy in provoking crime. Alfred Randall, in his essay 'A Plea for the Medical Assessment of Crime' in *The New Age* in 1912, cites statistics that a number of prisoners are epileptic. He concludes:

> Of epilepsy, no one but a lawyer would argue responsibility . . .
> A murder by an epileptic should usually be looked upon as being
> as much a symptom of his disease as larceny by a general
> paralytic; and further, that if a man has been subject to regular
> epileptic fits, and commits a homicidal act in an impulsive and
> motiveless manner, the presumption would be very strong that
> he was not responsible for his actions. (610)

The inclusion of epilepsy in *Thou Art the Man*, therefore, is not for sensational purposes. Rather, Braddon is working to investigate the relationship of detection to medicine.

An additional factor involving epilepsy concerns Victorian and Edwardian masculinity. In his essay, 'Malingering', published in the *Strand* in March 1906, the physician Litton Forbes discusses males who counterfeit illnesses and diseases in order to avoid responsibility. Forbes defines 'malingering' as 'simulation of disease' (319). He observes that males use false epileptic fits as a way of avoiding duty or responsibility. He describes the 'real' epilepsy as 'indeed a dreadful disease'; after an attack, 'the hapless sufferer . . . lies where he fell, quiet, dazed, and apparently exhausted' (322), an accurate description of Mountford in the novel when he has a severe epileptic fit at the time Marie Arnold is murdered. But behind the idea that he is arrested as the murderer is the lingering doubt about males counterfeiting epilepsy.

Hence, Mountford's epilepsy in *Thou Art the Man* is part of a larger legal/medical/detectival debate about criminality and about masculinity. The reviewer in the *Athenaeum* (30 June 1894) stressed that 'the crimes of these three volumes . . . are complicated by a strain of epileptic tendencies, in the treatment of which Miss Braddon shows no slight skill' (833). This singling out of the details about epilepsy reveals that Braddon is engaging this larger cultural discourse involving crime, detection, masculinity, responsibility, law and medicine.

The verdict of coroner and jury, however, is 'wilful murder against Brandon Mountford' (126). When Sibyl visits him in the gaol, he tells her that 'there sometimes are two natures in the same man – the nature in calm and well-being – the nature in storm and madness' (131), as in Jekyll/Hyde. Convinced by Urquhart, the real killer of Marie Arnold, that Mountford will be executed for the murder, Sibyl assists Urquhart in removing Mountford and enabling what she thinks is her lover's escape. Having 'helped to get Brandon Mountford out of the clutch of the law' (152), Sibyl nevertheless wonders 'whether this first crime might not be the beginning of a series of murders?' (153). This is Braddon's direct evocation of the Jack the Ripper case of 1888.

Sibyl Penrith thinks it might have been better for Mountford to have been tried, for then 'the keenest intelligence in the land, the quick intellect of the trained advocate, might have been brought to bear upon crime and motive. The clue might have been found, the labyrinth threaded, and the real murderer discovered. By his disappearance Brandon had left the mystery dark, and his name disgraced' (173). Such words as 'clue', 'crime' and 'motive' make it clear that Sibyl Higginson, soon to marry the Earl of Penrith, will be the female detective when the occasion presents itself. The pages devoted to her speculations about the case confirm that her interrogation of the 'case' is ratiocinative in nature, not merely emotional.

That occasion for the beginning of detection is the strange message Sibyl is handed on the heath in the first chapter. She takes the message to Andrew Orlebar, the old family retainer at Ellerslie House, and receives confirmation that the handwriting is similar to that in her lover's letters. She then begins to scour the area to locate Mountford, eventually coming to the vicarage of St Jude's.

Meanwhile, Coralie Urquhart is not wrong to record in her diary: 'There is a feeling in the air as if it were not the end of the century, but the end of the world' (205). Coralie overhears a violent interview between her father and the Earl of Penrith, concluding that 'Providence can't expect much good out of any woman who starts in the race of life handicapped with such as a father as mine' (254). Coralie confronts her father, wondering if it is certain that Mountford was the murderer of Marie Arnold. She records: 'The horror of that murder haunts me' (271).

After seeing her father in hunting dress the same day her uncle is killed, supposedly in a hunting accident, Coralie Urquhart ceases to resort to her diary: 'I shall write no more in this journal. I close the book for ever this miserable night. My heart is frozen' (286). She repudiates writing altogether, since it was commanded by her father and is male-identified. Although she has no positive proof of her father's guilt, she strongly suspects he has killed both Marie Arnold and the Earl of Penrith. This rejection of writing, furthermore, comes at a devastating personal cost. In the same chapter, just before seeing her father in the hunting dress, Coralie had felt the opposite about writing: 'I find an undiminishing interest in this volume [her personal diary], and the facility with which my pen runs along the page makes me think that I shall some day blossom into a novelist . . . I see myself ten years hence a spinster novelist, in a snug little house – in Mayfair' (281). Braddon strongly implies that the circumstantial evidence of her father's criminality destroys any ambition the daughter might have had to become a writer – or even have financial security (Mayfair) from her own independent efforts. It is a crushing defeat of any attempt to survive outside the patriarchy.

Sibyl Penrith, however, becomes a female detective in earnest. When the Carpew family and the vicar resist her attempts to locate Mountford, who she suspects is incarcerated at the vicarage, Sibyl enlists the help of the Church of England priest John Coverdale, who is familiar with all kinds of human failings from his service in the East End of London. Hearing the details of her suspicions, Coverdale tells her 'there can be no doubt it is a case for investigation' (238). Coverdale as clergyman/detective anticipates G. K. Chesterton's famous Father Brown in the early twentieth century. Coverdale tells Sibyl: 'I have had to hunt for people in the East End' (288).

Eventually, John Coverdale tracks down Mountford and reunites him with Sibyl, who is confirmed in her belief that her lover is the victim not only of epilepsy but of 'a diabolical conspiracy' (293) devised by the killer, her brother-in-law Hubert Urquhart. A doctor confirms that Mountford 'has been cruelly treated, kept in worse seclusion than if he had been in a madhouse' (302). Sibyl confronts Urquhart, telling him he is 'twice a murderer' (310), once for killing Marie Arnold and then for condemning Mountford to a living death. For her part, Coralie confesses to Sibyl that she was 'tainted' with her father's 'bad blood' and 'venom' (322), but wishes to remain with her rather than with her father.

The Christian names and surnames given to the characters in *Thou Art the Man* also prove intriguing. To her disgrace, Coralie learns she was named after a French burlesque actress. In its melange of Italian and English, the name means 'the heart is a lie', which connotes her initial dislike and resentment of Sibyl Penrith. It also suggests that her nature would evolve the system of two diaries, one public and one private. More significantly, Coralie recognizes she never loved her father, Hubert Urquhart:

> That interview between her father and her uncle had left a sense
> of bitter degradation in her mind. She had never really loved her
> father; there had been nothing between them but the bond of
> relationship – a bond which he had shown himself very glad to
> loosen . . . It tortured her to think of degradation that reflected
> upon herself. To be the daughter of such a father! There was the
> sting! (258)

At the end of the novel, she will leave her father, having forged a separate identity for herself. The surname Urquhart recalls that of David Urquhart

(1805-1877), who had bitterly opposed Palmerston's foreign policy in the Crimean War. Like the fictional Urquhart who had been in a cavalry regiment, David Urquhart had been in the military. It is also 'to irk the heart', which Hubert Urquhart does to women, both his daughter Coralie and to the woman he desires and murders, Marie Arnold. Ebenezer Carpew's name evokes that of Ebenezer Scrooge of Dickens's *A Christmas Carol* (1843) with a similar coarse miserliness. Mountford's surname is particularly ironic, since the doomed and confined epileptic can neither 'mount' nor 'ford' anything at all.

After Brandon Mountford's death, Sibyl Penrith is summoned to Urquhart's deathbed, where he is being ravaged by cancer of the face. The disfigured and dying Hubert Urquhart has already refused to accept any religious consolation from Coverdale:

> 'I know your craft . . . You sneak to my bedside under the guise of friendship – a man with whom I never had one thought or feeling in common – and presently you will bring a little black book out of your pocket, and drop on your knees, and pray me into worse horrors than those I suffer now. I don't want you or your Mumbo-Jumbo, your Abracadabra.' (331)

In a message to Sibyl Penrith, Urquhart reaffirms his atheistic beliefs:

> 'Don't be afraid that you will hear a puling death-bed repentance. I believe in neither pardon nor pity. I die the victim of an inexorable scheme of Creation which includes the horrors of diseases that torture and kill, damnable maladies which no human skill can cure. Do you think that any man, doomed as I am doomed, is likely to go out of this life listening to twaddle about Divine Beneficence?' (332)

Having no belief in God and rejecting any deathbed confession, Urquhart instead recounts to Sibyl that he did murder Marie Arnold when she did not requite his desire: 'Passionate love like mine was to be valued or to be feared' (334). However, '[Marie] laughed at my passion and my threats' (335). Urquhart killed her not only out of frustrated love but out of patriarchal authority challenged and defied. Only Coralie, however, knows her father killed her uncle in the putative hunting accident.

There is an issue of considerable complexity about this final episode in *Thou Art the Man*. Having been given the facts of the case by the detecting Sibyl Penrith, Coverdale proceeds to act as detective, finding the ruined Mountford. His services as a detective are successful, but those as a priest are not so far as Urquhart is concerned. Urquhart's allusion to 'damnable maladies' which defy human cure certainly includes the epilepsy which Mountford inherited and which drove him to mental torment. In effect, not only Urquhart's crime but equally Mountford's own inherited stain destroyed his life, certainly causing one to question the benevolence of God – or the existence of God.

Braddon's structuring of the conclusions of the three volumes of her triple-decker confirms the importance of this metaphysical issue to her. Urquhart's repudiation of God is a perfect gloss to the strategically placed final paragraphs of the first volume (chapter 10), which conclude with the arrest of Mountford for the murder of Marie Arnold. Sibyl remembers that 'only a few hours before' Mountford had told her that epilepsy might lead to eruptions of murderous violence:

> He had painted in strongest phrases the horror of his hereditary malady. He had told her that there was no limit to the dark possibilities of that dread disease. He knew not what phase it might assume. It might be murder.
>   Yes, those were the very words which he had spoken, when he tried to cut himself off from her sympathy – a doomed wretch, worse than a leper, since with him physical malady might pass into moral delinquency . . . And now she heard how he had been found with blood-stained hands beside the murdered girl, unable even to assert his innocence, allowing himself to be led off to gaol without protest or remonstrance. (121)

Braddon intends the reader to remember these concluding words of volume I when hearing Urquhart's denunciation of incurable maladies as proof of the non-existence of a benevolent God.

In addition, at the conclusion of volume II (chapter 22), Sibyl is told that the evil vicar Carpew is unavailable and cannot provide either statement or evidence about the disappeared Mountford – all of which is a lie. Volume III opens with a first sentence mentioning John Coverdale, who will uncover that lie. Urquhart's rejection of Providence at the end of Volume III is undoubtedly reinforced by discovering how disgracefully a clergyman like Carpew can be purchased to contribute to the death-in-life confinement of an innocent man for ten years. Evidently, the vicar Carpew does not trust at all that God will provide for his large family. These strategic demarcations in the triple-decker format confirm Braddon's intention to force discussion about the detective supplanting the priest in the modern world.

Therefore, in solving a secular crime by tracking down Mountford, Coverdale, although a priest, has supplanted Providence, a Providence often invoked in sensation fiction but irrelevant to detection as practised by

Holmes, where emphatically the detective supplants the priest as society's preserver, rescuer and saviour. It is central to Braddon's argument that it is Sibyl Penrith who brings the priest/detective Coverdale and the atheist/murderer Urquhart into juxtaposition. Acting herself as detective, Sibyl Penrith provokes this metaphysical clash at the end of the Victorian age, for if God existed, in a perfect world there would be no need for a detective, only a priest. The example of Coverdale, however, demonstrates that it is not such a world: his toils in the East End as a priest catalyze his skills as a detective tracker of missing persons. His success in the latter means he has moved beyond the priestly to the detectival role. Muscular Christianity has evolved into secularized muscularity.

Maio observes about the conclusion of the novel: 'The women [Sibyl Penrith, Coralie Urquhart] are active survivors, while the restrictive men [Hubert Urquhart, the Earl of Penrith] are eliminated' (94). Sibyl Penrith marries Coverdale, and Coralie Urquhart marries Nicholas Hildrop at the end of the novel. Braddon disposes of the two marriages in a Postscript, thereby indicating she is merely going along with novelistic convention in both instances. One wonders, however, about Maio's statement that the women end up 'choosing their own men — both of whom are of the easily managed, nonauthoritarian variety' (94). Neither Coverdale nor Hildrop seems to be 'nonauthoritarian.'

The former Sibyl Penrith finds herself in an intense urban environment 'in the thick of the bitter battle, among the revolts and conspiracies of labour against capital, and the exactions and injustices of capital against labour . . . Here she must live through seasons of fear and sadness . . . Here she has to learn the lesson of life in all its stern reality' (339). As for Coralie, she is valued as a horsewoman and has that house in Mayfair, but she is married to the hunt and in the house at Mayfair, contrary to her fantasy, she will never be a novelist.

As Heidi Johnson observes about *Thou Art the Man*, 'Braddon is little concerned with the father's legal guilt or its public identification and punishment; instead, . . . she focuses on the more insidious psychological crimes that take place within the family and can only be resolved with the transformation of familial dynamics' (267). As can be seen in Coralie Urquhart's rejection of writing after discerning her father's criminality, these 'psychological crimes' can be devastating and decisive. These dynamics, however, affect not only Coralie Urquart but also Sibyl Penrith.

Sibyl never learns that Marie Arnold was the illegitimate daughter of her father Sir Joseph. In other words, she never becomes aware that her own father, albeit not a murderer, was a sexual predator like Hubert Urquhart. This fact adds a new significance to Sir Joseph Higginson's remark to Urquhart, when Urquhart asks for Marie Arnold's hand:

'It is not your wild oats I am thinking about, so much as the character of the sower . . . I have heard stories of your unkindness and neglect as a husband . . . To be frank with you once more, you are by no means the man I would choose [as husband for Marie Arnold].' (82)

In reality, Sir Joseph is protecting not only his ward but his illegitimate daughter. While he is being honest with Urquhart, he is also being a hypocrite. And Sir Joseph recognizes the contrasting masculinities of Mountford and Urquhart: 'You don't want to be in London, Mountford . . . You are not a man about town like Urquhart' (92). Sibyl Penrith had considered Marie an orphan companion. In this respect, the concealing of family secrets aligns *Thou Art the Man* with a range of Holmes narratives, especially in the short stories which began to appear in the *Strand* in 1891 and 1892 before the publication of *Thou Art the Man*.

Of these stories appearing the two years before Braddon's text, one thinks, for instance, of the diabolical step-father Mr Windibank in *A Case of Identity*, the renegade husband Neville St Clair in *The Man with the Twisted Lip*, the murderous step-father Dr Grimesby Roylott of *The Speckled Band*, the deceiving American woman Hatty Doran in *The Noble Bachelor*, the ghastly feud among sisters in *The Cardboard Box*, the inter-racial marriage of the American Effie Munro concealed from her English husband in *The Yellow Face*, and the sabotage of Percy Phelps by his future brother-in-law in *The Naval Treaty*.

In each of these instances, detection involves the exposure of dreadful family dissonances, as occurs in the murder of the Earl of Penrith by his half-brother Hubert Urquhart in *Thou Art the Man*. The mode of narration in the novel, furthermore, anticipates the complex strategy Doyle will employ in *The Hound of the Baskervilles* (1901-1902), where chapters 8 and 9 are letters from Watson to Holmes and chapter 10 is an extract from the diary of Watson.

In his famous evaluation of *Aurora Floyd* for the *Nation* in 1865, Henry James demarcated Braddon from other writers such as George Eliot or William Thackeray. James notes that while 'bigamy, murder, and arson are exceptional . . . Miss Braddon distributes these materials with a generous hand' (745). It is significant that of these three staples of the sensation novel, only murder appears in *Thou Art the Man*, an indication of Braddon's true intentions in this text.

The review of *Thou Art the Man* in the *Athenaeum* (30 June 1894) evaluated the story as a crime novel rather than as a detective text:

> The last of Miss Braddon's plots is not one of the most ingenious or natural. The new murderer [Hubert Urquhart] is a little too undiscriminating and the new mysteries [the murders of Marie Arnold and the Earl of Penrith; the confinement of Mountford for ten years] are too elaborately artificial. But there is plenty of them; the author never stints her readers of plot and developing incidents. The crimes of these three volumes (exceptionally atrocious ones) are complicated by a strain of epileptic tendencies [in Mountford], in the treatment of which Miss Braddon shows no slight skill. Of course there are some gruesome passages in *Thou Art the Man*. (833)

The reviewer then proceeds to quote Mountford's perception of Marie Arnold's dead body, isolating the most grim details:

> His hand touched another hand, his fingers closed automatically on the soft fabric of a woman's gown . . . He clutched that cold and stiffening hand . . . The hand that had been lying on her breast was wet and dabbled with blood . . . that thick and viscous fluid which covered his clammy fingers and trickled about his wrist. (107-8)

The use of ellipses in the review renders the discovery of Marie Arnold's body all the more gruesome, stressing the physical action rather than the psychological reaction which Braddon intersperses in the description, especially when Mountford wonders if the body is that of Sibyl Pentrith and slowly recognizes it is not.

This stress in the *Athenaeum* review on the criminous incidents rather than the detection is surprising, since the entire Volume III (chapters 23-32) is devoted to the detectival efforts of Sibyl Penrith and John Coverdale. Braddon signals this detectival intention in chapter 23 when Coverdale, after hearing the facts recounted by Sibyl, remarks: 'There can be no doubt it is a case for investigation' (238). In chapter 28, Coverdale will tell Sibyl: 'I have had to hunt for people in the East End, and I have found out there is only one way of doing it [searching on foot]' (288). Both of Coverdale's remarks could have been made by Sherlock Holmes. Coverdale designates the new genre which Braddon is attempting by emphasizing 'case' and 'investigation', words applied to secular detection, not to spiritual ministry.

In its review of *Thou Art the Man* on 28 July 1894, the *Spectator* believed the work to be 'far below her best' and 'hardly less conspicuously inferior to such early attempts as *Lady Audley's Secret*' (118). The review, however, ignores the new genre to which Braddon was aspiring after the Holmes manifestations of the early 1890s. The review continues: 'That the book has a certain quality of readableness is matter of course, for to genuine dullness Miss Braddon – who is a born teller of tales – could not possibly descend' (118). The animus of the reviewer to *Lady Audley's Secret* after three decades makes it impossible to recognize Braddon's new experiments in genre, the transition from sensation to detection, in *Thou Art the Man*.

This ability to tell tales, however, is put to new purposes in *Thou Art the Man*, which Braddon signals by evoking the famous title of Poe's story. As is clear from its contrast with *Lady Audley's Secret* (and its bigamy, impersonation, arson and male amateur sleuth), *Thou Art the Man* is Braddon's generic and narratological experiment to contribute to the tradition of the female detective at the end of the century. She is transforming female sensation into female detection – hence, in *Thou Art the Man* there is no bigamy, Providence, impersonation or arson, all former trademarks of sensation fiction.

Conan Doyle's Sherlock Holmes spurred Mary Elizabeth Braddon to new inflections of narrative, inflections reinforced by her strategizing of the triple-decker format. Braddon's fame did not deter her from making a transition from sensation to detection. She did it by creating a powerful female sleuth in Sibyl Penrith – a sibyl indeed.

Catherine Louisa Pirkis (1839-1910): *The Experiences of Loveday Brooke, Lady Detective* (1894)

One of the most important female detectives at the end of the nineteenth century in England was Loveday Brooke, created by Catherine Louisa Pirkis in six stories presented in the *Ludgate Monthly* from February through July in 1893. The book version of the tales was published as *The Experiences of Loveday Brooke, Lady Detective* in 1894, with a second edition published in 1895. The book version of the tales contained one narrative not included in the original six. As Michelle Slung notes in her introduction to the Dover edition, Pirkis had published previously, and she also took to some social activism. She and her husband, Frederick Pirkis, were ardent in the work of the National Canine Defence League, of which he became chairman. Slung notes that Catherine Pirkis 'wrote energetically in support of the anti-vivisection movement' (xiii). *Loveday Brooke* was to be her last work of fiction.

Like many female detectives who will come after her, Loveday Brooke often goes under a different identity or in disguise. She appears as someone's niece, as an amanuensis, a nursery governess, as an interior decorator, and, in the added final tale, without disguise as a lady detective. As Slung comments, her name 'Loveday' is a translation of the Latin *dies amoris*, which 'signifies a day set aside for the peaceful settling of disputes' (x). According to Slung, it was a name applied to both men and women in the Middle Ages, so there is a remnant of gender blurring in the name itself. Loveday Brooke is employed by Ebenezer Dyer, the 'chief of the well-known detective agency in Lynch Court, Fleet Street' (1). She and Dyer have a spirited, sometimes disputatious, relationship. Pirkis introduces some additional connotations in his surname, which might be read as 'die-her' or 'dye-her', the former suggesting potential oppression, the latter a compulsion to change the woman.

As Slung observes, Loveday Brooke is one of the century's 'odd women', so denominated in George Gissing's novel *The Odd Women* of 1893, the same year in which the Loveday Brooke series appeared. Like some of the women in Gissing's novel, Brooke is unmarried, self-sufficient, engaged in a profession, without attachments which might hinder or delay her work. In fact, Pirkis presents Loveday as not having any romantic interest in anyone. Even more striking is the fact that Loveday has no female friend or companion. She is completely self-defining and self-determining. In this respect, she differs from a detective like Dorcas Dene, created by George Sims in 1897, who must work to support her artist husband, whose blindness has made it impossible for him to pursue his career. The Loveday Brooke narratives have no Watson, so Pirkis manages to differentiate her detective from the Holmes texts not only by her sex but also by the narratology of the tales. As the denomination 'lady detective' indicates, however, Loveday Brooke negotiates the contradictory categories of being a lady while pursuing her own professional occupation. It is significant that only a few years later, in 1897, George Sims could entitle his series *Dorcas Dene, Detective*, no longer needing to append 'lady' to the title.

In the first case, *The Bag Left on a Door-step*, Loveday Brooke is defined, unusually, by what she is not:

> Loveday Brooke, at this period of her career, was a little over thirty years of age, and could be best described in a series of negations.
>
> She was not tall, she was not short; she was not dark, she was not fair; she was neither handsome nor ugly. Her features were altogether nondescript; her one noticeable trait was a habit she had, when absorbed in thought, of dropping her eye-lids over her eyes till only a line of eyeball showed, and she appeared to be looking out at the world through a slit, instead of through a window.
>
> Her dress was invariably black, and was almost Quaker-like in its primness. (2)

The narrative establishes the manner in which she came to 'the profession she had chosen' (3):

> Some five or six years previously, by a jerk of Fortune's wheel, Loveday had been thrown upon the world penniless and all but friendless. Marketable accomplishments she had found she had none, so she had forthwith defied convention, and had chosen for herself a career that had cut her off sharply from her former associates and her position in society. For five or six years she had drudged away patiently in the lower walks of her profession; then chance, or, to speak more precisely, an intricate criminal case, threw her in the way of the experienced head [Ebenezer Dyer] of the flourishing detective agency in Lynch Court . . . [Her] work . . . brought increase of pay and of reputation alike to him and to Loveday. (2-3)

Her employer, Ebenezer Dyer, is quick to defend her and her profession. In this defence, Pirkis, writing in 1894, feels it necessary to confront in the first tale the issue of the 'lady detective' as well as the unique qualifications she holds to be in the profession of detection:

> 'I don't care twopence-halfpenny whether she is or is not a lady. I only know she is the most sensible and practical woman I ever met. In the first place, she has the faculty — so rare among women — of carrying out orders to the very letter; in the second place, she has a clear, shrewd brain, unhampered by any hard-and-fast theories; thirdly, and most important item of all, she has so much common sense that it amounts to genius.' (3)

Pirkis feels it is necessary to defend the concept of a woman detective, and she is adroit in putting the defence of the profession in the declaration of a male character.

As will occur frequently in the tales, Loveday and a male frequently disagree. The narrator observes: 'There were occasions on which [Loveday Brooke and Ebenezer Dyer] were wont, so to speak, to snarl at each other', and Loveday asks Dyer in this instance not to be in 'such a hurry', making the request 'calmly' (3). One of the illustrations by Bernard Higham shows Loveday and Dyer across from one another at a desk, as she thrusts a newspaper cutting to him. As the cases represented underscore, Pirkis makes a point of showing Loveday in professional discussions with Dyer and with various policemen and detectives, often correcting their assumption of male superiority in reasoning. Pirkis does not make Loveday Brooke either eccentric or exotic, but she does make her emphatic.

In the first case presented, *The Black Bag Left on a Door-step*, published in the *Ludgate Monthly* in February 1893, Loveday Brooke undertakes to solve a robbery which occurred at Craigen Court, the residence of Sir George and Lady Cathrow. A young French maid, Stephanie Delcroix, has been suspected of the robbery. In contrast to the calm Loveday, the French maid is said to go 'from one fit of hysterics into another' (2). It turns out that one Harry Emmett is guilty of the robbery, having disguised himself as a curate to enter the house. The black bag refers to his leaving his disguise at the door of a spinster lady.

When Loveday Brooke arrives at Huxwell, she meets a detective, Jeremiah Bates, from Scotland Yard, who tells her they can solve the case easily with him working outside and she working 'inside the castle walls' (5). Bates believes that the French maid, being attractive, had a number of lovers, so she opened the window and unlocked the safe to enable one of these lovers to rob her mistress. This is presented as typical male, gender-biased commentary.

The housekeeper, Mrs Williams, also subscribes to male superior doctrines. When Loveday wishes to see a room in the home, the housekeeper cuts her by stating the 'gentlemen detectives' (8) have already been in the location. Loveday insists, changing 'from gossiping friendliness to that of the business woman hard at work at her profession' (8). Pirkis emphasizes that both males and many women will not concede that a female has equivalent or superior reasoning powers.

Brooke has to confront Jeremiah Bates again, when he gives a long explanation of the case, declaring that the French maid will be hunted down along with her lover accomplice. Bates decides to capture the woman at the train station, bragging that this deduction 'relieves my mind from all anxiety on the matter' (9). Loveday Brooke will not let this pass. She states: 'I can see another possible destination for the girl – the stream that runs through the wood' (9). By discovering that Harry Emmett had been a footman in the neighbourhood and also had a proclivity for recitations, and by figuring out it was Emmett's curatorial disguise left in the black bag, Loveday Brooke solves the case and brings in Dyer for the arrest. The French maid is found nearly drowned at the verge of a stream by the young farmer, Holt, who loves her.

Loveday Brooke demonstrates her ability to see through cabman's slang to trace Emmett to his current employer, the United Kingdom Cab-drivers' Beneficent Association. Her method is a 'chain of reasoning . . . step by step in her usual methodical manner' (11). Brooke's employer Dyer can only exclaim: 'You've surpassed yourself this time!' (14). Pirkis stresses in this initial story the rationality of her detective, her calm, her self-assurance and her ability to read evidence despite male interference. As a woman, she can create a narrative about crime different from that concocted by prejudiced, gender-biased male professionals, even ones like Jeremiah Bates from Scotland Yard. There is certainly a sub-textual advocacy that women ought to be admitted as detectives to Scotland Yard in *The Black Bag Left on a Door-step*.

The Murder at Troyte's Hill engages homicide. The lodge-keeper to Mr Craven of Troyte's Hill, Cumberland, one Alexander Henderson, is found murdered. It becomes clear that 'robbery was not the motive for the crime' which people suspect 'has been perpetrated by some lunatic, escaped or otherwise' (15). The household consists of the older Craven and his young son Harry, at nineteen 'as much a gentleman-blackleg as it is possible for such a young fellow to be' (16). Loveday is compelled to work with police inspector Griffiths of the Newcastle Constabulary, who thinks that Henderson and the younger Craven often disagreed and that therefore the young man is the suspect in the murder.

Loveday Brooke goes to Troyte's Hill as an amanuensis to the elder Craven, who is working on a multi-volumed project about comparative philology. When she arrives at the estate, Loveday discovers the young man is too ill to be seen, being kept upstairs and overseen by his vigilant mother. In the end, Loveday hears the rambling statements made by the old man, and she leads him into confessing that he is the murderer of Henderson. In his past, Craven had married a barmaid and then went to Natal and married again. Although the first wife had died, the fiendish Henderson had kept alive the idea that she was living, blackmailing Craven for thirty years. To learn this secret, Loveday had imperilled her life by being 'locked in with this lunatic' (28). She had perceived the deranged state of Craven's mind when he killed his retriever Captain in a philological experiment to learn if a dying dog let out a yelp or a groan.

Loveday is rescued by detectives for whom she had sent, suspecting that Craven was a madman. She admits 'I thought I was conducting my very last case – I never had such a narrow escape before!' (29). To avoid giving evidence against his father, young Harry Craven is shipped out to Natal by his mother, the typical case of exporting wastrel sons to the colonies. The person locked up in the sick-room at Troyte's Hill turns out to be the daughter, persecuted and forced into this masquerade by the mother to save the errant son. The locking up of women occurs in many nineteenth-century texts, from Maria Edgeworth's *Castle Rackrent* (1800) and Charlotte Brontë's *Jane Eyre* (1847) to Mary Elizabeth Braddon's *Lady Audley's Secret* (1862). The instance is especially disturbing in this tale, since the 'gaoler' is the young woman's own mother.

The Murder at Troyte's Hill makes the reader wonder if the surname 'Brooke' has any affinity with the Dorothea Brooke of George Eliot's

Middlemarch (1872). The aging obsessive scholar Craven in this tale evokes the similar case of Casaubon in Eliot's novel. There may be an echo as well of Eliot's heroine. Both Dorothea and Loveday strive to remedy difficult cases of hardship, at the same time attempting an independence. In Eliot, however, Dorothea marries Will Ladislaw, submerging her own strengths within his. Loveday Brooke, on the other hand, is the more independent woman of the two. It is possible that Pirkis's tale is a commentary on Eliot's novel, stressing that a woman can exist apart from the marriage plot of Victorian texts. The fact that *Middlemarch* contains crimes and a hidden past in the case of Bulstrode is another parallel that might align *The Murder at Troyte's Hill* with *Middlemarch*.

Loveday Brooke's next case, *The Redhill Sisterhood*, published in April 1893, concerns a group of non-denominational nuns who care for crippled children. When they appear in the neighbourhood, there is a string of gang robberies in the area. A group of male gang members contrives to make the authorities think the sisterhood is guilty of these thefts. One member of the sisterhood is Anna Lee, and it evolves that her father Arthur and her brother George are criminals and burglars. At one point, George Lee masquerades as a reporter, George White, to delude Loveday Brooke. In fact, he tells her he was present at the trial of Craven of Troyte's Hill, the killer from the previous case. Although he is her brother, George passes himself off as Anna Lee's lover.

Anna Lee is a victim of her criminal father and brother, having fled to the sisterhood to avoid them. Loveday thinks of her as an Andromeda, 'tied to my stake, helpless and hopeless' (36), an association pervasive in Victorian neoclassical paintings by such artists as Edward Poynter, William Richmond and Frederic Leighton, as has been examined by Kestner (1989, 1995). There is little doubt that Pirkis expects the reader to be familiar with some examples of this pictorial representation of Perseus and Andromeda. The striking feature of this case, however, is that it is a woman – Loveday Brooke – who plays the role of Perseus in freeing Anna Lee of these dreadful male relations.

Loveday travels to Redhill in a 'dreary November' (31) as a nursery governess. Inspector Gunning of the police believes the sisterhood is involved in the crimes, primarily because the face of one of the sisters, Sr Monica, is so repellant: 'Of all the lowest criminal types of faces I have ever seen, I think hers is about the lowest and most repulsive' (33) he tells Loveday. Loveday agrees the woman is very unattractive, but she also notices, as only a woman might, that Sister Monica is tender with the crippled children for whom she begs charity.

Another member of the gang, John Murray, had tried to get Loveday to believe the Redhill Sisterhood was the criminal gang, but Loveday refuses to follow the line that physiognomy indicates criminality. Through her investigation, and an adroit use of invisible ink, Loveday enables Mr Jameson and his two sons to apprehend the gang when they attempt to rob his house at North Cape. This house is interesting because it is lighted by electricity, which the gang thinks to cut at the time of the robbery.

Several elements are of importance in this case. First of all, *The Redhill Sisterhood* allows Pirkis to question the system by which physical appearance indicates criminality. Brooke tells her employer Dyer: 'I would like to ask some rabid physiognomist how he would account for Sister Monica's repulsiveness of feature as contrasted with young [George] Lee's undoubted good looks – heredity, in this case, throws no light on the matter' (44). As a female detective, she discounts a woman's features as a sign of innocence or guilt, unlike male counterparts with their gendered predispositions about women's physical appearance. About George Lee, the rogue brother, Brooke had noticed his hands were 'coarse and grimy as only a mechanic's could be' (45) although he pretended to be a reporter. She also noticed that the volume of Tennyson he carried with him was uncut.

Bernard Higham included an illustration of George Lee meeting Loveday Brooke, depicting him as a good-looking man. Surely this picture was completed to make Pirkis's point. Even the newspaper account of the capture of the gang states about George Lee: 'The boy is a handsome young fellow, but appears to have in him the makings of a first-class criminal' (44). So the press learns a valuable lesson from Loveday Brooke's investigation of this fake reporter. She had noticed when she first met the cyclist: 'The young man who thus accosted her had not the appearance of a gentleman' (37). He manages to take in everyone else, however.

Inspector Gunning praises electric lighting as a possible means of reducing criminality, but Loveday Brooke has other ideas:

> 'The burglars would find some way of meeting such a condition of things, depend upon it; they have reached a very high development in these days. They no longer stalk about as they did fifty years ago with blunderbuss and bludgeon; they plot, plan, contrive and bring imagination and artistic resource to their aid.' (33-4)

Loveday Brooke then muses: 'It often occurs to me that the popular detective stories, for which there seems so large a demand at the present day, must be, at times, uncommonly useful to the criminal classes' (34). This is quite a remarkable statement, in which Pirkis wonders if the genre in which she is working contributes to cultural malaise, even as she recognizes that crime has passed into a new phase of sophistication.

Dyer tells her at the beginning that women detectives are being more respected: 'The idea seems gaining ground in many quarters that in cases of mere suspicion, women detectives are more satisfactory than men, for they are less likely to attract attention' (31). In this story, however, Loveday undertakes surveillance, but she is also much under the surveillance of the criminal gang, such as the good-looking but dangerous George Lee. Nevertheless, Dyer's enthusiasm for women detectives is shown at the conclusion to be tempered, as he is 'not paying much heed to Loveday's digression' (45) about physiognomy and criminality, even though this is one of the key elements of the case of *The Redhill Sisterhood*. Its ultimate purpose is to contend that a woman is better off in a sisterhood than in a family of criminal males.

Loveday Brooke's next case is that of *A Princess's Revenge*, a narrative which allows Pirkis to introduce Victorian Orientalism. The Turkish Princess Dullah-Veih and a Mrs Druce induce her Swiss secretary Lucie Cunier to marry the butler, Pierre Lebrun, so that the Princess's fiancé, Major Druce (a callow flirt) will not lose his affection for her. The Princess wanted Lucie out of the way, since the Major was attracted to her. Mrs Druce, for her part, knows the Major must marry a rich woman, since he has debts: 'Knowing her son's extravagant habits and his numerous debts, it must have been patent to her that a rich wife was a necessity to him'; 'his attentions to the little Swiss girl [are] ill-advised' (48). The Major is described as 'a tall, handsome young fellow' who is 'well turned out' with 'moustache waxed, orchid in button-hole, light kid gloves and patent leather boots' (48). He appears suitably stylist and rakish in Bernard Higham's illustration.

Loveday Brooke takes the Major to the marriage ceremony at the Swiss Protestant Church to convince the Major that any overtures to Lucie Cunier are pointless. In any event, the secretary does love the butler: 'Lucie has married Lebrun of her own free will . . . Your evident admiration for [Lucie] disturbed the equanimity of the Princess, who saw your devotion to herself waning' (55) Loveday informs the Major.

In addition to introducing the Middle East into the narrative, Pirkis manages to make the tale almost a social satire. Mrs Druce is a woman capriciously devoted to one charity or rescue mission after another, as with the Harem Mission to help 'our sisters in the East' (47). The Major notes that at his mother's house there are 'Jews, Turks, heretics and infidels – all there' (48). The illustrations to the story by Bernard Higham are replete with women in Middle Eastern dress, an element undoubtedly captivating to readers, since these people are set in London drawing-rooms. Mrs. Druce is described as 'that essentially modern product of modern society – the woman who combines in one person the hard-working philanthropist with the hard-working woman of fashion' (50). The story implies that this combination is both calculated and frivolous.

The Middle Eastern characters are described with prejudicial epithets. The Princess 'with Eastern blood in her veins' has 'a violent and jealous temper' (47). The son of the Princess's guardian, Hafiz Cassimi, in love with the Princess, is 'a swarthy, well-featured man, with bold, black eyes' (50). It is intriguing that the Higham illustration of Cassimi bears a resemblance to the first illustration of Major Druce. One wonders whether Pirkis and her illustrator want to suggest that a predatory male – whether English or Eastern – is still the same undisciplined male. The Major calls Cassimi 'the Beast – Iago' (50), totally unaware that he and Cassimi are the same type.

When the Major asks Loveday Brooke what 'role [she] will take up this afternoon', Loveday decides to be what she is, a lady detective. Mrs Druce states the frequent objection to detectives: 'I am not accustomed to the presence of detectives in my house; . . . How do you mean to begin your investigations – by going over the house and looking in all the corners, or by cross-questioning the servants?' (52). A ring with Genevese associations, the milliner's label on a lady's hat and Loveday's observation of the drawing-room reception on a hot June afternoon all lead to her deductions. At the conclusion, Major Druce denies feebly any flirtation with Lucie Cunier: 'I only moved in the matter at all out of – of mere kindness to a young and friendless foreigner' (57). *A Princess's Revenge* indicts this callow and callous young man, and the ultimate revenge is that he is forced because of his wastrel habits to marry a wealthy Middle Eastern woman for whom he has no affection. The Major becomes the commodified object, as the Princess will use him to gain access to English upper middle-class society. Major Druce 'drawls' that this is 'like a fairy tale' (57), but in his case it is a potential nightmare.

In *Drawn Daggers*, the focus is again on a marriage plot, but now literally so. Miss Monroe, an heiress, has an Irish girl, Mary O'Grady of Cork, impersonate her in London so she can meet and marry her lover (whom she knew in Peking) William Wentworth Danvers in the interval. The three principals (Monroe, Danvers, and O'Grady) communicate by drawing daggers – really heraldic crosses, to communicate by letters. Loveday Brooke, having seen letters with a single dagger and with two daggers, deciphers this little code by cleverly using a letter with three heraldic daggers to expose the plot.

Her client is a Reverend Anthony Hawke, a clergyman of the Church of England. Monroe's father, Sir George Monroe, has planned to 'get her out of the way of a troublesome and undesirable suitor' (58), but the young woman manages to foil her father. The commentary about marriage extends to the Rev Hawke, who throughout the narrative (60-63, 65, 71) makes constant reference to his termagant wife. Although he tells Dyer that he is 'master in his own house' (60) for example, he confesses that his wife 'has a very firm, resolute manner' (61). Loveday quickly discovers that Miss Monroe is 'a young lady of independent habits' (61). Those two nations dreaded by Victorians contribute to this independence, since Miss Monroe was educated 'by a succession of French and American governesses' (61).

In contrast to the previous tale, Loveday in *Drawn Daggers* goes to Hawke's home as a 'lady house decorator' (62), a role peculiar to the lady detective, since Dyer wants her 'to begin her work inside [the] house' (62). On investigating the room of the supposed Miss Monroe, Loveday concludes it is too neat and orderly to be a real lady's. Instead, she deduces that Mary O'Grady is a lady's maid, impersonating Miss Monroe. This detail is one, of course, only a female detective could perceive. However, to decipher the communication by drawn daggers, Loveday Brooke does research at the British Museum about 'the various crosses borne on armorial shields' (67). Loveday also notices the Irish pronunciation of a word, which betrays that the young woman in Hawke's house is not Miss Monroe but Mary O'Grady.

Most striking about the case is that it begins with what appear to be two separate cases, the instance of the drawn daggers and also that of a lost necklace. Dyer argues that the two are unrelated: 'The episode of the drawn daggers . . . should be treated entirely on its own merits, considered as a thing apart from the loss of the necklace' (59) he stresses to Loveday Brooke. As with Jeremiah Bates of Scotland Yard in *The Black Bag Left on a Door-step* and Inspector Griffiths in *The Murder at Troyte's Hill*, Brooke draws a conclusion different from those of men, who mis-read and mis-interpret the evidence.

Loveday Brooke is not afraid to assert: 'I think we are bound to look at the other side of the case, and admit the possibility of these daggers being sent in right-down sober earnest by persons concerned in the robbery' (60). Brooke proves that the necklace was given by Miss Monroe to her lover Danvers to get money to obtain passage to follow her to England. In *Drawn Daggers*, Loveday Brooke reveals the true state of marriage in middle-class homes: the renegade daughter marries her love against the father's wishes, and the clergyman is scarcely master in his own house. Each instance demonstrates the newly independent status of the married woman in the last decade of the nineteenth century, resulting from legal protections such as the various Married Women's Property Acts, which induce a novel freedom of inclination.

One of the most unusual elements of the next Loveday Brooke tale, *The Ghost of Fountain Lane*, is its subject – religious fanaticism linked with crime. In this story, Brooke proves that the former Wesleyan now millenarian preacher Richard Steele, and one of his congregation, Maria Lisle, stole a blank cheque from the Rev Charles Turner, Vicar of East Downes. In reality, Steele and Lisle were defrauding the congregation by pretending the money was for resettlement of the saved to Judea. Loveday Brooke, 'overtaxed in mind and body' (72), has taken a holiday to Brighton. Inspector Clampe, of the Local District Constabulary, interrupts Brooke's holiday.

As in *Drawn Daggers*, where the two cases involving the missing necklace and the daggers are in reality one, here also the case involves two elements, the theft of the cheque and the appearance of a ghost who resembles Napoleon. Steele has turned many in the area into millenarians with his forceful but fanatical preaching that the world will end in 1901.

Inspector Clampe's suspicion falls on Turner's wife, who is both hard-featured and a Roman Catholic, which means that she and her husband have frequent quarrels about religion and money, making the marriage uneasy. To Clampe, the case is clear: 'Three parts cunning to one of simplicity is precisely what lady criminals are composed of' (75) he informs Brooke. Brooke, however, trails Maria Lisle to a summer-house, where she finds the diary of the woman along with fanatical books. Brooke also learns that among millenarians Napoleon is often identified with Apollyon and the 'great battle of Armageddon' (81). Steele tells his congregation: 'A Napoleon it will be who, in that day, will stand as the embodiment of Satanic majesty' (81).

Brooke recognizes that for this sect, the 'evil Apollyon' is embodied 'in the person of a descendant of the great Emperor' (83). The ghost, seen by Martha Watts in the house of Freer the shoemaker, a fervid Wesleyan/millenarian, is the product of these wild sermons and the girl's imagination. Steele and Lisle are arrested while Steele is haranguing his flock. As Brooke notes, 'I came to connect a stolen cheque with a "ridiculous ghost"' (82). The story condemns 'the mischief that the sensational teaching of these millenarians is doing at the present moment' (82). The cultural critique comes in Brooke's final assessment of the case:

> 'The world, it seems to me, abounds in people who are little more than blank sheets of paper, on which a strong hand may transcribe what it will – hysteric subjects, the doctors would call them; hypnotic subjects others would say; really the line that divides the hysteric condition from the hypnotic is a very hazy one.' (83)

Brooke thinks that Maria Lisle is 'not one of the criminal classes, but a religious enthusiast' (82) who needs to be put away at Broadmoor for some rational correction. Relatively few detective stories link crime with religion or religion with hysteria, but Pirkis obviously feels, at the end of the century, that this millenarian thinking is dangerous in its irrationality and can be discussed within the parameters of a tale like *The Ghost of Fountain Lane*. 'Ghost-seeing is quite as catching as scarlet-fever or measles . . . Don't you think the converse of the saying is true also, and that "believing is seeing"?' she speculates (84).

The Ghost of Fountain Lane was Pirkis's last Loveday Brooke story published in the *Ludgate Monthly*. When the book version of the tales appeared in 1894, Brooke added a final story, *Missing!*, to the collection. It is a story of an unpleasant marriage and its consequences. Loveday Brooke proves that the dead woman, drowned on the estate of Langford Hall, is a Mr Richard Golding's first wife, the Italian Irene Mascagni, who had left him years before. Their daughter, René, had fled the country to see her dying mother in Italy. It results that the mother had left Italy, dressed as her daughter, to make amends with her husband, Golding. This woman 'had been cruelly treated alike by husband [Golding] and [her] father' (97), Count Mascagni of Alguida in southern Italy.

When the wife returns to Langford Hall, she sees Golding with the woman he intends to marry, the unpleasant Clare Greenhow, and leaves in a rainstorm. She falls into or deliberately throws herself into a pool. She had always disliked 'the rigid conventionality of English domestic life' (98), having many years before left her husband to become an actress back in her native Italy, although her maid led Golding to believe his wife was dead. Lord Guilleroy brings the daughter René back from Italy. This reunion probably means that Golding will not marry Clare Greenhow, about whom Brooke had thought 'the velvet paw and the hidden claw' (88). For her part, Clare Greenhow believes that 'lady detectives . . . were a race apart' (93).

Pirkis stresses the professional circumstances of Loveday Brooke in this final tale. Loveday declares that the local detective, Ramsay, is 'the country inspector to the backbone! He'll keep a case in his own hands so long as there's a chance of success; then, when it becomes practically hopeless, hand it over to you just to keep his own failure in countenance by yours' (85). Dyer agrees but urges her to take the case: 'Business has been slack of late – expenses are heavy' (95). Loveday tells Dyer sharply that with ten days having passed since the disappearance of the daughter, 'it would have been better, for the credit of the office, if you had declined such a hopeless affair' (86). Exasperated, she explains her theory to Dyer, who should know better:

> 'After ten days! . . . when the house has settled down into routine, and every one has his story cut and dried, and all sorts

of small details have been falsified or smudged over! Criminal cases are like fevers; they should be taken in hand within twenty-four hours.' (85-6)

Brooke goes to the estate as herself: 'In the circumstances no disguise as to her name and profession had been deemed necessary' (87).

As Brooke's rebuke to her employer Dyer indicates, in *Missing!* this female detective is all business. The local inspector, Ramsay, had strictures about her 'leisurely handling of the case', which 'had put [Loveday] upon her mettle, and she had decided that Ramsay and his colleagues should be taught that Lynch Court [Dyer's agency] had a special way of doing things, and could hold its own with the best' (93). At the conclusion of the case, Loveday Brooke tells Ramsay: 'To be quite frank with you, I would have admitted you long ago into my confidence, and told you, step by step, how things were working themselves out, if you had not offended me by criticising my method of doing my work' (95).

Pirkis intended to conclude the book version of *The Experiences of Loveday Brooke, Lady Detective*, with the strongest possible assertion of the detective's professionalism and independence. Her frank discussion of the profession with both Dyer and Ramsay reveals she is completely unafraid to assume an equal place with them. Unlike other female detectives to follow her, who will be married or who wish to aid husbands, Loveday Brooke is indeed an 'odd woman.'

But this is so not merely because she is a woman and unmarried and professional. It is the result of her repudiating male cultural gendered expectations about women by being assertive, courageous, defiant and self-reliant when confronting murder (*The Murder at Troyte's Hill*), embezzlement, (*The Ghost of Fountain Lane*), theft (*The Black Bag Left on a Door-step*), criminal gangs (*The Redhill Sisterhood*), impersonation (*Drawn Daggers*), or male harassment of women (*A Princess's Revenge*). Her independence, indeed, is striking among female detectives of her era, extending to willingness to confront male colleagues as an indisputable equal. Catherine Louisa Pirkis merits inclusion among the most forward-thinking of writers about the female detective – and about late-Victorian culture.

Elizabeth B. Corbett (1846-c. 1922): *When the Sea Gives Up Its Dead* (1894)

In addition to Braddon's *Thou Art the Man* and Pirkis's *Loveday Brooke*, the year 1894 saw the appearance of a third text of importance to the tradition of the female detective in fiction of the late Victorian period. This volume was *When the Sea Gives Up Its Dead* by Elizabeth Burgoyne [Mrs George] Corbett. Its protagonist, Annie Cory, is one of the most significant of female amateur detectives in the literature. By the time of the publication of *When the Sea Gives Up Its Dead*, Corbett had already produced several dramas as well as novels, including *Mrs Grundy's Victims* in 1893 about the white slave trade (Blain 237). As with other narratives about female detectives during the era, Annie Cory's adventures contain certain established motifs, such as the ability of the female detective to engage in disguise and her easy reception into domestic spaces.

Corbett's narrative concentrates on the situation of Harley Riddell, who is unjustly accused of and convicted of having stolen diamonds from the firm where he has been the manager for 8 years, owned by two brothers, David and Samuel Stavanger, and another partner, Edward Lyon. As the reader learns through Annie Cory's earliest detection, the guilty party is Hugh Stavanger, David Stavanger's son, who stole the diamonds to pay off debts. Harley Riddell is sentenced to five years' penal servitude.

Annie Cory, Harley Riddell's fiancée, determines to prove his innocence. When Harley's twin brother, Hilton, proposes that a 'principal lady detective' from a private inquiry agency be sent as governess to the home of David Stavanger to gather information, instead Annie Cory, aged 20, declares: 'Not another word, I will turn detective, and beard these lions in their own den' (16-17). Her father, John Cory, endorses this idea, upon which he 'found himself enrolled as an amateur detective, liable to be called upon for active service at any time' (17). While Annie Cory receives assistance from her father and her lover's twin brother Hilton Riddell, eventually she strikes out on her own as a detective.

Corbett stresses that Annie Cory is unlike a woman being raised as another Angel in the House: 'Annie, instead of moping at home and giving way to melancholy, was bent upon yielding efficient help as a lady detective' (17). Cory's aunt, Margaret Cory, advises her that 'when one takes up detective work, one has not to be too squeamish about the ways and means' (17). Cory takes the position as governess in the Stavanger household.

David Stavanger's wife treats Cory as the governess with contempt: 'She apparently imagines that a woman who is compelled to earn her living in any shape or form is no longer deserving of respect or civility' (20).

Ignoring this scorn, Annie Cory conceals herself behind the window draperies and overhears an interview between David Stavanger and his rogue son Hugh, in the course of which she learns that Hugh Stavanger stole the diamonds and that the parlour-maid, Wear, saw the stones and is now blackmailing the family. Perceiving that Hugh Stavanger will make an escape by sea, Annie urges Hilton Riddell to sign on board the ship regardless of his inaptitude for sea duties.

Two elements of significance emerge from this designation of the guilty party. First, the fact that the son is the thief demonstrates that there can be no separation of public from private morality: crime in the figure of the son has invaded the middle class home. Second, that Corbett reveals the true criminal so early in the text (chapter 3) discloses that its purpose is not to name the scoundrel but to detail the operations of its female detective. The stress is not on the product of the investigatory practise but on its process.

Early in *When the Sea Gives Up Its Dead*, moreover, Corbett addresses the ambiguity of this entire process of detection, especially its association with spying and surveillance. As Anthea Trodd (1989) has studied in careful detail, the anxiety about servants spying on the household was extensive in Victorian England. 'The middle-class home often appears as a beleaguered castle . . . Many fears of endangered privacy and resentments of the individual's exposure to internal surveillance are concentrated on the servants' (6). Servants are viewed 'as fifth columnists in the home' (8). In Corbett's text, scarcely has the robbery been committed than the parlour-maid is blackmailing her employer. Trodd observes:

> Servants were the necessary guarantors of social status. They were also an unacceptable obstacle to the growing demand for privacy. On this contradiction the domestic crime intrigues of Victorian fiction situate themselves . . . Servants were seen as the weak point . . . [They] might aggressively manipulate their knowledge of the family for their own ends. (49, 53)

Dickens in *David Copperfield* (1850) and *Bleak House* (1853), Braddon in *Lady Audley's Secret* (1862) and *Aurora Floyd* (1863) and George Eliot in *Felix Holt, the Radical* (1866) reveal this anxiety about servants as spies. Trodd rightly stresses the importance to this motif of Conan Doyle's Holmes short story *The Musgrave Ritual* published in May 1893 in the *Strand Magazine*, where Brunton the butler and Rachel the housemaid obtain knowledge sufficient to bring down the house. Mrs Henry Wood's *East Lynne* (1861) has the former lady of the house return as governess, in effect a spy on/in her own household. Pirkis's Loveday Brooke, previously discussed, disguises herself as a nursery governess in *The Redhill Sisterhood*. The governess who takes a position to learn secrets is central to Conan Doyle's Holmes tale *The Copper Beeches* published in June 1892 in the *Strand*.

In Corbett's novel, Annie Cory as governess does learn the vital secret of Hugh Stavanger's guilt, but the young detective demonstrates her aunt's dictum about the need to be daring rather than scrupulous when undertaking detection. When she first arrives at the Stavanger house, Annie reflects when she learns information from her young charge, Fanny Stavanger: 'I am, I suppose, not yet quite inured to my duties as detective, for I felt downright mean when listening to Fanny' (22). She thinks of herself as 'playing the eavesdropper' (26). Corbett endorses Annie's activities, but she is careful to modulate her success by noting the element of spying involved in detection. The parallels between Annie Cory as the spying detective governess and Wear the blackmailing parlour-maid are unmistakable.

Later, through Annie's information, Hilton Riddell follows Hugh Stavanger, who uses the alias 'Paul Torrens', aboard the *Merry Maid* in the thief's flight from England. Masquerading as a steward 'William Trace', Riddell observes through a peephole the cabin of Captain Cochrane, who demands from Stavanger a share of the stolen diamonds. But Cochrane in turn spies on Riddell removing his disguise and reflects: 'The steward had evidently been officiating as spy, or detective, whichever he might like to call himself' (58), and even Riddell regards his work as 'espionage' (59). Thus, while Annie and Hilton are trying to save an innocent man, they learn that in detection the end sometimes justifies the means.

The Captain and Hugh Stavanger murder Hilton Riddell and toss him overboard soon after Hilton leaves a message about his discoveries in a bottle which eventually washes ashore, unluckily found and destroyed by David Stavanger, the thief's father. Before leaving England, Hugh Stavanger has poisoned the parlour-maid, Wear, to prevent her from divulging his guilt. He leaves with the connivance of his father, David Stavanger. Corbett's amateur detective Annie Cory is up against fiendishly professional antagonists in the Stavangers and the Captain. Annie is described as 'plucky' (32), but she is also in a dubiously moral universe.

In no other novel involving female detection during the period is the motif of disguise and transvestite costume so prevalent. Annie and her father pursue Stavanger to Malta under the assumed names of Mr and Miss Waine. Soon, however, Annie resorts to disguising herself as a young man, when their initial pursuit of Stavanger is foiled. 'We must disguise ourselves effectually' she advises her father; 'we have a great stake to play for, and we intend to win' (111). Corbett describes the consequence:

> The result of the conversation that now ensued between father
> and daughter was a complete change in the appearance of both
> of them, and those who could recognise Mr Cory or his daughter
> in the elderly clergyman who was supposed to be the tutor and
> travelling guide of the rather delicate-looking young Englishman
> who accompanied him would have to be extremely wide-awake.
> There was no cessation of watchfulness on the part of the so-
> called Rev Alexander Bootle and Mr Ernest Fraser. (111-12)

In male attire, Annie Cory assumes new confidence: 'As time wore on, she
became more brave, nay, positively daring, and showed such skill in safely
following up clues that her father no longer felt any uneasiness about her
. . . She had retained her masculine clothing, without which it would not
have been so easy for her to penetrate unobserved into all sorts of places'
(121). In having her detective resort to male disguise, Corbett follows the
model of Irene Adler in Conan Doyle's famous Holmes tale *A Scandal in
Bohemia* published in the *Strand* in July 1891. This transgression of gendered
borders serves to empower Annie Cory, as it had Irene Adler. Corbett
indicates that gendered behaviours are questions of culturally-determined
scripts rather than innate nature and that gender is a matter of performance.

Particularly unusual about this transvestism in *When the Sea Gives Up Its
Dead* is the fact that Annie Cory is not the first woman to don male attire in
the novel. Her father's sister and her aunt, Margaret Cory, wears some of
her brother's clothes to go to the docks to find the ship, *Merry Maid*, on
which Hugh Stavanger intends to sail. As she narrates:

> 'Women, at least respectable women, don't hang about the dock
> gates at night unless they are on the look out for some particular
> ship. I am not one to stick at trifles, but I did not want to be
> mistaken for somebody who wasn't respectable, and I did want
> to be as unnoticed as possible. So I just got dressed in one of
> your suits, put my hair out of the way – there isn't much of it –
> donned a long top-coat and took an old hat, and set off for
> Millwall. I took the Underground, and changed at Mark Lane. At
> Fenchurch Street I just caught a train starting for the docks.' (42)

Thus, a woman of a generation previous to the detective's has already
engaged in this transgressive practise.

Corbett underscores this component of her narrative by indicating that
Annie's assumption of male attire influences not only her appearance but
also her responses. When Annie asks an investigating detective, John Gay
(who had arrested her lover) a hazardous question, the narrator notes:
'[Annie's] assumption of masculine garb made it more imperative upon her

to keep her composure than would have been the case had she been figuring simply as Annie Cory' (130). When Gay leaves her, he 'went away with a higher admiration of Annie Cory's pluck than he had ever felt for that of any woman in his life' (132). Even this tough detective acknowledges that Cory does not conform to gendered expectation:

> 'She is game to the core . . . and if anybody can help the poor fellow [Harley Riddell] in gaol, it is his sweetheart, who, it seems to me, cannot be daunted. She is one in a million. Most girls would have sat down and fretted, instead of trying to remedy the evil. Well, good luck to her, say I. If a girl like that doesn't deserve to succeed, nobody does.' (132)

As Ernest Fraser, Cory appears 'a rather handsome young fellow, with short, dark hair, bright dark blue eyes, and a dark moustache' (135). By this time, Annie is intercepting mail – blatantly illegal – in her pursuit of Stavanger. Corbett makes a slip in calling the disguised Annie 'Ernest Bootle' (137) from this point on in the narrative. Nevertheless, her aunt can note her 'pluck' (139). Corbett appropriates this quality, usually attributed to males, without hesitation to apply to her female detective. Both women and men acknowledge Annie Cory's daring.

To demonstrate her intention in *When the Sea Gives Up Its Dead* to interrogate gendered behaviours, Corbett also addresses several cultural models of masculinity. One of these is the template of St George. A Portuguese ship captain, Quaco Pereiro of the *Halcyon*, hears a shriek from the waters and rescues Hilton Riddell. Pereiro had called on his patron saint, St George, to aid him in the rescue. It turns out that Captain Cochrane and Hugh Stavanger had not killed Hilton, whose life is saved by an inflatable waistcoat. Corbett shows the fluidity of gender markers beyond nationality, applying the saint's ability to rescue to a Portuguese navigator.

Evoking St George in her novel, Corbett suggests the location of her text in the broad cultural interest in St George. The figure of the saint appears extensively in literature, prominently in texts ranging from Braddon's *Lady Audley's Secret* to Thomas Hardy's *The Return of the Native* (1878). Conan Doyle had used the saint as patron of a charity where Nancy Barclay works in *The Crooked Man*, a Holmes tale published in June 1893, a month after *The Musgrave Ritual*. In her depiction of the servant Wear, Corbett probably draws on the latter story, just as the references to St George draw on the former. The saint had also figured in Grant Allen's short story *The Prisoner of Assiout* published in August 1891 in the *Strand*. Given that Grant Allen was to write two famous texts about female detectives, *Miss Cayley's Adventures* and *Hilda Wade*, within a few years, it is probable that he had perused Corbett's text, as both of Allen's protagonists travel extensively in their investigative pursuits.

Furthermore, as Corbett must be aware, St George figures significantly in the fine art of the period (Kestner 1995, 103-104, 118-120). As early as 1857, Dante Gabriel Rossetti was depicting the saint, and William Morris finished a cabinet painted with motifs of the saint's life in 1862. His friend Edward Burne-Jones undertook a series of panels about the saint for the dining room of Myles Birket Foster's house The Hill from 1865 to 1867. Later, Burne-Jones finished two canvases of the triumphant saint in 1877 and 1898. Other artists who completed canvases or sculptures of the saint include George Hitchcock (1897), Henry Fehr (1898), Briton Riviere (1900), and Solomon Solomon (1906). In his *Scouting for Boys* in 1908, Robert Baden-Powell designated St George as the patron saint of scouts, a model of their chivalrous tenets.

Many of these images depict the rescue of a woman by the male saint. In *When the Sea Gives Up Its Dead*, Corbett adopts the model to a Portuguese ship captain, applying the English masculine paradigm to a foreigner who rescues an Englishman. This shading of national pre-eminence corresponds to the larger narrative revealing the rescue of another Englishman, Harley Riddell, by a woman detective, Annie Cory. Where the role of rescuer was previously associated with males, Corbett subverts this gendered expectation in *When the Sea Gives Up Its Dead* when the woman rescues the man.

On the other hand, Corbett does not allow Anglo-Saxon manhood to be outshone in her text. She describes Captain Pereiro as follows:

> Short, stout, of stolid feature; black-haired, rough-bearded, and carelessly shaven; with dark eyes, whose kindly light was almost obscured by bushy, overhanging eyebrows; of the swarthiest complexion; with big, coarse hands, and a rough gait, and with all the eccentricities of his appearance accentuated by a sublime indifference to the advantages of becoming attire, Captain Pereiro was not one to strike the casual observer with enthusiastic admiration. (147)

When they see the body of Hilton Riddell, the sailors remark: 'He is a beautiful man, as beautiful as the fabled gods must have been' (147). When he recovers, the crew notices his physical distinction:

> Some of them – indeed, all – used as they were to swarthy skins, and dusky locks, looked upon his smart, upright physique, his clear, fair skin, just relieved from effeminacy by being slightly

tanned, his finely-cut features, his wavy, flaxen hair, his expressive grey eyes, and his small hands and feet, as the perfection of all that was gallant and beautiful in man. By-and-bye [sic] they also began to admire him for other than his physical qualities. (151)

Since Hilton is the twin brother of Harley Riddell, his physical beauty must also be attributed to the unlucky prisoner. Annie Cory's efforts on behalf of her fiancé, therefore, are also inspired by racial motives to preserve Anglo-Saxon purity. Corbett's stress on Hilton Riddell's physical beauty reinforces this pre-eminence in the face of considerable concerns about the racial degeneracy of Englishmen during the 1890s and later. In 1902 and 1903 John Frederick Maurice, for example, published two essays in the *Contemporary Review*, the first with the ominous title 'Where to Get Men' (Kestner 2000, 7). In that essay, Maurice argued that about 60 per cent of those presenting themselves for military service were rejected by doctors as unfit. Thus, if Corbett's agenda is to empower women by the daring of Annie Cory, it is also to reinforce white predomination.

This agenda of reinforcing white and specifically English superiority, male and female, is underscored by the title Corbett selects for her text, *When the Sea Gives Up Its Dead*, which derives from the theme of the Apocalypse based on the Revelation of St John the Divine (Revelation 20:13): 'And the sea gave up the dead in it, Death and Hades gave up the dead in them, and all were judged by what they had done.' Corbett refers to her title six times in the course of the text. The title, with its stress on revelation and judgement, is astutely suitable to a detective text.

The first allusion to the biblical passage is in a letter from David Stavanger to his evil son Hugh, which records the death of the firm's partner Edward Lyon in a collision at sea: 'He himself [Lyon] is powerless to do you further injury unless the sea gives up its dead' (103). Hugh Stavanger reflects: 'The sea can't give up its dead, at any rate not in such a condition as to be able to speak against me' (105). Hence, initially it is the evil men who take consolation from the biblical lines. Annie Cory's aunt and father note that old Mrs Riddell must 'awaken to the bitter truth that the sea will not give up its dead [Hilton Riddell]' (141). The narrator comments that Stavanger and Captain Cochrane, in supposedly murdering Hilton Riddell, felt 'secure in the reflection that, as the sea was not likely to give up its dead, they were not likely to be confronted with Hilton Riddell again' (146). The complicit David Stavanger, in the delirium of brain fever at the conclusion of the novel, still raves: 'Neither he nor you can prove aught against my son – unless the sea gives up its dead!' (218).

At the novel's conclusion, Hugh Stavanger and Captain Cochrane are indicted and tried for theft and murder. Here, Corbett's title merges with the issues of gender raised by the novel. The presiding judge, unnamed, is the same individual who oversaw the conviction and sentencing of Harley Riddell at the beginning of the narrative. By this time, Annie Cory's exploits have been given wide circulation in the popular press. The judge is prejudiced against the case because of Annie Cory's fame:

> He had read all about Annie's adventures, and had at once dubbed her in his own mind an unwomanly schemer. He didn't like unwomanly women. They set a bad example to others. Therefore an example must be made of them, and they must be shown that the dictum of one of her Majesty's judges cannot be lightly upset. Poor man! He was but human, and he could hardly be expected to view with favour an attempt to upset the judgment he had himself given when Harley Riddell was tried for the diamond robbery. (225)

When all seems lost because of the judge's gender bias, Hilton Riddell, restored from the sea, reappears to give the testimony that frees his brother Harley and confirms the success of Annie Cory. The narrator stresses that Hilton Riddell 'had been given up by the sea for their [Hugh Stavanger's and Captain Cochrane's] undoing . . . Hilton's opportune return wrought the condemnation of villainy' (226). The 'revelation' is that the innocent and guilty are appropriately judged.

In selecting her title, which resolves issues of both gender and justice, Corbett may have been specifically invoking an event of 1894. In that year, Henry Tate had presented to the Tate Gallery a canvas by Frederic Leighton, painted c. 1892, entitled *And the sea gave up the dead which were in it*. Leighton had been elected President of the Royal Academy in 1878 and been knighted the same year. The canvas was well known from exhibition reviews of 1892, and Leighton's pre-eminence made it conspicuous. Corbett undoubtedly knew the painting.

Corbett's description of the plight of Hilton Riddell cast on the sea evokes the depiction of the dead rising out of the ocean at the Apocalypse in Leighton's canvas: 'Not only was it evident whence the cry proceeded, but the hands of the supposed corpse were thrown up imploringly, yet feebly, as though by one from whom the vital spark had nearly fled' (144). In particular, this description would appear derived from the male figure in the mid-distance at the right of the canvas, who is represented with upraised arms emerging from his shroud. He has the tanned skin and impressive form Corbett ascribes to Hilton Riddell. The body, inspired by Michelangelo, appears resurrected from deterioration, its nobility of form confirming the resurrection of the white race from any degeneration.

Furthermore, the roundel form of the canvas suggests both the eye (spying/surveillance) and a peephole, the latter figuring in the fates of Captain Cochrane and Hilton Riddell in the narrative.

This association of males with the sea is also part of a larger Victorian pictorial tradition of painting the male nude, often in connection with mythological episodes involving men and water (Kestner 1995, 235-289). Some examples include Leighton's *Daedalus and Icarus* of 1869, Herbert James Draper's *The Lament for Icarus* of 1898, William Blake Richmond's *Hermes* (1886), and Briton Riviere's *Prometheus* (1889) and *Dead Hector* (1892). Each of these combines a male nude with some marine component. While several of the legends involve catastrophe, the aspiration associated with each legend is admired, very parallel to the daring if rash investigation undertaken by Hilton Riddell on behalf of his brother. Corbett's emphasis on Hilton's body and his ultimately fortunate and heroic survival is contextualized in the fine art of the period.

Such emphasis on dimensions of gender construction is strongly marked in the final episodes of *When the Sea Gives Up Its Dead*. In tracking Hugh Stavanger to Spain, Annie Cory is compelled to dual impersonations, one male (Ernest Bootle) and one female (the artist Una Stratton). Cory's final disguise as a female artist suggests the correlation of the novel with contemporaneous subjects in painting. Staying in the same boarding house as Stavanger, who now uses the alias Gregory Staines, Cory transforms herself back and forth from male to female to observe him. As a male she accompanies Stavanger to gambling hotels; as a female she flirts with him at the boarding house dining table. She thinks of herself as both 'a modified Delilah' and 'a syren' (175), deploying 'a wonderful assumption of ingenuousness' (176) to deceive Stavanger.

For his part, Staines/Stavanger behaves as a self-involved male, believing Stratton is 'struck with' him (175), reflecting: 'I can have things pretty much my own way with women, if I like to lay myself out to please them' (178). For her part, Cory notes: 'It doesn't take much manoeuvring to throw dust in the eyes of a vain man' (179). Staines regards her as 'his willing prey' (181), while she becomes used 'to the necessity for a certain amount of deception' (181).

The wavering of gendered disguises prompts some linguistic contortion on the part of the narrator. For example:

> But he, or rather she, would have braved much greater inconveniences than these. (170)
> 'Mr Bootle' prepared to sally forth on her evening's adventures, of which she by no means underestimated the possible peril. (199)

> Had 'Mr Bootle' looked round, he, or she, if the reader prefers, might possibly have seen a mortal enemy. (199)

The narrator focuses on the implications of the female detective's disguises, which call into question the construction of gendered behaviours by the culture.

When Annie Cory notes she might be a 'syren' (175), the novel suggests another dimension of its marine title. Victorian painting was replete with figures of sirens and mermaids luring unwary males to disaster in canvases by such artists as William Etty (1837), William Frost (1849), Frederic Leighton (1858), Edward Burne-Jones (1870), Arthur Hacker (1897) and John William Waterhouse (1901). Representations of the legend of Ulysses and the sirens by such artists as Waterhouse (1891) and Draper (1909) alluded to women's empowerment and male fears of this process (Kestner 1989 *passim*). As a female detective, Annie Cory assumes powers she did not imagine she possessed in order to save her lover from an unjust sentence.

In *When the Sea Gives Up Its Dead*, Corbett establishes this empowerment as the text advances. In the beginning, Annie Cory is joined in her detection by her father John and her fiancé's brother Hilton. Once she adopts the disguise of the woman painter Una Stratton, however, she is working alone: Corbett withdraws male involvement. Like other detectives from 1888 to 1894, Annie Cory exhibits a daring, intelligence and skill which delineate a breaking away from patriarchal systems of control. In moving beyond the insularity of England, as does her predecessor Miriam Lea of *Mr Bazalgette's Agent*, Annie Cory anticipates the global range of female detectival activity that will appear in the final years of the nineteenth century.

Corbett's female detective attests that, on the brink of the twentieth century, the culture will give up some of its dead – its dead conceptions. Blain (237) records that Elizabeth Corbett was angered by the women's anti-suffrage movement at the end of the century. *When the Sea Gives Up Its Dead*, therefore, advances a progressive agenda in the person of its female detective, Annie Cory, whose determination to act in the face of intimidation serves as a model for women.

3 The Victorian Female Detective, 1897-1900

After the publication of Braddon's *Thou Art the Man,* Pirkis's *Loveday Brooke* and Corbett's *When the Sea Gives Up Its Dead* in 1894, there is a conspicuous gap in fictional narratives involving the female detective until 1897. In the tradition of the detective narrative in English, there is an explanation for this temporary hiatus. In effect, the disappearance of Sherlock Holmes led to a temporary absence of Sherlock's sisters.

The Memoirs of Sherlock Holmes was published as a book in December 1893, in effect 1894. The last tale in that volume was *The Final Problem,* which had also appeared in December 1893 in the *Strand.* In that story, Doyle presents the diabolical criminal mastermind Professor Moriarty. After being assaulted by Moriarty's thugs several times in London, Holmes goes to the Continent with Watson. He is pursued by Moriarty. They finally engage in a deadly encounter at the Reichenbach Falls near Meiringen in Switzerland. As the horrified Watson, being waylaid by one of Moriarty's lieutenants, returns to the Falls, he witnesses a struggle between Holmes and Moriarty, at the end of which they are 'reeling over, locked in each other's arms' (267) plunging down the Falls. Watson assumes that both men have died. In 1901-1902, Doyle presented *The Hound of the Baskervilles* as a case occurring before the supposed death of Sherlock Holmes at the Falls. Only in *The Empty House* published in the *Strand* in October 1903 did Doyle officially resurrect Holmes, who in fact had not died in Switzerland.

It took writers a year or two after 1894 to absorb the consequences of Doyle's decision to have Holmes supposedly die at the Falls. In effect, the putative death of Holmes opened the way for writers to advance the female and male detectives in fiction. In March 1894, the *Strand* published the first of Arthur Morrison's tales involving the detective Martin Hewitt. The six stories in the series were published in book form in 1894 as *Martin Hewitt, Investigator.* However, the second and third series of tales about Hewitt appeared in 1895 and 1896 in the *Windsor Magazine,* a slight demotion from the *Strand.* These were collected as *The Chronicles of Martin Hewitt* and *The Adventures of Martin Hewitt* respectively in 1895 and 1896. By 1897, there was a genuine possibility for the reappearance of the female detective when George R. Sims published *Dorcas Dene, Detective.*

In the interval from 1895 to 1897, several historical events occurred which deflected public attention from the detective story. Oscar Wilde's two trials for sodomy in 1895 aroused intense interest. Also, the publication of *Fingerprint Directories* by Francis Galton in 1895 indicated a new advance in forensic detection. It was the first statement in print of digital classification. By 1897, a criminal conviction was secured in India on the basis of fingerprinting. In 1897 as well, the National Union of Women's Suffrage Societies was formed, reinforcing an acute emerging movement for women's increasing independence during the final years of the century.

Modifications of the tradition of the Holmes tales in narratives about female detectives from 1897 to 1900 are interesting in several particular instances. Some of these texts in this chapter follow the model of having an admiring narrator/observer record the exploits of the female detective: Saxon in *Dorcas Dene*, Hubert Cumberledge in *Hilda Wade*, Lonsdale in *The Detections of Miss Cusack* are such examples. Even here, however, there is an important change, as in each instance it is a male observer/narrator, a subtle shift in the balance of gendered power, as the gaze of the male is used not for male empowerment but for male growth through observing the valour of a woman. This model, with a female narrator, is advanced in 1910 by Emmuska Orczy, where Mary Granard narrates the activities of the protagonist in *Lady Molly of Scotland Yard*. This change reflects the influence of the suffrage movement and the need for women as sisters to band together.

However, in the late nineteenth century texts to be examined in this chapter, there is also a striking sign of female independence in having the female sleuth narrate her own activities. This is not only a departure from the Holmes model. It signifies a striking independence which one can associate with the New Woman. Mollie Delamere in Beatrice Heron-Maxwell's *The Adventures of a Lady Pearl-Broker* in 1899 records her activities, which occur at various locations throughout the globe. This use of the female first person narrator is pursued in the twentieth century with the protagonist of Richard Marsh's *Judith Lee, Some Pages from Her Life* in 1912. In this respect, these tales go beyond the Holmes model. In only two of the sixty Holmes narratives is Holmes himself the narrator, both among the last of his adventures: *The Blanched Soldier* published in November 1926 and *The Lion's Mane* of December 1926. Hence, the use of the first person female narrator by Heron-Maxwell and Richard Marsh is particularly innovative, as there is no Holmes model for such a practise.

George R. Sims (1847-1922): *Dorcas Dene, Detective* (1897)

During his lifetime, George R. Sims was one of the most prolific writers of
the Victorian and Edwardian eras. A successful journalist, novelist, reporter,
dramatist and fiction writer, Sims was important for exposing social evils of
the late nineteenth century, among them child abuse, slum conditions and
urban blight. As a social reformer, he 'campaigned against false
imprisonment', for instance in 1904 proving a man had been 'wrongly
convicted of fraud' (Kemp 363). In the history of the female detective, Sims
is important for his 1897 *Dorcas Dene, Detective*. These narratives were of
sufficient interest that a second book of Dorcas Dene's adventures
appeared in 1898. Composed of eleven tales, the 1897 series actually
encompasses only five cases. These five cases, however, comprise
interesting material: bigamy, jewellry theft, attempted murder, false
indictments and murder.

In the initial story, *The Council of Four*, Sims establishes Dorcas Dene's
uniqueness. The narratives are recounted by a Mr Saxon, a dramatist who
knew Dorcas Dene as Dorcas Lester when she was an aspiring young
actress. Saxon records that Dorcas Lester was 'a young and handsome
woman' (1). After an interval of eight years, Saxon encounters her again,
recognizing her when she has not yet lowered her veil. He learns from a
solicitor that she is 'Dorcas Dene, the famous lady detective . . . With our
profession and with the police, she has a great reputation' (2). Saxon learns
she has no official position with the Criminal Investigation Department;
instead she 'works entirely on her own account' (3).

Dorcas Lester, Saxon learns when he re-encounters her, is now Dorcas
Dene, living in St John's Wood with her husband Paul, her mother and her
bulldog Toddlekins. Saxon learns her rather distressing history from her,
including the fact that her artist father had died and 'left her and her mother
nothing' (5), hence compelling her to the stage. Then, she marries:

> 'A young artist, a Mr Paul Dene, who had been our friend and
> constant visitor in my father's life, fell in love with me. He had
> risen rapidly in his profession, and was making money . . . Paul
> proposed to me, and I accepted him. He insisted that I should
> leave the stage . . . For two years we were very happy. Then a
> terrible misfortune happened. Paul had an illness and became
> blind. He would never be able to paint again.' (6-7)

Dorcas was compelled to find a means of earning a living. She hears about
the work of criminal investigation from a neighbour, a retired
superintendent of police who had become a private investigator. Dorcas

became interested in cases 'which seemed to defy the efforts of Scotland Yard' (8).

This neighbour, Johnson, asks Dorcas's assistance in a case. At first, Dorcas Dene resists: 'You – you want me to be a lady detective – to watch people?' (10). Johnson reassures her:

> 'I have too much respect for you and your husband to offer you anything that you need be afraid of accepting. I want you to help me to rescue an unhappy man who is being brutally blackmailed ... That is surely a business transaction in which an angel could engage without soiling its wings ... You have plenty of shrewd common sense, you are a keen observer, and you have been an actress.' (10-11)

Dorcas acquiesces: 'I accepted – on one condition. I was to see how I got on before Paul was told anything about it. If I found that being a lady detective was repugnant to me – if I found that it involved any sacrifice of my womanly instincts – I should resign, and my husband would never know that I had done anything of the sort ... That was how I first became a lady detective. I found that the work interested me' (11). This situation is intriguing: Dene recognizes the ambivalent attitude in the culture about detectives, that they are beneficial but also potentially malevolent because their work might be construed as spying. Then, she is concerned about two gendered issues: that her work not violate the expected behaviours of women and that her husband not know of her first professional ventures. In other words, the business has great transgressive potential.

Dene becomes a partner with Johnson and, when he retires, she becomes 'a professional lady detective' (12) working on her own. Dorcas Dene negotiates her professionalism with some care. Saxon recognizes that 'in all business matters she invariably consulted' Paul Dene (16). Dorcas consults him and her mother, described by her son-in-law as 'a plain, straightforward, matter-of-fact' woman. 'Detectives are only human, you know, and, like the rest of the world, they frequently go looking about in every direction' (17). Implicit in the remark is the fact that Dorcas Dene needs the corrective of this straightforward approach. Dorcas Dene's mother, however, claimed that Johnson's stories personally made her nervous and that 'she would soon begin to believe that every man and woman she met had a guilty secret' (8-9). As many critics have noted, the appearance of a detective causes one to wonder if everyone is potentially criminal. Furthermore, there is a strong suspicion that the entire culture is permeated by concealed criminality and guilt, that morality is a veneer. When Dorcas Dene asks that Saxon assist her, he observes: 'Not even in the days of my youthful romance had I waited so eagerly for the hour and the lady, as I waited that evening for eight o'clock and Dorcas Dene' (19).

Dorcas Dene's first recorded case involves the disappearance of the son of Lady Helsham, whom his mother believes is on the point of suicide. The son is in love with the actress Nella Dalroy, while the mother wishes him to marry her ward, which he refuses to do: 'His lordship informed his mother that the idea was entirely repugnant to him' (26). However, Dorcas Dene notes that the mother is almost relieved to hear about the son's potential suicide, and she suspects fear of a damaging discovery is disturbing the mother as well as the son. A newspaper account records the disappearance of the young lord while bathing in the sea. Dene disguises herself as a gypsy to get on stage to observe Nella Dalroy. Then, Dene visits the actress Nella Dalroy, who shows her letters in which Lord Helsham stated 'a terrible discovery' (32) made it impossible for him to marry her. 'I *knew* what the skeleton in the Helsham family cupboard was' (32) Dene tells Saxon.

Dene confronts Lady Helsham's sister in Scotland. She learns that this sister had had a son at the same time Lady Helsham had had a daughter. To secure the title and estates, the two sisters had switched children. As Dene recounts:

> 'Had [Lady Helsham] confessed that her child was a girl she would have had to give up everything – except her allowance under the will – to her husband's brother . . . The sisters had by that time agreed on the fraud . . . Lady Helsham had, it seems , in her rage at her supposed son's refusal to marry her real daughter, whom she loved and desired to benefit, involuntarily revealed her secret, threatening the young fellow with the loss of everything if he refused . . . Thereupon he quitted the house, but he feared to tell the truth, because he would be giving up his own mother to a long term of penal servitude.' (36-7)

The 'son' had 'discovered that he has unwittingly dispossessed another of the title and estates' (35). After Dene arranges the false suicide and disappearance of the young man, the real Lord Helsham, the Hon. John Farman, settles an income on him and allows him to go to America with Nella Dalroy; Lady Helsham leaves England to live abroad.

Dorcas Dene, however, connives in the entire concealment of the guilt of Lady Helsham and her sister. Dene decides about 'the best to be done to avoid scandal' (34):

> 'No good purpose would have been served by prosecuting the two women. The new Lord Helsham insisted on a written confession from all concerned, which he retains for his own

protection. As I was employed by one of the guilty parties, it would have been unprofessional of me to give them to justice.' (38)

Saxon, however, recognizes that under the arrangement 'the new Lord Helsham is compounding a felony' (38). Dorcas Dene 'shrugged her shoulders' he records, explaining; 'My dear Mr Saxon, . . . if everybody did the legal thing and the wise thing, there would be very little work left for a lady detective' (39). As the first case in the series, this case is complex. Dorcas Dene conceals the fraud and guilt of a titled woman, endorsing the real Lord Helsham's solution which does constitute the compounding of a felony. Despite the fact that her neighbour Johnson had assured her she would not soil her wings, eventually Dene connives at concealment. Left unstated is whether Paul Dene has known about this circumstance. Presumably, since she consults him in everything professional, the answer is yes.

Sims includes several observations of Dorcas Dene by Saxon which attempt to reinforce her femininity. Saxon sees her reading to her blind husband and observes: 'I could not help thinking how far removed the loving and tender wife devoting herself to the blind husband seemed from the woman who had unravelled the mystery of the tragic fate of young Lord Helsham' (28). Later, Dorcas Dene admits she was apprehensive: 'I made my way up the pathway with a fluttering heart, for in spite of my profession, I have still that feminine weakness in moments of excitement' (33).

These attempts at making Dorcas Dene a conventional middle-class woman, however, are belied by her complicity in concealment. Under the guise of being the Angel in the House, Dorcas Dene in reality is the opposite: she engages in an impersonation which suggests her affinity with Lady Helsham's deceptive strategy to retain her title and income. Saxon's awareness of her complicity, however, becomes the reader's. If he wished, he could have concealed his final conversation with her about the case.

The next two tales in the series, *The Man with the Wild Eyes* and *The Secret of the Lake*, concern Maud Hargreaves, the daughter of a Colonel who had served in India. She has been found by the side of a lake at the family's home, Orley Park. A doctor examining Maud Hargreaves notes bruises on her wrists which could not have been caused by a fall; rather, they result from an assault, although at first suicide was suspected. As in *The Helsham Mystery*, there is a desire to keep the matter from the police. The Colonel tells Dene: 'I have not been to the police . . . The police inquiries would make the whole thing public property . . . It was the doctor who advised me to come to you and let the inquiry be a private one' (48).

Dorcas Dene goes in disguise as a trained nurse to the home, partly to prevent the servants from discovering her motive. She takes Saxon with her, as he is now her official 'assistant': 'I was sometimes able to assist her by going about with her in cases where the presence of a male companion was a material advantage to her' (40). When Saxon had appropriated the designation 'assistant', Dorcas Dene did not object.

From the lodge-keeper Peters, Dene learns that a man with 'wild, staring eyes' (53) had been peering in at the gates. Dene tricks Maud, who is sleeping, to utter the name Victor. By tracing a photograph with the assistance of Saxon, it is learned that there is a young man in the case, Victor Dubois, the son of Maud Hargreaves's French tutor, who had had to be committed to a lunatic asylum. It evolves that when the Colonel was serving in India, Maud Hargreaves had met Victor Dubois in England and secretly married him. He had met with an accident which had severely injured his head, and the son, like his father, had become insane and was likewise taken to an asylum. Maud resolved to keep the marriage a secret from her father, for 'she knew how bitterly it would distress him to learn that his daughter was the wife of a madman' (74).

Victor Dubois, released from the asylum, returns to find his wife. When Maud refuses to leave with him, he attempts to strangle her. When he hurls her into the lake, he believes she is drowned. Thinking he is a murderer, he drowns himself. Dene reflects: 'Suicide – insanity. The father was taken to a lunatic asylum . . . Son doubtless inherited tendency. Looks like a case of homicidal mania' (72).

In *The Man with the Wild Eyes* and *The Secret of the Lake*, Dorcas Dene is daring. It is she who finds the corpse of Victor Dubois in the lake. When she tells Saxon she has searched the male corpse, her assistant is shocked. Nevertheless, Saxon is genuinely used as an assistant in this case. It is he who is commissioned to visit the London Stereoscopic Company to confirm the identity of a young man in a photograph obtained by Dene. Furthermore, Saxon is entrusted with tracing at Somerset House the record of the secret marriage of Victor Dubois to Maud Hargreaves.

This adventure is also important because Saxon realizes he will not be able to resist recording his experiences with Dene: 'There was only one drawback to the pleasure I felt at being associated with Dorcas Dene in her detective work. I saw that it would be quite impossible for me to avoid reproducing my experiences in some form or other' (40). He asks Dene if she objects to 'the assistant one day revealing the professional secrets of his chief', to which she declares: 'I am quite sure that you will not be able to resist the temptation . . . with this stipulation, that you will use the material in such a way as not to identify any of the cases with the real parties concerned' (41).

At the conclusion of the case, Dorcas devotes herself to her husband Paul. Saxon notes 'that evening [she] had eyes and ears for no one else – not even her faithful "assistant"' (77), revealing perhaps a more than professional interest in her. The Colonel takes his daughter abroad after the conclusion of the case which, like *The Helsham Mystery*, camouflages the secret torments of marriage, here in the bourgeoisie in contrast to the aristocracy of the previous case. Again, this camouflage flags the unusual nature of the Dene marriage, where the wife is the source of the income in a profession not entirely free of suspicion.

In the next two stories of the Dorcas Dene series, *The Diamond Lizard* and *The Prick of a Pin*, Sims reiterates a number of elements now evident in the tales. There is the concern by the second Mrs Claude Charrington about going to the police: 'She explained that her suspicions pointed to a member of her own family as the thief, and she was terrified to go to the police for fear their investigations should confirm her suspicions' (82). Dorcas Dene, the former actress, wears no less than three disguises in the course of the investigation: first as an American tourist (78), then as a parlour-maid (81) and finally as an old German woman visiting an Italian gambling den, The Camorra (96-8).

As in two previous investigations, a son figures prominently, not like the mother's victim in *The Helsham Mystery* or like the lunatic son in *The Man with the Wild Eyes*. Here, it is the figure of the slightly wastrel son, Claude Charrington Jr, who has and then loses money with regularity. 'Mrs Charrington tells me that her stepson has lately caused his father considerable anxiety owing to his extravagance and recklessness. He has just left Oxford, and is going to the Bar, but he has been very erratic' (83). Claude Charrington Sr accuses Dorcas Dene of 'spying' (107) in his house, reflecting the ambivalent perception of detectives in an accusation heard before in criticisms of detectives, as Anthea Trodd has demonstrated.

Saxon's role as the John Watson narrator is confirmed, as he operates with Dorcas Dene like a member of the Greek chorus in his question/answer relationship with his chief (93). Hence, this is one significance of the reference in the narration by Dorcas Dene: 'There is a mystery and a romance behind it – a tangled skein which a Lecoq or a Sherlock Holmes would have been proud to unravel – *and I think I have a clue*' (94).

The two stories recount inter-familial tension in the Charrington family. The second Mrs Charrington discovers she has lost a pendant, bracelet and diamond lizard pin, given to her for her birthday by her husband, Claude Charrington Sr. Claude Jr is in love with a Miss Dolamore, a singer lodging in Fitzroy Street in apartments kept by an Italian, Carlo Rinaldi, who is married to an Englishwoman. As Dorcas Dene learns in her investigation,

Claude Sr had given the jewels to Rinaldi's English wife when she was his mistress. She had had to pawn some of them to get money for Rinaldi, who gambles at The Camorra.

Furthermore, the former mistress had sold the diamond lizard to Claude Jr to give to Miss Dolamore. Through an unfortunate accident, a clerk had given these jewels, pawned by the former mistress in Charrington's name and then redeemed to provide cash for Rinaldi, to the second Mrs Charrington when Claude Sr was out of town on her birthday. This mistake led to a dangerous situation: 'When her husband returned to dinner he was horrified to find his wife wearing his former mistress's jewellery' (111). In the process of taking these dangerous pieces of evidence from his wife's jewel-box, Charrington pricked his finger on the lizard, leaving traces of blood in the drawer and on his bed sheet. Charrington has a second set made to conceal his theft, but in the end he manages to get these as well from his wife, claiming they were imitation.

When Dorcas Dene confronts Charrington, she tells him; 'I have come here not to make a scandal, but to avoid one' (108). Paul Dene inquires of Dorcas: 'And the wife? . . . You did not make her unhappy by telling her the truth?' (112). Instead, Dorcas Dene concocted the story by which Charrington confessed the set was imitation. Thus, she connives at the thief's deception of his wife and the Charrington family is preserved, with the wastrel Claude Jr proved innocent and Claude Sr's past indiscretions concealed.

The implications of the story are more than disturbing, as both father and son have given the same diamond lizard pin to their lovers, respectively the mistress and Miss Dolamore. Even though the son becomes engaged to Miss Dolamore at the tale's conclusion, he exhibits all the deceiving tendencies of his father and will probably be engaged in similar deceptions and connivances. As with the marriages presented in the first two cases, the marital institution is gerryrigged to remain standing.

The next three tales, *The Mysterious Millionaire*, *The Empty House* and *The Clothes in the Cupboard*, present Dorcas Dene saving Lady Anna Barraclough from her bigamous husband Judkins Barraclough, an abusive criminal who had made his fortune in South America. In these three narratives, Saxon's character is more revealed. While he retains his function as interrogator of Dorcas Dene, he is shown as less courageous than she. At one point, when they have gained access to a suspicious house: 'I am ashamed to say that in my overwrought nervous condition I couldn't help giving a little cry of alarm' (141).

Saxon assists Dorcas Dene in getting keys to this house, rented by Judkins. Saxon learns at the beginning that Dorcas will have to be 'under a lamp-post in Berkeley Square at midnight' (116), and Paul Dene encourages

Dorcas Dene to accept Saxon's company, to which she responds: 'Of course, if *you* wish it, dear . . . Honestly I shall be glad of your company' (122-23). Kathleen Klein construes this exchange as Dorcas 'abandon[ing] her independence, her judgment, and her conclusions' (64):

> The functions of both the detective as formulaic character and the protagonist as one of the novel's structuring elements are reduced in this novel as Sims replaces them with the combined presence of the male team – narrator and husband. Dorcas Dene, woman and detective, is submerged within the confines of patriarchal marriage. (64)

However, a closer reading of the text reveals that Dorcas Dene is accepting the assistance with total self-awareness of, even self-irony at, her role as Victorian wife – she mocks her own acquiescence.

Dorcas Dene in fact takes the case to rectify the evil men do in marriage. Lady Anna suspects bigamy when she confides in Dene:

> 'If I am really this man's wife, . . . I have no right to go to the police, for he is my husband. I have come to you to find out everything for me first. Oh, if you can only tell me that I am a free woman, that I owe no further allegiance to this wretch whom I despise – whom I loathe – you will have done me the greatest service one woman can do another!' (119)

Dorcas Dene recognizes the frauds at the base of so many marriages:

> 'Oh . . . how horrible it must be, to have to go about before the world with a smiling face bearing the name of a man you detest – to have to submit alike to the curses and the caresses of a man whom in your heart you believe to be the husband of another woman!' (119)

Far from being submissive, Dorcas Dene forms an alliance with her client to save her from a brutal marriage. Dene also enunciates that 'Chance is the most successful detective the world has ever known' (127), demonstrating not reliance upon men but a determined professional aspiration to confront whatever is yielded by circumstance. Dorcas Dene even makes an error about Barraclough being disguised as an Indian gentleman: 'I've been off the track a little, but I'm on it right enough now' (154), adapting to circumstance.

Dorcas Dene in this investigation confronts a situation quite horrible. It evolves that Barraclough had chloroformed his first wife, Marian Judkins, and locked her in a cage in the middle of a room at the house in Berkeley Square. He planned to give her only liquor to drink so she would die in an alcoholic stupor. Despite the obvious echoes of Charlotte Brontë's *Jane Eyre*, the very brevity of the episode has its terrifying dimension, causing the reading to think not only of Brontë but also of the orangutan in Edgar Allan Poe's *The Murders in the Rue Morgue*.

> As the light illuminated the apartment an extraordinary sight met our eyes. The centre of the room was entirely occupied by what looked like a huge wire cage. Wire netting nearly six feet high was stretched from side to side of the room on ropes which were fastened in the walls by iron rings . . . In one corner of the cage, on a rug, covered over by a scarlet blanket, lay a woman. (147-8)

Dorcas tells Saxon:

> 'She is caged in order to keep her from beating the walls, and she is dosed with chloral in order to keep her from moving about . . . She might in an access of delirium tear down her cage and get free. No – kept here without food and with a plentiful supply of brandy she will die slowly of alcoholic poisoning. But she must die quietly – hence the chloral.' (150)

Sims here outdoes Brontë in this depiction of female imprisonment, determined to show the extent of the malevolence of some men under the guise of marriage.

At the conclusion of this episode, Barraclough is arrested for attempted murder of his first wife and Lady Anna is 'a free woman' (171). Dorcas Dene uses the assistance of Inspector Bartlett of the C.I.D. to effect the arrest. Bartlett states: 'I am always delighted to work with the famous Dorcas Dene . . . My only regret is that she is not one of us' (157). These three tales, *The Mysterious Millionaire*, *The Empty House* and *The Clothes in the Cupboard*, are important in revealing not only the false but the brutal nature of some men in Victorian marriages. Far from showing a submissive Dorcas Dene, the episode about Lady Anna Barraclough has a strong proto-feminist element which links it to the evolving rights established by the various Married Women's Property Acts. The title of the second part of the narrative, *The Empty House*, may well have been used by Conan Doyle when he resurrected Sherlock Holmes in October 1903.

The final case presented in *Dorcas Dene, Detective* is contained in two connected stories, *The Haverstock Hill Murder* and *The Brown Bear Lamp*. The case is similar to the previous one, as Dorcas Dene forms an alliance with

Mrs Hannaford, who asks her to investigate the murder of her son's wife, for which the son, a stock-jobber, has been committed for trial. Hannaford had been in 'an irritable, nervous condition' (179), 'worried lately over business matters' (180). Having quarrelled with his wife, the marriage being an unhappy one, he had 'thought perhaps if he went to his mother for a day or two he might get calmer and feel better' (180). After being committed for trial, Hannaford's 'reason gave way, and, the doctors certifying that he was undoubtedly insane, he was sent to Broadmoor' (181), with the result that 'his life had probably been spared by this mental breakdown' (183).

In the course of her investigation, Dorcas Dene learns that the murdered wife had been married previously to Charles Drayson, a financier in partnership with Thomas Holmes. Drayson was thought to have died in a fire in Paris. However, a turf crook, Flash George, had been seen at the murder site and had also been passing some bills from a cheque originally cashed by the first husband, Charles Drayson. Dorcas Dene discovers that Drayson, who in reality did not die in the Paris fire, had concealed cash in the back of a brown bear lamp, now in the Hannaford home. He had broken in to get the cash, had been surprised by his former wife and had killed her with a poker.

Disguised as an Italian street musician, Dorcas Dene, with the assistance of Drayson's former partner Thomas Holmes, captures Drayson on Hungerford Bridge, where he goes to meet Flash George and just as Drayson is about to commit suicide by jumping into the water, realizing he is finished. Thomas Holmes identifies Drayson, his former partner, who had let him go to prison. Once identified, Drayson succeeds in committing suicide from Hungerford Bridge.

It is in fact Saxon who first seizes Drayson, disguised as an old man to meet the turf crook, so he proves his worth as Dorcas Dene's 'assistant' (186). Hannaford, 'completely recovered and in his right mind, was in due time released from Broadmoor' (209). Again, as in the previous case, Dene's alliance with another woman ultimately saves a wronged party, in this case a son. This circumstance explains Dene's remark to Saxon when he suggests they go to the police: 'I'm going to carry this case through on my own account' (193), keeping the womanly alliance apart from male official intervention. When she reads the mother's letter of gratitude, Dorcas Dene declares; 'These are the *rewards* of my profession . . . They compensate for everything' (210).

At the beginning of this final case, Saxon records that 'Paul [Dene] had not been very well lately' (171). This glancing remark reinforces the pressure on Dorcas Dene, female detective, to persist in her career, one designated in the final line of the book very distinctly as a 'profession.' But given that in the final two cases Dene forms an alliance with distressed women as clients, one a wife, the other a mother, this profession becomes indeed a feminist 'calling.' Kathleen Klein, while correctly noting that Paul Dene's blindness echoes that of Brontë's Rochester, contends:

> Sims holds his married couple to the traditional pattern . . . She is doubly secondary and submissive as she bolsters his self-confidence by deliberately minimizing her own independence. Her self-effacing behavior, however, is taken for granted by the narrator and author as though a natural and reasonable attribute of married women. (64)

In fact, there is a marked progression from the early stories, where Dorcas Dene was concerned about being a female detective, to a vaunted professionalism by the conclusion of the cases narrated by Saxon. The assessment by Craig and Cadogan seems more accurate: 'Apart from the sentimentality of the introduction . . . , the stories have a fairly vigorous, forward-looking tone . . . Dorcas is capable of analytical reasoning, and she is also a mistress of disguise' (23).

Sims supplies an additional excuse for Dorcas Dene's being a lady detective. When Saxon wonders if Toddlekins is 'the baby', 'a shade crossed Dorcas Dene's pretty womanly face, and I thought I saw her soft grey eyes grow moist.' She tells Saxon 'We have no family' (12). One can only speculate if Paul Dene's blindness implies infertility. By this detail, however, Sims suggests that Dorcas Dene's real family results from her profession, above all through her assistance to women involved in crime by the activities of male members of their families: Maud Hargreaves in *The Man with the Wild Eyes*, Lady Anna Barraclough in *The Mysterious Millionaire*, or Mrs Hannaford in *The Haverstock Hill Murder*. While Dorcas Dene saves endangered marriages, as in *The Diamond Lizard*, or enables a desired marriage, as in *The Helsham Mystery*, she does so completely aware of the frequently distressing and potentially criminous nature of the marital institution. Dorcas Dene acts outside official institutions, marking her independence as well as indicating George Sims's animus against institutions, often expressed in his journalistic investigations of urban malaise. Dorcas Dene is unafraid of illegality so long as she facilitates justice. As her Christian name indicates, Dorcas Dene is engaged in self-realization through service to others. Sims's *Dorcas Dene, Detective* is therefore justifiably important as a key late-Victorian text not only about the female detective but about constructions of gender, especially of sisterhood, at the end of the nineteenth century.

Fergus W. Hume: *Hagar of the Pawn-shop* (1898)

When Fergus Hume published *Hagar of the Pawn-shop* in 1898, he was already a famous man. Hume in 1886 had produced the 'most sensationally popular crime and detection novel of the century' (Sutherland 454), *The Mystery of a Hansom Cab*, set in Melbourne, featuring no less than two detectives, Gorby and Kilsip. When published in Australia, the novel had not achieved much fame, but the following year, with its publication in England, the novel became a phenomenon. Although born in England, Hume had been raised in New Zealand and had moved to Australia after being called to the New Zealand bar in 1885. In 1888, the year after Conan Doyle had published *A Study in Scarlet* in *Beeton's Christmas Annual*, Hume emigrated to England, having published another great detection novel, *Madame Midas*, the same year. It was inevitable that he would return again to the detection genre. In the process, he created one of the most intriguing of all amateur female detectives, a gypsy woman named Hagar Stanley. Hume's focus on a gypsy protagonist is the culmination of an extensive nineteenth-century literary tradition, represented by such works as G. P. R. James's *The Gipsy* (1835), Matthew Arnold's 1853 poem 'The Scholar-Gipsy', George Borrow's *The Romany Rye* (1857) and Charles G. Leland's scholarly study *The English Gipsies and Their Language* (1874); beginning in 1888, the Gypsy Lore Society published a journal.

The twelve episodes contained in *Hagar of the Pawn-shop* sharply exploit the nature and the occupation of its protagonist, as Slung has observed:

> A gypsy pawn-broker of considerable spirit, she is more of a problem-solver than a detective. Though she is untaught, her Romany heritage makes her naturally shrewd and quick-witted, and her adventures follow the appearance of unusual pawned objects. (361)

To differentiate his 'problem-solver' who is sometimes a detective, Hume makes her not only a woman but a gypsy and eliminates any narrator figure. Because the pawn-shop where Hagar pursues her trade is in Lambeth, the series permits Hume to present an image of the cityscape of London at its most grimy and unappealing, in fact a parallel to the world made infamous by Jack the Ripper, one which had already been delineated in Somerset Maugham's *Liza of Lambeth* in 1897. Undoubtedly, Hume set his gypsy heroine in this environment to capitalize on the notoriety of Maugham's novella.

Hume makes it clear that the pawn-shop is a microcosm of the world in the first tale, *The Coming of Hagar*. He presents the old miser Jacob Dix of

Carby's Crescent, Lambeth, who had had a gypsy wife named Hagar Stanley, who died, but not before giving birth to his dreadful son James, a red-headed thug who has taken up with gypsies. Hagar is the niece of this dead woman, bearing the same name. The shop she enters is straight out of Blue Books:

> The pawn-shop – situated in Carby's Crescent, Lambeth – furthermore resembled an ogre's castle inasmuch as, though not filled with dead men's bones, it contained the relics and wreckage, the flotsam and jetsam, of many lives, of many households. Placed in the centre of the dingy crescent, it faced a small open space, and the entrance of the narrow lane which led therefrom to the adjacent thoroughfare . . . The contents of Dix's window typified in little the luxury, the meanness, the triviality and the decadence of latter-day civilisation . . . Wreckage of many centuries; dry bones of a hundred social systems, dead or dying! What a commentary on the durability of empire – on the inherent pride of pigmy man! (3-4)

One can only surmise the appearance of this locale on the 'foggy November night' (5) when Hagar Stanley, the niece of Dix's deceased wife, appears. Dix's only 'friend' is the corrupt, dreadful solicitor Vark, 'more like a worm than a man made in the image of his Creator' (6). Vark attempts to get Dix to disinherit his son James.

Hagar's entrance is worthy of the Victorian stage:

> Out of the fog and darkness a young girl of twenty years stepped into the shop . . . Her head [was bare], save for a scarlet handkerchief, which was carelessly twisted round her magnificent black hair. The face was of the true Romany type: Oriental in its contour and hue . . . Face and figure were those of a woman who needed palms and desert sands and golden sunshine, hot and sultry, for an appropriate background; yet this Eastern beauty appeared out of the fog like some dead Syrian princess. (9)

Dix calls her a 'jade' (10) and a 'Jezebel' (11), but Hagar instead reveals she fled the gypsy camp in the New Forest to avoid the attentions of a brute called Goliath, who at the end of the first chapter is revealed in fact to be Dix's son James. The chief of the tribe 'would have forced me also to be this man's rani' (12), Hagar states, so she fled this male tyranny. Although Dix once tries to strike her, she confronts him and prevents it ever happening again. Dix takes her on in the business, teaching her everything, until 'the untaught gipsy girl became a connoisseur' (13). Vark offers her marriage, in order to get Dix's inheritance by compelling the man to disinherit the son (via a forged note pretending that the son wished to kill the father). Hagar prevents this transaction, even though the money would come to her. When Dix drops dead, Vark tells Hagar that Goliath, the man she loathes, is Dix's son and will inherit the property.

In her first case, which does involve solving a riddle, *The Florentine Dante*, Hagar after one year in the shop exhibits a 'keen business instinct' (27). Set in June 1896, the tale recounts that a young man, Eustace Lorn, had come to the shop to pawn a fourteenth-century Florentine edition of Dante's *Commedia*. Hagar is attracted to Lorn, 'tall, slim, fair-haired and blue-eyed' (28). Later, a stout elderly man, Jabez Treadle, brings the pawn ticket to the shop, but Hagar refuses to give him the book. When Lorn returns, Hagar hears the story of his uncle Benjamin Gurth, who had made a fortune in the West Indies. Eustace Lorn's uncle supposedly left the secret of where his money is in the Florentine Dante.

Hagar thinks the clue is written in lemon juice, heats a flat iron and finds the clue, an underscored passage with a date in the margin. Hagar and Eustace go to the uncle's house in Woking, only to find Treadle anticipating them. Hagar figures out the numbers translate to *il fico*, and Treadle begins digging frantically under a fig tree. When the box turns up, they find only a note inside, in which Gurth states he had no money, was poor, but got every luxury from those who thought he had money and curried his favour during his last ten years of retirement in England. Apparently, Gurth sought to teach the greedy fortune-hunters a lesson. Lorn had debated whether to marry Hagar: 'He had neither birth nor money, yet he drew back from mating himself with such a one' (40), but he decides to ask Hagar. Instead, Hagar returns the Dante to him, telling him to sell it, make his fortune and find Goliath, that is, her cousin James Dix. Lorn determines to do so, resolved to marry Hagar Stanley.

In *The Amber Beads*, Hagar again functions like a detective. An ostensibly black woman named Rosa pawns an amber necklace, but Hagar copies the number of the bank note she gives this woman. She then learns from Luke Horval of the detective police of the murder of a woman, Mrs Arryford, the widow of a West Indian; she also learns that Frederick Jevons inherits the money. Hagar goes with Horval to investigate, leaving the shop in charge of a sixteen-year-old hunch-backed devil named Bloker. Hagar meets Jevons and takes the negress Rosa to the pawn shop to shelter her, as she is thought to be the murderer of the widow. Hagar had noticed, however, that the person pawning the necklace had missing the little finger of the right hand, like Jevons and unlike Rosa.

Hagar concludes that Jevons masqueraded like a black woman. Confronting the woman's companion, Miss Lyle, Hagar learns that Jevons is her son. When she killed Mrs Arryford, the son, in order to save her, pawned the amber beads while he was disguised as a woman. After writing her confession, the woman commits suicide by jumping from Westminster Bridge. Jevons, who had been arrested, is released from prison and gets the widow's money, thanks to his mother's persistent harassment of Mrs Arryford.

The Amber Beads is an important text in the Hagar chronicle. First, Hagar actually joins with Horval of the detective police to solve the crime. This association confirms her detecting credentials. However, in this tale Fergus Hume confronts the issue of the woman as detective in this exchange between Horval and Hagar:

> 'You ought to be a man, with that head of yours', he said; 'you're too good to be a woman!'
> 'And not bad enough to be a man', retorted Hagar, laughing. 'Be off with you, Mr Horval, and let me know when you want me up West.' (61)

Hagar's perception of the detail of the missing finger indeed solves the case. This proto-feminist exchange between the professional male detective and the unofficial female detective makes an argument that in fact women should be members of the detective police.

Hagar's role in the next tale, The Jade Idol, however, is far less significant. It is curious that Hume, after defending and demonstrating her expertise in the previous tale, relegates her to so small a role in the subsequent narrative. In this text, the sailor Nathaniel Prime pawns a jade idol of the Chinese god of war, Kwan-tai, fearing the Chinaman Yu-ying. From what turns out to be the fatal 'vice . . . which ruins the female sex, . . . curiosity' (74), Hagar places the idol in the shop window, from which it is stolen. Hagar regrets her error. Prime meets another corrupt friend, one Dr Dick. They want the idol so they can find instructions to locate the small gold images worth 50,000 pounds, brought to England by the Chinaman Poa. Yu-ying, who stole the idol from Hagar's shop, returns it.

Hagar gives the object to Prime and Dick, who find instructions in it to go to an opium den run by the merchant Yeh in Whitechapel. When Dick and Prime open the box, it explodes, killing them and the merchant. Yu-ying reports to the Chinese priests of Kwan-tai's temple back in Canton that he had taken the sacred images from the box and substituted dynamite. He declares his motive:

> 'I wished to punish Yeh for his sacrilege in conspiring with Poa against Kwan-tai; and also to kill the foreign devil [Prime] who

had thieved the jade god . . . The foreign devil and a friend
[Dick] were shattered, and also the house of Yeh was destroyed
. . . Thus did I lure the foreign devils to their deaths.' (86)

Prime and Dick had exhibited 'a wholesome mistrust of the race' (82)
earlier. The narrative, which leaves Hagar waiting for Prime to return to tell
of the conclusion, is an indictment of Western imperialism and racism.
However, in diminishing the role of Hagar Stanley, who is more or less an
observer and auditor, Hume reduces her status.

The next tale, *The Crucifix*, set in April 1898, is a grim melodrama which
has its roots in the Renaissance. Bolker, Hagar's assistant, is at the shop
when Gemma Bardi pawns a silver crucifix 'in the style of Cellini' (90). The
clever Bolker figures out that it is in reality a dagger, when the image of
Christ slides down the object. A man comes to redeem the ticket, one
Carlino Bardi. He tells Hagar that his wife Gemma has run off with his best
friend, Pietro Neri. The crucifix, he states, is related to a revenge killing
during the Renaissance, when a man named Guido was deceived by his wife
Bianca, who had run off with her lover Luigi da Francia. Bolker
inadvertently reveals that the crucifix is a dagger, at which Bardi runs off to
kill his wife and her lover. He finds them at Daleminster. Performing in the
street, his wife is held by his gaze but later his look deceives her, when he
claims to have no weapon, only the crucifix. Gemma leads him to Pietro
Neri, who is ill. Carlino Bardi then produces the dagger in the crucifix and
murders Gemma and Pietro.

After the murders, to make it appear as if he were assaulted and acted
in self-defence, Carlino Bardi inflicts on himself a slight gash at his throat
with the dagger. In doing so, he is ignorant that the tip has been anointed
with poison, and he dies. It turns out Bolker, the rogue assistant to Hagar,
had removed from the dagger a slip of paper which the original wronged
husband, Guido, had left around the blade of the poniard. Although Hagar
learns this secret, she never learns that Guido had wounded himself: 'Hagar
never learnt that Bardi had inflicted the wound on himself to save his life,
hereby slaying himself as surely as the law would have done' (105) the text
concludes.

The Crucifix again relegates Hagar to a relatively minor role in the
tragedy. However, in engaging the Victorian debate about the nature of the
Renaissance – whether it was wonderfully beneficent or brutally violent –
the story finds a context in everything from the essays of Walter Pater to
the paintings of Frederic Leighton, the poems of Robert Browning
(especially *The Ring and the Book*) and the chronicles of John Addington
Symonds's *The Renaissance in Italy* (1875-1886) about what constituted the
essence of the Renaissance. Hume uses the detective genre to intersect with

this Victorian speculation, which exhibits urgency because the Victorians modelled themselves, among other cultures, on Renaissance civilisation.

So far as the case relates to Hagar, it suggests the violence that James 'Goliath' Dix might inflict on her because of his erotic obsession with her. The murders, whether in the past or present, affirm the correctness of her suspicions of violent males. Furthermore, Hagar reads a record of the case which notes 'the deadly ingenuity of the weapon used, which was at once a dagger and a crucifix' (104). Such a comment suggests an extension of the debate about the Renaissance, that is, the ambiguous nature of religion, in the name of which so much violence has been perpetrated.

The most bizarre feature of the tale is that Carlino Bardi had stolen the crucifix in the first place, because it was believed that if its possessor had a faithless wife, 'the Crucifix of Fiesole would give him power to slay her and her lover' (95) because of its past. He even admits to Hagar: 'As I had then married Gemma, and thought that some day she might be faithless, I stole the crucifix from Signor Ancillotti' (95). All along, in other words, the man had suspected his wife, with the model of revenge derived from a Renaissance example. Religion itself is no safeguard against male erotic obsession.

In *The Copper Key* Hume again gives Hagar genuine prominence. The tale opens with Hagar's situation as pawn-broker:

> To find that strange stories were attached to many pawned articles; to ascertain such histories of the past; to follow up their conclusions in the future – these things greatly pleased the girl. (109)

In fact, Hume associates Hagar's ability to 'deduce' with the expertise of Georges Cuvier, the French naturalist, who 'could construct a marvellous and prehistoric world' from a bone or footprint (109).

A copper key is brought to the shop by Luke Parsons, the steward on the Danetree estate. It is a key with numbers on it, a cryptogram in the form of a simple numerical substitution cipher. Hagar goes to Danetree Hall. Out on the open country, 'her gipsy blood sang in her veins' the reader learns (113). At the Hall, she learns from Parsons that the Danetrees had lost everything from the recklessness of the Squire during the Regency, except one painting, *The Nativity* by Andrea del Castagno, a Renaissance canvas which is missing. Hagar figures out the cipher, which tells the location of the picture.

The key opens through the eye of a cherub in a carving to a secret storage place in a wall, where the painting is located. Hagar tells the steward's son, Frank Parsons, who is in love with Marion Danetree, the descendant of the wastrel Danetrees. Marion now is left with nothing but the Hall itself. Luke Parsons did not want Frank to learn of the location of the picture, since it would only enrich Marion Danetree, who he thinks does not love Frank, even though Frank loves her. Frank tells Hagar that he and Marion cannot marry because of their mutual poverty.

After Frank finds the picture, the father determines to destroy it. In this he is thwarted by Marion Danetree, who tells the father that she does love his son Frank: 'I love him better than all the world! . . . I shall bring that picture to Frank as my dowry. He shall take my name, and there will once more be a Squire Danetree at the Hall' (126). The bitterness between social classes is resolved when Frank achieves this hypergamous marriage, a telling acknowledgement of the shifting class parameters in late Victorian society. In *The Copper Key*, the outsider Hagar through her deduction is able to effect this redefinition of class boundaries.

If *The Copper Key* facilitates a marriage, the subject of *The Silver Teapot* is a marriage destroyed by a malign friend. Margaret Snow, a blind old maid who makes baskets, brings to Hagar a silver teapot, telling her there are letters in the soldered teapot. Hagar learns, when she goes to help the ill old woman, that the letters are the correspondence between Miss Snow and John Mask, her lover, who had gone to India and eventually broke off their engagement. Instead, he married Snow's close friend, Jane Lorrimer, when she went to India.

When Hagar gets access to the letters and reads them to the old woman, she discovers that Jane Lorrimer and the servant Lucy Dyke had contrived the correspondence. John never in these letters rejected Margaret Snow. Jane Lorrimer and the servant deceived the blind woman because Jane loved John Mask, making up letters which the blind woman could not possibly verify. Hagar reveals this to the old and dying woman. Hagar brings the now penitent faithless friend Jane Lorrimer Mask to confront the dying and destitute Margaret Snow. However, Snow compels Hagar to promise not to inform John Mask about the deception. Although Mask comes to Snow's lodging the instant she has died, Hagar never tells him the truth about his wife: he leaves 'ignorant and happy' (149).

In this tale, of course, the man's name 'Mask' symbolizes for Hagar and probably for Hume the actual state of the marital institution, that it is built on deception and delusion. Hagar ponders the situation: 'That he should have ceased to love Margaret was not uncommon, as men, particularly when absent, are only too often prone to forget those they leave at home; but it was curious that he should have married Jane Lorrimer' (139). She wonders 'if treachery and woman's wiles had parted the lovers, or if the story was merely one . . . of a faithless man and a broken-hearted woman' (139). When the truth is learned, Hagar in fact urges Margaret Snow to 'punish these vixens! . . . Ruin her! She ruined you' (144-5). When Mask praises his wife, Hagar laughs cynically about the falsity at the base of the Mask marriage.

The next case confronted by Hagar is *The Mandarin*, a narrative marked by considerable violence. A brutal man, William Smith, pawns a statue of a mandarin at Hagar's shop. When he gets out of prison, he comes to get the mandarin statue and discovers that diamonds, stolen from Lady Deacey's residence in Curzon Street, which he had placed in the statue, are missing. In the interval while Smith was imprisoned, Bolker, Hagar's assistant, had left the shop to work at a bookseller's in Leicester Square. Smith tracks down Bolker, and in a frightening scene grabs the young hunchback in the back alleys of Lambeth after the young man has paused to admire the sunset on Westminster Bridge. Vark, Bolker and Hagar plan to catch Smith. Bolker had been asked by one of Smith's acquaintances, Monkey, to steal the mandarin and hand over the diamonds. Instead, Bolker takes the diamonds to Scotland Yard. In the final scene, set in Vark's office, the solicitor levels a revolver at Smith, who is caught by two policemen.

It is in this story that Hagar is labelled by the dreadful solicitor Vark with her titular designation 'Hagar of the Pawn-shop' (167), with the implication that she is so immersed in crime, only this corrupt man and rejected suitor could name her. Vark himself is designated as 'a latter-day Fagin' (167) after the sinister gang leader in Dickens's *Oliver Twist* of 1838. Much of this tale evokes Dickens's text, with its descriptions of London's back alleys and bridges. The fact that Fagin dealt with stolen goods only puts him one step below those who pawn objects in Hagar's establishment.

Clearly inspired by the Bill Sykes of Dickens's tale, Bill Smith is one of Hume's most violent villains. When he first appears in the shop, Hagar responds: 'Hagar did not like the man's looks at all, although she was by no means exacting on the score of personal beauty – especially with regard to the male sex. Still, there was something brutal about this fellow which revolted her every sense' (154). When Smith exits the shop for Whitechapel (155), no reader would not think of Jack the Ripper. Bolker the renegade assistant is 'an arab of London city' (156), a rogue who would not be out of place in *Oliver Twist*.

The Pair of Boots concerns a love affair which leads to murder. Sir Leslie Crane of Welby Park, Marlow, is found murdered, and it is thought that his gamekeeper, George Kerris, has committed the crime. In this tale Hagar works with a detective, one Julf, who has respect for her: 'Julf always believed that two heads were better than one, especially when the second head was that of a woman. He had a great respect for the instinct of the weaker sex' (177). This opinion reflects the grudging admiration given to detecting women, categorized as the weaker sex but granted 'instinct.' After

Hagar surveys the scene of the crime and draws conclusions, Julf is quite 'confounded by [her] reasoning' (185), confounded not by her explanation only but by the fact she 'reasons' at all.

Hagar learns that a farmer's daughter, Laura Brenton, was loved by Kerris and by the young baronet Sir Leslie. She interviews Sir Lewis Crane, who had succeeded to the title after the murder of his cousin. Sir Lewis is another one of Hume's dreadful old men, perhaps a comment on the decline of the aristocracy. Indeed, Hagar is reminded of the dreadful Jacob Dix, the original owner of the pawn-shop. Sir Lewis suspects she is a detective, stating: 'I did not know that the Government employed lady detectives', to which Hagar replies: 'I am not a detective, but the owner of the shop' (180). After Hagar finds a pistol belonging to Sir Lewis in an urn at Queen's Pool on the estate, she confronts Laura Brenton, who has been desired by the gamekeeper, Sir Leslie, and Sir Lewis. Brenton is described as 'somewhat masculine in her looks' (186).

When Hagar visits the gamekeeper Kerris in gaol, she tells him that he 'is screening someone. Who is it?' (188). When it is learned that Laura Brenton gave the young Irish lad Micky the boots to pawn, Hagar then tells Kerris:

> 'You wish to screen her, as you have tried to do all along. But you are wrong. Laura Brenton is not worth your sacrificing your life, my man. She is the guilty person who killed Sir Leslie. And why? Because he had cast her off, and was about to marry another woman.' (189)

One woman has indicted another woman. Julf tells Kerris that 'she loved herself' (189) and no one else. Laura Brenton confesses and is given penal servitude for life, with leniency because of her beauty. Kerris decides to take 'himself into exile' (191) to Australia.

The Pair of Boots gives Hagar a new role. She becomes a defender of men against the unscrupulous nature of women. The narrator observes:

> But for Hagar and the episode of the pawned boots, which Laura had given to Micky to get rid of, she might have succeeded in her vile plans, and have escaped free, to ruin other men. (190)

Hagar asks Kerris at the conclusion, 'Why did you do all this for Laura — that worthless woman?', and Kerris responds: "Worthless she is, I know . . . but — I loved her!' (191). The tale concludes with this larger mystery of male erotic obsession, even when it leads to self-destruction, unexplained albeit not unexplored. The gamekeeper George Kerris recalls Carlino Bardi of *The Crucifix*, with his similar obsession with a faithless woman.

It is difficult to determine if this abasement is another component of the Victorian concern with the decline of white manhood at the end of the century. On the other hand, Laura Brenton could be construed as enacting a classist revenge when she, a farmer's daughter, is cast off by the aristocratic Sir Leslie Crane, who used his power to victimize her. Alternatively, the tale might signify that Laura Brenton is punished for rejecting the gamekeeper and transgressing class barriers.

The Casket opens with a statement about female detection:

> Hagar had almost a genius for reading people's characters in their faces. The curve of the mouth, the glance of the eyes – she could interpret these truly; for to her feminine instinct she added a logical judgment masculine in its discretion. She was rarely wrong when she exercised this faculty; and in the many customers who entered the Lambeth pawn-shop she had ample opportunities to use her talent. (195)

Twice later, however, Hagar is recorded as having 'instinct' (197, 201), this epistemological blurring reflecting the indecision of the culture about female detectives.

In *The Casket* the subject of the Renaissance, already dealt with in *The Florentine Dante* and *The Crucifix*, reappears. The Florentine casket pawned by a valet, John Peters, exhibits several sides of the Renaissance:

> Renaissance work certainly, for in its ornamentation there was visible that mingling of Christianity and paganism which is so striking a characteristic of the re-birth of the Arts in the Italy of Dante and the Medici . . . [The casket has] its odd mingling of cross and thyrsus; its hints of asceticism and joyous life. (197)

In a secret drawer of the casket, Hagar discovers love letters, written by Peters's master Lord Averley. Although she has a 'pure and virginal soul' (199), Hagar understands that 'in every line there was divorce' (199). She removes the letters, thinking that the valet 'was quite capable of making capital out of them at the expense of the unhappy woman or his own master. He had the face of a blackmailer' (200).

When Peters returns, Hagar accuses him: 'You would steal the letters, if you could, to extort money from a woman . . . You are a scoundrel' (202). Peters admits he learned about the letters when he 'heard my lord say to a friend of his that there were letters to him from a married lady in the secret place of the box' (204), a fact guaranteed to terrify individuals with servants who might become blackmailers because of their masters' indiscreet conversations. Learning the identity of the woman involved as a Mrs Delamere, Hagar confronts her. Hagar tells the woman the letters will lead to 'the Divorce Court with Lord Averley as co-respondent' (207). Mrs Delamere offers Hagar money, but she refuses to accept it: 'I take nothing from a woman who betrays her husband' (208) she declares. When she visits Lord Delamere, however, she discovers that she has given the letters to the wrong married woman. If Hagar defends men in *The Pair of Boots*, she defends even an errant woman from blackmail in *The Casket*.

Hagar Stanley's final case is recorded in *The Persian Ring*. The tale is disappointing because Hagar essentially does nothing in it. The narrative involves a man Alee, a Persian, who pawns a turquoise ring, which has quite a history. Alee had loved a woman, Ayesha, who wished to be in the Shah's harem. In exchange for her, the Shah had given Alee the turquoise ring. Instead of surrendering his wife, Alee had tried to escape with her, but she is apprehended, willingly, by the Shah's men. Then Alee gets involved with a conspiracy against the Shah, but he is betrayed by a man who hates him, Achmet. Hence, Alee had to flee Persia for England. Friends had sent jewels to Alee in England, to be surrendered when the ring identifying him is produced. However, another Persian, Mohammed, gets the ring from Hagar's shop. Alee goes to Southampton to try to find the jewels and runs into an Englishman, Carthew, who gives him a job as a translator. It evolves that Ayesha and Achmet, back in Persia, want Alee dead. In the end, when Mohammed takes the ring to the ship in Southampton to obtain the jewels, he is thought to be Alee and is captured by the Shah's men. Destined to be beheaded on arrival back in Persia, this man throws himself into the sea instead. Since the Persians think Alee is dead, he is free to live in England. The obvious theme is that living in the West is far better than trying to survive in the dreadful political climate of the East.

The Persian Ring, basically melodramatic and scarcely involving Hagar, nevertheless is intriguing for its relationship to contemporary history. The Persians had desired to grab Alee even if he were in their Embassy in London. Carthew states, however, that embassies are not neutral territories and that the English would not have permitted the man to be extradited. Then Carthew links this issue to an actual case: 'The Chinese Embassy tried on that game with Sun Yat, and had to give him up. The English Government do not recognise the Embassies as so many neutral territories in London' (229). In fact, the Chinese revolutionary Sun Yat (1866-1925) had been held for ten days in 1896 in the Chinese embassy before the Chinese were forced to free him. Hume gives this otherwise unremarkable tale a genuine political point by contrasting Eastern tyranny with British freedom.

Fergus Hume concludes the series with *The Passing of Hagar*, bringing together the key individuals in the series and evoking previous cases. After two years Hagar 'was getting very tired of the shop and the weary life of Carby's Crescent' (235). James Dix, alias Goliath, escapes from prison, where he had been incarcerated for horse-stealing, bringing along another convict, the evil Bill Smith of *The Mandarin*. Loved by Hagar, Eustace Lorn returns, having become successful as a travelling bookseller by establishing himself from the profits of the Florentine Dante, Hagar's first case. Smith, picked up by Lorn, escapes from Lorn's caravan, at which Lorn goes to Scotland Yard to tell them about Smith.

Vark reveals to Hagar and Lorn that Goliath had escaped with Smith and concocts a plan to turn in Smith. At his mansion by the river, Vark demands half of Goliath's inheritance. When Smith arrives, he shoots 'the wretched solicitor' (248) Vark dead; Smith then jumps out the window and drowns in the Thames. As he had hoped, Goliath is pardoned for helping in the arrest of Smith, but he wastes his inheritance in drinking and dissipation. Bolker, the assistant to Hagar, buys the shop from Goliath with the money he received from Lord Deacey for recovering the jewels in the episode of *The Mandarin*. Hagar thinks he is well on his way to becoming another Jacob Dix, the original despicable proprietor of the pawn-shop.

After Hagar Stanley marries Eustace Lorn, they travel the country as itinerant booksellers. Hagar admits to Lorn:

> 'I am glad to leave dirty Lambeth for the green fields of the
> country. I am a gipsy, and not used to the yoke of commerce . . .
> I am Mrs Lorn now, and Hagar of the Pawn-shop, with all her
> adventures, is a phantom of the past.' (252).

The narrator records that

> [Lorn and Hagar] passed down the lane, across the dancing
> shadows, and went away hopefully into the green country
> towards the gipsy life. Hagar of the Pawn-shop had come to her
> own at last. (252)

The conclusion of the series is striking, in that instead of Hagar being assimilated to conventional urban and commercial life, she and Lorn, who is not a gypsy, repudiate middle class existence for the pleasures of roaming. All other female detectives of the period remain in their social class during their investigations. As Craig and Cadogan note, Hagar 'refuses a salary throughout this period, and keeps only just on the right side of the breadline' (32). Her existence at the pawn-shop is one of precarious economic survival.

Craig and Cadogan are correct when they note that Hagar Stanley 'probably set the fashion for a touch of the bizarre in the field of twentieth-century female sleuthing' (33). One cannot deny their evaluation that 'there is often a Victorian heaviness of tone in the stories' (33) despite the intriguing character of the protagonist. Some of the tales, such as *The Florentine Dante* or *The Amber Beads*, are quite successful. Others, such as *The Persian Ring*, are failures. The stories engaging the Renaissance, such as *The Crucifix* or *The Casket*, indicate the detective story intersecting with important cultural debates of the late Victorian era.

In *Hagar of the Pawn-shop*, the period of detection occurs in a context which the protagonist abandons at the conclusion. Although Hagar exhibits the traits of combined intuition and rationalism of other female detectives, in the end she channels these abilities to live more like a gypsy than an established middle class woman. In the final episode, Hagar is surrounded by criminous men – Vark, Smith, James 'Goliath' Dix, Bolker. Indisputably aware of this male oppression, which had driven her to the pawn-shop in the beginning, as her final decision she rejects the urban world predominantly populated by such males, choosing instead a freedom of definition beyond male constraints.

Still, Hagar Stanley does not return to a gypsy group, where she would re-experience male domination. Hagar selects an itinerant way of life, but only with one man, the single decent male she ever encounters, Eustace Lorn. As his surname indicates, this promising young man was 'forlorn' before knowing her. Hagar enables Eustace to come to a respectable manhood, but one which ultimately she defines and determines.

Grant Allen (1848-1899): *Miss Cayley's Adventures* (1899)

'I knew a woman who did', said I; 'and this is her story.'

Perhaps no novel published in the Victorian period has so memorable or so notorious an epigraph as this one from Grant Allen's famous New Woman novel *The Woman Who Did*, published in 1895. Already known as a prolific writer about science, sociology and travel (see Cominos 21, 231), the Canadian-born Grant Allen was to write this definitive New Woman novel about a daring individual, Herminia Barton, a Girton College graduate who has a love affair with a bohemian artist Alan Merrick and bears an illegitimate daughter Dolores, who rejects her mother's unconventional ways; Herminia takes prussic acid in an act of defiant suicide. Despite the achievements of George Gissing's *The Odd Women* (1893) and Thomas

Hardy's *Jude the Obscure* (also 1895) which exhibit dimensions of the New Woman, it is Grant Allen's *The Woman Who Did* which remains distinctive in the sub-genre of New Woman fiction.

Critical focus on *The Woman Who Did* is understandable, and yet it has led to the neglect of Allen's achievements in depicting New Women in other novels. In particular, Grant Allen is justly known for his two texts which involve detection by women, written after *The Woman Who Did*: *Miss Cayley's Adventures*, twelve stories serialized in the *Strand Magazine* from March 1898 through February 1899 and published as a volume in 1899; and *Hilda Wade*, serialized in the *Strand* as well and published in 1900, with its final chapters completed by Arthur Conan Doyle, who promised the dying Allen, his friend, he would complete the work. (On the individual instalments, see Beare 1982, 4-6.)

Both *Miss Cayley's Adventures* and *Hilda Wade* focus on independent women who engage in detection amidst their professional responsibilities, Lois Cayley as journalist and typist and Hilda Wade as a nurse. *Miss Cayley's Adventures* is of particular interest because of the diversity of the occupations held by its protagonist and its conflation of several sub-genres in its development. Lois Cayley engages in sporadic amateur but clever detection in the stories.

By the time Grant Allen produced *Miss Cayley's Adventures*, he had already achieved distinction in the short story involving criminous activity. These short stories began appearing in the *Strand* in 1891, beginning in January with the first issue, that is, even before Conan Doyle began producing the Sherlock Holmes short stories in the same publication beginning in July 1891 with *A Scandal in Bohemia*. Grant Allen's short stories about crime prepare the reader for the treatment of crime and detection in his later female detective texts.

A story such as *A Deadly Dilemma*, which appeared in the *Strand* in January 1891, represents the kind of narrative to which Allen was attracted. In the story, Ughtred Carnegie quarrels with his fiancée, Netta Mayne. After they separate, she falls unconscious on the railway tracks. After he throws a pole on the track to stop an oncoming train, he realizes that he is destroying the train and its passengers. He removes the pole, and after the train passes over him between the rails, he rescues the still unconscious Netta Mayne. The dilemma which he faces is whether to rescue Netta or to save the train. The train is in fact derailed by the end of the pole, and hence both Carnegie and Netta survive. He is both the potential murderer of many and the rescuer of everyone. Grant Allen concentrates on the mental reactions of Carnegie, not his actions, a focus typical of Grant Allen. Carnegie turns out to save everyone, yet he might have been the killer of everyone as well. This ambiguity of character is a sharp mark of Allen's short stories.

In March 1891, Allen published in the *Strand* the short story now known as *Jerry Stokes*, although its original title in manuscript was *The Law's Delay*. The hangman, Jerry Stokes, of Canada, decides that Richard Ogilvy, condemned to death for poisoning his wife, is innocent. He determines not to hang him. In the end, a physician, Wade, confesses to the murder after Stokes sends him a letter stating he would hound him forever if he did not admit his crime. Stokes based his conclusion on his study of visages during the trial. Stokes gives up being a hangman at the conclusion of the story, arguing against capital punishment. As the manuscript title indicates, the issue engaged here is not peripheral to the culture.

Two short stories from 1892 reinforce Allen's interest in the ambiguity of crime and the potential for anyone to engage in crime. In *The Conscientious Burglar* from June 1892, the struggling painter Guy Lethbridge goes to Germany to paint landscapes. There he runs out of money and steals the purse of Sir Richard Lavers during the night. He then returns it, admitting he stole it. Sir Richard ultimately buys his first big picture to help him, since he admires his candour in admitting the theft (although Lethbridge actually took nothing from the purse). As in other Allen stories, the mental processes of the characters are the focus here, especially with the artist debating whether to take the money, whether to return it and his remorse. At the conclusion, Guy Lethbridge has become an Associate of the Royal Academy.

This same ambiguity appears in one of Allen's most famous short stories, *The Great Ruby Robbery*, published in the *Strand* in October 1892. Persis Ramenet, an American heiress, has her rubies stolen by the detective Mr Gregory. Gregory tries to throw suspicion on the Irish man about town Sir Justin O'Byrne, whom Persis in the end marries. The maid, Bertha, helps solve the case. Persis claims to read Robert Browning to soothe her nerves, and in fact on the final page of Allen's *Hilda Wade* the two lovers quote from Browning's 'Grammarian's Funeral' of 1855. What is striking about the story is that the detective is the thief. Again, Grant Allen never accepts the superficial quality as a guarantee of validity. *The Great Ruby Robbery* has illustrations by the immortal artist who created the definitive images of Holmes and Watson in the *Strand*, Sidney Paget.

It is Allen's distinct achievement to weld the New Woman novel to the detective narrative in a work such as *Miss Cayley's Adventures*. This amalgamation is signalled in the text by references to George R. Sims (269), the author of *Dorcas Dene, Detective* of 1897, and to Eliza Lynn Linton (113). Linton was the writer of the most famous denunciations of the New Woman in essays such as 'The Wild Women as Social Insurgents' and 'The Partisans of the Wild Women', published in *The Nineteenth Century* in 1891 and 1892 respectively. When the elderly Lady Georgina Fawley exclaims 'I don't know what girls are coming to nowadays', Lois Cayley replies 'Ask Mrs Lynn-Linton [sic] . . . She is a recognised authority on the subject' (113).

Many critics, including Cunningham, Ledger and Showalter, have discussed the emergence of the New Woman during the latter part of the nineteenth century in England, due to such factors as the increased opportunities for education for women (as with the founding of Girton College, Cambridge, in 1869), the various Married Women's Property Acts (1870, 1882, 1884), the repeal of the Contagious Diseases Acts (1886), the circulation of information about birth control, and the formation of women's organizations such as the Women's Trade Union League in 1890 or the National Union of Women's Suffrage Societies in 1897. (On the changing status of women during the nineteenth century, see the anthologies of documents edited by Bauer, Murray, Pike and Read.) In addition, the perfection of the typewriter around 1867, a machine crucial to *Miss Cayley's Adventures*, opened an opportunity for women to gain employment during the latter part of the century.

Allen's text engages many of the essays which debated the New Woman during the era. There is little doubt, furthermore, that interest in female detection was reignited during the 1890s by the failure of males in the detective and police forces to solve the Jack the Ripper murders of 1888. Allen had, furthermore, made his mark in the literature of crime with his renowned series of tales, *An African Millionaire* of 1897, about a rogue swindler, a prototype of several men who appear in *Miss Cayley's Adventures*.

There is one additional factor crucial to assessing Grant Allen's *Miss Cayley's Adventures*. While Lois Cayley is an amateur detective/sleuth, such behaviour marks her as independent indeed, since in fact no woman was officially part of the Criminal Investigation Department (C.I.D.) until 1922 (Rawlings 16, 151). As with the other texts previously studied in this book, the representation of a woman engaging in detection during the nineteenth century constituted a profound fantasy of female empowerment. By this strategy, a woman was conceived as not only *subject* to the law but as an *enforcer* of the law. This linkage of New Woman novel with the detective novel reveals Allen's genuine ideological agenda.

Grant Allen's engagement in *Miss Cayley's Adventures* with New Woman discourses begins with its title, with the stress on 'adventures', for the word has two implications in the series of stories: first, the experiences of the narrator, Lois Cayley; and second, the suggestion that 'adventures' implies an 'adventurer' or in this specific instance, an 'adventuress', a word which carries considerable ambiguity. Lois tells her friend Elsie Petheridge, 'I am going out, simply in search of adventure' (5). However, in the second tale *The Supercilious Attaché*, in which Lois Cayley meets Harold Tillington, the nephew of the elderly Lady Georgina Fawley, to whom she is a companion, the old woman gives the word 'adventures' a new inflection: 'What I'm always afraid of is that some fascinating adventuress will try to marry him out of hand' she declares; Lois responds: 'I don't think Mr Tillington is quite the sort that falls a prey to adventuresses' (48). 'That evening Lady Georgina managed to blurt out more malicious things than ever about the ways of adventuresses, and the duty of relations in saving young men from the clever clutches of designing creatures' (52-53).

Instead of repudiating the slur, Lois Cayley tells Harold Tillington her reason for leaving his aunt: 'The world is all before me where to choose. I am an adventuress, . . . and I am in quest of adventures' (55). By the end of the second story, therefore, Grant Allen has inflected the word both in its negative aspect and in its newer application to the independence of the New Woman. When Harold dismisses his aunt's attitude, Lois refuses to see him: 'I cannot – I am a penniless girl – an adventuress' (56). Even after Lois rescues Harold from a dangerous mountaineering accident in *The Impromptu Mountaineer*, the fifth tale, she refuses to marry him while he is rich, although she loves him: 'We are still ourselves; you rich, I a penniless adventuress' (145).

By the time she makes that statement, however, Lois has won a bicycle race and become a commission agent for an American inventor's bicycle. Her independence is established as an adventuress in the positive sense by this demonstration of the economic freedom of the New Woman. In the seventh tale, *The Urbane Old Gentleman*, Lois Cayley re-encounters Lady Georgina, who informs her that Harold has encountered an 'adventuress' (171). The old woman is amazed when Lois Cayley states that she herself is that woman (173). At this point, Lois has formed a typewriting service in Florence. Thus, throughout the text, the New Woman as 'adventuress' is addressed.

Allen confronts the attitude of those opposed to the New Woman that she is nothing but an adventuress, a common accusation among essayists of the period. Specifically, however, amidst writers who deployed such charges was Eliza Lynn Linton, referred to by name in *Miss Cayley's Adventures*. Linton, who died in 1898, was of considerable interest to supporters of the New Woman because she was so outspoken an opponent. Her name was prominent at the time of Allen's text not only because of her death but also because her memoir *My Literary Life* had been published posthumously in 1899. In debating the label 'adventuress', Allen appears to repudiate a specific essay by Linton, 'The Wild Women as Social Insurgents', which she published in October 1891 in *The Nineteenth Century*. Linton argues that the New Woman 'does all manner of things which she thinks bestow on her the power, together with the privileges, of a man' (597).

Linton then writes: 'About these Wild Women is always an unpleasant suggestion of the adventuress. Whatever their natural place and lineage, they are of the same family as those hotel heroines who forget to lock the chamber door . . . Under the new *régime* blots do not count for so much' (601). Allen would expect his readers to know this specific passage from Linton, which is the clearest indictment of the New Woman as sexually transgressive. Although Lois Cayley is decidedly not transgressive as is Herminia Barton in *The Woman Who Did*, her economic independence, her refusal to marry Harold Tillington for money and her economic success on the Continent leave her open to Linton's charge, so far as opponents of the New Woman are concerned.

In fact, in the same essay, Linton observes: 'With other queer inversions the frantic desire of making money has invaded the whole class of Wild Women; and it does not mitigate their desire that, as things are, they have enough for all reasonable wants' (599). After graduating from Girton, Lois refuses to be a teacher or a milliner, although she states: 'As a milliner's girl; why not? 'T is an honest calling. Earls' daughters do it now' (3), an observation directly repudiating Linton, who states: 'Women who, a few years ago, would not have shaken hands with a dressmaker . . . now open shops and set up in business on their own account' (599). The fact that Lois Cayley 'sets up in business' as a typist in Florence and continues that business for over a year is Allen's way of answering Linton, who herself ignores the economic imperatives which compelled women to work, however 'unladylike' it might be.

Many aspects of Lois Cayley's character seem created to challenge the predispositions of opponents of the New Woman. As a 'Girton girl', Lois is suspect. For instance, S. P. White, writing in *Blackwood's*, declares in 'Modern Mannish Maidens': 'The Girton girl emulates the Oxonian in the liberty accorded to her at her collegiate establishment . . . What means this modern craze for mannish sports and mannish ways?' (252-3). George J. Romanes, writing in 1887, remarks about Girton: 'When I was at Cambridge, the then newly established foundations of Girton and Newnham were to nearly all of us matters of amusement. But we have lived to alter our views' (666).

Likewise, Lois Cayley's physical strength is another challenge to opponents of the New Woman. She tells Harold Tillington: 'I am a fairly good climber . . . You see, at Cambridge, I went on the river a great deal – I canoed and sculled; and then, besides, I've done a lot of bicycling', at which Harold labels her 'a wholesome athletic English girl' (50). Cyrus W. Hitchcock, the American inventor of the four-speed bicycle she will market, is impressed by Lois's athleticism. Cayley observes: 'I like to intersperse culture and athletics. I know something about athletics, and hope in time to acquire a taste for culture. 'T is expected of a Girton girl, though my own accomplishments run rather towards rowing, punting, and bicycling' (78). In the course of the stories, Cayley will demonstrate her ability at mountaineering, hunting and above all cycling, especially in the episode of *The Inquisitive American* when she wins a race in Germany against all male opponents as she rides Hitchcock's four-speed bicycle.

The stress on cycling throughout *Miss Cayley's Adventures* is intended as a refutation of the opponents of the New Woman. Denouncing 'mannish maidens', S. P. White in 1890 remarks: 'What, now, shall be said of the modern popular mode of locomotion, at once a recreation and convenience to those who can afford no better – cycling? We will dismiss the bicycle from consideration, as, so far, the most enterprising of females has abstained for obvious reasons from adventuring herself thereon; though what the future may have in store in this way it is hard to say' (255). In her essay 'Why Women are Ceasing to Marry' published in the same year as *Miss Cayley's Adventures*, Ella Hepworth Dixon notes 'the amazing changes in the social life of women . . . Someone has boldly laid it down that it is the bicycle which has finally emancipated women, but it is certain that there are other factors besides the useful and agreeable wheel' (86). As does Lois Cayley, the protagonist of Grant Allen's other female detective tale *Hilda Wade* also uses a bicycle, memorably on the veldt in Rhodesia.

In 1894, M. Eastwood in the essay 'The New Woman in Fiction and Fact' had noted that detractors of the New Woman had pointed to 'the audacious young person who, seated astride a bicycle . . . shoots past them on the public road', but the writer continues that 'if she assumes certain articles of masculine garb on occasion, it is solely on account of their superior utility; if she rides out on a bicycle it is for the purpose of strengthening her muscles and expanding her lungs for the great work she has before her': 'The New Woman of today will be the woman of the future' (91). Allen's stress on bicycling in the stories *The Inquisitive American* and *The Amateur Commission Agent* emphasizes Lois Cayley's New Woman athleticism. In addition, she proves adept at climbing in the episode of *The Impromptu Mountaineer.*

Grant Allen addresses another charge against the New Woman, noted in Eliza Lynn Linton's essay 'The Partisans of the Wild Women' of 1892, that the New Woman travels brazenly abroad: 'We will give to these restless wild creatures all the honour to which they are entitled for their mischievous interference in politics, their useless tramps abroad – which are only self-advertisements and which do not add a line to our knowledge of men or countries' (462). In *Miss Cayley's Adventures*, the protagonist travels to Germany, Italy, Egypt, India, Asia and across Canada. In the initial tale, *The Cantankerous Old Lady*, Lois Cayley overhears Lady Georgina Fawley lamenting the lack of a companion to travel abroad with her; Lois Cayley offers to do so, which initiates her subsequent 'adventures.'

During her global travels, Cayley has various occupations: commission agent for Hitchcock's bicycle, typist and journalist. Cayley leaves Lady Georgina and travels alone to Germany in the third tale, *The Inquisitive American*. Although Elsie Petheridge joins her in Italy, she leaves Lois Cayley at the beginning of the tenth tale, *The Cross-Eyed Q.C.* Cayley then travels through Asia and Canada alone to return to England and aid Harold Tillington in repudiating accusations he is a forger. This stress on global travel marks Lois Cayley's 'adventures' as entirely appropriate for a Girton girl/New Woman. In all, she remains away from England, as noted in the eleventh story *The Oriental Attendant*, for three years (297). Lois Cayley labels her book her 'confiding memoirs' (261), which appear to validate her status as an independent woman, at least until her marriage to Tillington at the book's conclusion. At the same time, the label of 'confiding memoirs' shields the book from the 'self-advertisement' indicted by Linton.

Of the twelve stories in *Miss Cayley's Adventures*, seven have a criminous or detectival element, but the point of Allen's text is to integrate all twelve tales on the basis of Lois Cayley's New Woman enterprise, ingenuity and intelligence, whether or not these are directed at solving or preventing crime. In effect, the text subsumes the detectival genre within the New Woman narrative, a principal component of its distinction. This dual nature of the text is stressed in the first narrative, *The Cantankerous Old Lady*, which appeared in March, 1898, in the *Strand*.

The beginning of the story stresses its New Woman agenda, the conclusion its detectival dimension. Cayley admits that it was her mother's imprudent remarriage which drove her to be the woman she is, since she was given barely enough money to study at Girton by the stepfather. After her graduation, when her friend Elsie Petheridge suggests she teach, Cayley responds: 'Did you say *teach?* . . . No, Elsie, I do *not* propose to teach' (2). In the Long Walk at Kensington Gardens, Cayley overhears Lady Georgina Fawley lamenting her need of a companion. She tells the old woman she is 'a Girton girl', to which the woman replies: 'What are girls coming to, I wonder? Girton, you say; Girton!' (12).

Despite this reservation, Cayley travels to the Continent with the old lady. In the train, Cayley becomes suspicious of a glib man in the compartment, who, she correctly surmises, plans to steal Lady Georgina's jewel case. She foils him by removing the steel box with the jewels from the case. It will evolve that the man, pretending to be a Count, is in reality a corrupt butler/valet named Higginson, in the service of Lady Georgina's brother Marmaduke Ashurst. This initial story links detection with the New Woman, demonstrating that a Girton girl is capable of perceptive action in and out of the university. Lady Georgina praises Cayley's 'courage and promptitude' (31). The narrative also introduces the first of a string of deceiving, scheming males.

In the second story, published the following month, *The Supercilious Attaché*, Cayley is in Schlangenbad, Germany. This locale allows Grant Allen the opportunity to express typical later nineteenth-century contempt about Germans via the words of Lady Georgina:

> 'They're bursting with self-satisfaction – have such an exaggerated belief in their "land" and their "folk." And when they come to England, they do nothing but find fault with us . . . Nasty pigs of Germans! The very sight of them sickens me . . . They all learn English nowadays; it helps them in trade – that's why they're driving us out of all the markets . . . They're a set of barbarians.' (34)

Grant Allen's desire to contextualize the New Woman and detectival components of his text is exhibited here, as suspicions about German hegemony became very prominent in Britain during the period.

While at the spa, 'a loose-limbed, languid-looking young man, with large, dreamy eyes' appears to be following Cayley and the old lady. Cayley especially notes his 'superficial air of superciliousness' (36). When she describes the man's 'large, poetical eyes; an artistic moustache – just a trifle Oriental-looking' (40), she learns this is Lady Georgina's nephew Harold Tillington, an attaché in Rome. Tillington acts the role of a supercilious man, but Cayley is impressed with his knowledge of Europe and his 'epigrammatic wit, curt, keen, and pointed' (42). When he asks if she is 'medieval or modern', Cayley responds that she is modern; he is from Oxford, she from Cambridge. 'Thenceforth we were friends – "two 'Varsity men", he said. And indeed it does make a queer sort of link – a freemasonry to which even women are now admitted' (46), she observes.

Cayley learns that Tillington will inherit all his uncle Marmaduke Ashurst's money. In one of their discussions about marriage, Tillington observes that 'a man ought to wish the woman he loves to be a free agent, his equal in point of action' (52). When he expresses his love, Lois Cayley rejects him, fearing to be construed an adventuress merely after his inheritance. She tells his aunt, Lady Georgina: 'I am a lady by birth and education; I am an officer's daughter; but I am not what society calls a "good match" for Mr Tillington' (58). While not wishing to be construed an adventuress, Cayley also desires independence: 'I must work out my life in my own way. I have started to work it out, and I won't be turned aside just here on the threshold' she advises Lady Georgina (61). She records: 'Next morning I set out by myself . . . I went forth into the world to live my own life, partly because it was just then so fashionable, but mainly because fate had denied me the chance of living anybody else's' (61). *The Supercilious Attaché*, albeit it contains no overt detection, expands Grant Allen's evaluation of the beliefs of the New Woman.

At the beginning of the third narrative, *The Inquisitive American*, Cayley admits that parting from Tillington 'left a scar . . . but as I am not a professional sentimentalist, I will not trouble you here with details of the symptoms' (62). If German competition is a concern in the previous story, here it is the Americans and their competitive spirit that are displayed in the person of Cyrus W. Hitchcock, who has invented a four-speed bicycle that easily ascends hills. Declaring 'an adventuress I would be; for I loved adventure' (63), Cayley states her manifesto, contrasting herself with unmarried German women:

> I prefer to take life in a spirit of pure enquiry. I put on my hat; I saunter where I choose, so far as circumstances permit; and I wait to see what chance will bring me. My ideal is breeziness . . .
> I prefer to grow upwards; the frau grows sideways . . .
> Adventures are to the adventurous. They abound on every side; but only the chosen few have the courage to embrace them. And they will not come to you: you must go out to seek them. Then they meet you half way, and rush into your arms, for they know their true lovers. (64, 71)

Lois Cayley has the opportunity to demonstrate this credo when Hitchcock asks her to ride his bicycle in a contest with Germans, who 'were all men, of course' (79). When a German objects to her competing, Cayley whips out a copy of a law which permits women to race. Seizing the chance, Cayley competes, despite 'a look of unchivalrous dislike, such as only your sentimental German can cast at a woman' (86). Cayley wins the race, receiving fifty pounds from Hitchcock: 'I was now a woman of means' (88). Particularly significant in this story, beyond its cross-cultural comparison of America, England and Germany, are the illustrations by Gordon Browne, some of which (66, 67, 69, 82, 86, 87), showing Cayley on bicycles competing with men and confronting German officers, underscore the agendas of the New Woman. Gordon Browne would also illustrate Allen's other female detective series for the *Strand*, *Hilda Wade*. There the illustrations, as in *Miss Cayley's Adventures*, advance their own argument for greater female independence, parallel to the printed text itself.

The American inventor Hitchcock is so impressed with Lois Cayley that he makes her his commission agent for the four-speed bicycle on the Continent. Cayley accepts his offer, 'for I beheld vistas' (93). Her eagerness to make money from an American entrepreneur runs counter to the position of the detractors of the New Woman. Cayley, however, rejects Hitchcock's offer of marriage. 'I set out on my wanderings . . . to go round the world on my own account' (97), recognizing 'the business half of me' (99). Joined by her friend Elsie Petheridge, Cayley encounters a Mrs Evelegh, an Englishwoman under the care of a faith healer, one Dr Fortescue-Langley, who supposedly treats her 'psychically' (107). This man dupes Mrs Evelegh by having her wear an Indian bracelet which turns dark when her 'inner self' (107) is disturbed. From her experience 'in the laboratory at college' (107), Lois Cayley discovers that the maid brings the woman an india-rubber hot water bottle, the material of which contains sulphur; the rubber discolours the silver bangle.

It evolves that this man is the rogue, the Count, who had tried to steal Lady Georgina's jewels in the first tale. Cayley confronts him and tears off his fake moustache, revealing Higginson, Marmaduke Ashurst's valet/courier, who retreats confronted by the New Woman/detective. Cayley is enabled in her detection because of her education at Girton. Earlier in the same story she had encountered male trickery in the persons of two German students, Ludwig and Heinrich, who bought bicycles directly from Hitchcock to avoid paying Lois Cayley's commission, which Hitchcock pays her anyway. Yet in showing the deceit of both English and German men, the narrative reveals that the New Woman must be enterprising in whatever cultural situation she encounters.

In the fifth story, *The Impromptu Mountaineer*, published in July 1898, Elsie and Lois, while on vacation, are visited by Harold Tillington, who professes his love for Lois. She nevertheless again refuses to marry him because of his potential inheritance, despite the fact she admits she loves him. She explains:

> 'Well, because I am modern . . . I can answer you No. I can even now refuse you . . . But *I* am modern, and I see things differently . . . We are still ourselves; you rich, I a penniless adventuress . . . I am a modern woman, and what I say I mean. I will renew my promise. If ever you are poor and friendless, come to me; I am yours.' (144-5)

This refusal is made particularly complicated because in the course of this story, Lois Cayley rescues Harold Tillington when he falls over a precipice in the mountains.

In tracing Tillington's footsteps in order to rescue him, Lois exhibits the detectival ability to follow tracks: 'the emergency seemed somehow to teach me something of the instinctive lore of hunters and savages' (133).

Noting that 'women are almost always brave in great emergencies' (139), Lois manages to haul Tillington up from the place of his fall. Her strength comes from her rowing at Girton, she observes (140). As in the previous story, the illustrations, especially one of Cayley descending the slope (138) and one of Harold Tillington falling (142), visualize the New Woman ideology of the text. Instead of the male rescuing the imperilled or endangered woman à la St George, so common in the Victorian construction of genders, Grant Allen depicts the rescue of a distressed man by a strong, resourceful woman. It has already been discussed that the St George rescue motif appears in Leonard Merrick's *Mr Bazalgette's Agent* of 1888, where the reversal of gendered expectation is evident, with the rescuer the woman and the rescued individual a male.

This enterprise is furthermore part of Lois Cayley's ability to conduct business, which proves distressing to her own aunt, who writes 'to expostulate with me on my "unladylike" conduct in becoming a bicycle commission agent' (124). Even Lady Georgina defends Lois Cayley being in business:

> 'What does the woman mean? Has she got no gumption? It's "ladylike," I suppose, to be a companion, or a governess, or a music-teacher, or something else in the black-thread-glove way, in London; but not to sell bicycles for a good round commission. My dear, between you and me, I don't see it.' (124)

Fortified in her beliefs about economic independence, Cayley refuses to be betrothed to Tillington, despite having rescued him. Such repudiation of the romance plot is striking.

The next story, *The Urbane Old Gentleman*, finds Lois Cayley in Florence, where she sets up a typewriting service with her friend Elsie. One of her clients is Marmaduke Ashurst, Lady Georgina's brother. Lois Cayley reasserts her decision not to marry Harold if he has money. However, she consents to type Ashurst's will. When Frederic Higginson, the rogue who had impersonated both a Count and a faith healer, turns up to retrieve the will for Ashurst, who has re-employed him, Cayley refuses to yield it, delivering it herself to Ashurst. Higginson had defamed without naming her to Ashurst as an 'adventuress' (171), and Cayley readily admits to Ashurst she is the woman so labelled.

Ashurst has a bizarre philosophy of life which aligns religion, economics and imperialism, betraying male folly and ignorance, which Lois Cayley perceives and circumvents. 'My fairy godmother's name was really Enterprise' (154) Cayley records. One illustration (160) by Gordon Browne shows Cayley at the typewriter as Ashurst sits in the client's chair, another example of the illustrations by Browne providing an ideological commentary on the narrative.

After Elsie and Lois have spent about a year in Florence in business, they go to Egypt in the episode of *The Unobtrusive Oasis*. Lois Cayley has been hired by Elworthy, millonaire editor of the *Daily Telephone*, to be a roving reporter, sending 'three descriptive articles a week' (181) to the newspaper. Aboard ship, the two women meet an Irish doctor, Macloghlen. Once arrived in Egypt, the three decide to visit an oasis, which requires a long camel ride. In the town, a woman whispers to them that she was captured after the fall of Khartoum (1885) and sold to an Arab, whose children she has borne. Lois and the doctor contrive to effect her escape. Lois Cayley defends the right of the woman to have her children with her, despite reservations by Macloghlen. Her assertive feminism overcomes his hardline masculine attitude that children should remain with their father. Macloghlen nevertheless exhibits 'the reckless and good-humoured courage of the untamed Celt' (204) when confronted by hostile Arabs. Grant Allen had argued in his 1880 essay 'Are We Englishmen?' for the *Fortnightly Review* that Celts, not Anglo-Saxons, have been the true colonizers in the Empire and the key figures in the administration of India. *The Unobtrusive Oasis* demonstrates Celtic and feminine enterprise, noting 'that the English were now in practical occupation of Egypt' (204). Grant Allen shows one Englishwoman rescuing and defending another, an incident repudiating arguments about 'the shrieking sisterhood' of women, as expressed for instance in the essay 'Modern Man-Haters' in *The Saturday Review* (528) in 1871.

In *The Pea-Green Patrician*, Elsie and Lois voyage to India via the Red Sea. On ship they encounter Lord Albert Southminster, another nephew of Lady Georgina's and hence a cousin to Harold Tillington. Southminster's courier and assistant is the rogue Frederic Higginson from previous stories. Lois Cayley spurns Southminster as a cynical clubman, declaring 'He isn't a man; he's a lump of putty!' (219). Southminster admits he inhabits music halls, attends horse auctions at Tattersall's and courts music hall performers. He tells Lois, 'As a rule I don't think much of women' (229). Nevertheless, he proposes to her, claiming he rather than the other nephew Harold Tillington will inherit Marmaduke Ashurst's money. Lois rejects him, denouncing his 'insulting proposal' (231) and 'degrading offer' (232). The narrative presents yet another undesirable Englishman, a telling contrast with the refined, Oxford-educated Indian of the next story.

In *The Magnificent Maharajah*, Lois Cayley arrives in Bombay as a successful special correspondent, where she is met by the Maharajah of Moozuffernuggar. The narrative is explicit in its critique of English racist attitudes. The captain of the ship receives the man 'with true British contempt for the inferior black man' (235). Lois is impressed by the man, although she notices the incongruity of his European dress with an Indian turban. The Indian comments:

> 'You treat a native gentleman, I see, like a human being. I hope you will not stop long enough in our country to get over that stage – as happens to most of your countrymen and countrywomen. In England, a man like myself is an Indian prince; in India, to ninety-nine out of a hundred Europeans, he is just "a damned nigger."' (240)

Lord Albert, who has trailed Cayley to India, calls the Maharajah 'a niggah . . . behaving for all the world as if he were a gentleman; it's reahhly too ridiculous' (241-2). Cayley counters by noting that the man's 'ancestors were princes while ours were dressed in woad and oak-leaves. But you were right about one thing; *he* behaves – like a gentleman' (242). She concludes Southminster is 'nothing more than a born bounder' (24).

In this episode, Lois Cayley goes on a tiger hunt, during which she rides an elephant and kills the tiger accidentally, drawing much acclaim. The Maharajah states he 'could never have believed a woman could show such nerve and coolness' (257). 'I dared not confess the truth – that I never fired at all' (261) Cayley admits in the text. This episode appears to be another charge against Eliza Lynn Linton, who in 'The Wild Women as Social Insurgents' had declared:

> Free-traders in all that relates to sex, the Wild Women allow men no monopoly in sports, in games, in responsibilities. Beginning by 'walking with the guns,' they end by shooting with them; and some have made the moor a good training-ground for the jungle. (597)

The tiger shoot seems deliberately included to comment on Linton's assertion. In *Hilda Wade* Grant Allen will send his nurse/detective to India, Nepal and Tibet, which provides an illustrator like Gordon Browne ample opportunity for imaginative drawing.

The final three tales of *Miss Cayley's Adventures* concentrate on a single sequence of events, involving Lois Cayley's attempts to clear Harold Tillington of charges of forgery brought by his cousin Lord Albert Southminster. He contends that Harold forged the will of their uncle Marmaduke Ashurst, whose death had been recorded at the conclusion of the previous story. This is the will that Lois Cayley typed at Florence in the sixth tale of the series. In these three tales, Lois exhibits all her amateur detection skills. It is quite possible that Grant Allen echoes the concluding trial scenes involving the titular character in Elizabeth Gaskell's *Mary Barton* (1848), who races to give testimony to save her lover. A reference to the Jubilee dates the trial to 1897. Lois Cayley travels alone through Asia and Canada to return to London.

In the tenth story, *The Cross-Eyed Q.C.*, Lois Cayley is ruthlessly examined by the Queen's Counsel, who constructs her as a scheming *femme fatale* who has collaborated with Harold in perpetrating the fraud. Cayley discovers that her Girton education and penchant for 'originality' (281) are against her. (As the 1887 essay by Romanes supposedly proves, women could not be genuinely original.) The Q.C. then labels her an 'adventuress' (285, 288) after Harold's money, despite her protestations to the contrary. This summation by the Q.C. demonstrates the prejudicial male construction of women in the most glaring manner. Lois reflects about the all-male jury (shown in an illustration 283): 'The jury could never understand my point of view. It could never be made to see that there are adventuresses and adventuresses' (287). In other words, the negative connotation of 'adventuress' destroys the value of her evidence. Lord Bertie Southminster wins and Harold Tillington is pursued on a charge of forgery.

In the penultimate tale, *The Oriental Attendant*, the Maharajah aids Harold by having Tillington disguise himself as the Maharajah's Indian attendant. This ruse allows Harold to escape London with Lois. Together they take the train over the Scottish border, get off (at her providential suggestion) at the first town in Scotland and convince a minister to marry them after she reveals the truth. Dressed in Indian costume, Harold, Lois writes, 'folded me in his arms. I allowed him, unreproved. For the first time he kissed me. I did not shrink from it' (297). On the train journey, Harold is labelled a 'nigger' (302) by a porter. Lois thus has the fantasy of transgressive sexuality with a racial Other while knowing he is in fact white. Yet even Lois reveals an element of racism: 'I felt myself blush at the bare idea that I was marrying a black man, in spite of our good Maharajah's kindness' (310).

Lois Cayley foils the detective trailing them. 'You can only get the better of a skilled detective by taking him thus, psychologically and humanly . . . I felt almost like a criminal' (305) she records. After the marriage, Harold Tillington turns himself in to the authorities. Lois Cayley then assumes the role of detective in order to clear her new husband: 'I see a way out. I have found a clue' (317), she assures Harold. The last illustration to this chapter shows Lois delivering this statement as she holds her hands to Harold, still garbed in his Indian costume, her stance ostensibly the very image of cross-racial sexual transgression (316).

In the final tale, *The Unprofessional Detective*, Lois Cayley, with the assistance of the solicitor Hayes, saves Tillington from conviction for forgery by noting discrepancies in the typed copy of the disputed will. She recognizes that although they are both typed on the same brand of machine, she made no errors on the original in Florence, while the will presented by Southminster is marked by a few mistakes. The typewriter she used in Florence also had an imperfect *x*, while the same letter on the copy is perfect. At Ashurst's home, Cayley finds the real will in a secret drawer of his desk. The old courier Higginson had forged the will and drawn Southminster into the plot against Harold Tillington. Because he did not actually forge the will, Southminster is allowed to leave for permanent residence in South Africa. Lois Cayley marries Harold Tillington, who in the final illustration is now shown in gentleman's street dress rather than in Indian costume. As a fugitive, Harold Tillington was an Indian in appearance; with his honour restored, he is an English gentleman.

This conclusion of the final tale raises a number of questions. Since the original will is found, Harold Tillington indeed inherits Marmaduke Ashurst's money, so Lois Cayley, despite her stated unwillingness to marry a rich man, in the end does so. The final instalment has it both ways: Lois marries for love but gets the money anyway when the real will is proved in her husband's favour. In her defence, however, Lois Cayley marries Tillington when he is a fugitive who, if convicted, would never inherit his uncle's money; she supports him in his decision to turn himself in to the authorities. Mona Caird, in her essay 'Marriage' in 1888, advised that a woman 'ought not to be tempted to marry, or to remain married, for the sake of bread and butter' (79), and emphatically when Lois Cayley marries in so constraining a circumstance she is not marrying for money. Is Lois Cayley still a New Woman? She probably will maintain an independence of attitude, but she has no need to work or pursue a career after her marriage. Nothing is recorded about it: all her expertise as agent, typist and journalist appears to have been subsumed by the role of wife. Pressure from the *Strand* undoubtedly compelled Grant Allen to accept narrative closure by having Lois Cayley marry Harold Tillington. In his history of the *Strand*, Reginald Pound labelled Grant Allen a 'distinguished contributor' (43) to the magazine.

But was the *Strand* uneasy about the New Woman agenda, such that it is dismissed or ignored in the concluding narrative? It may well be that the *Strand* felt Allen had satisfied the demands of the unadulterated New Woman novel in *The Woman Who Did*. *Miss Cayley's Adventures* represents an amalgamation of novelistic sub-genres: the detective narrative, the New Woman novel, the travel/adventure record. That Lois Cayley marries at the conclusion is wildly in contrast with the suicide of Herminia Barton at the conclusion of *The Woman Who Did*. Nevertheless, it is possible to regard the marriage conclusion as compatible with the defence of the New Woman, since it establishes that Lois Cayley is not 'unsexed', a common accusation of detractors of the New Woman such as Linton, who in her 1892 essay deployed this charge (461).

In *Miss Cayley's Adventures*, Grant Allen represents the contextualizing of New Woman ideology by exhibiting through the detectival element the functioning of the New Woman's education, originality and freedom in a variety of circumstances — foreign travel, business relations, legal procedures. The illustrations by Gordon Browne contribute to advancing New Woman ideology by depicting Lois Cayley riding a camel, racing a bicycle, taking typed dictation, speaking with a veiled Englishwoman at an oasis, descending a mountain precipice, giving testimony in court and holding hands with a black man, for example. Such illustrations underscore Grant Allen's ideolgical defence of the New Woman. Arthur Conan Doyle remembers that Grant Allen took 'a certain pleasure . . . in defending outside positions' (262).

If Allen rejects the sexual permissiveness associated with the negative inflection of the word 'adventuress' in *Miss Cayley's Adventures*, he advances beyond 'the woman who did' to recognize its positive dimension — for 'the woman who dares.'

Beatrice Heron-Maxwell (d. 1927): *The Adventures of a Lady Pearl-Broker* (1899)

In her discussion of female detectives, Michelle Slung discusses the protagonist, Mollie Delamere, created by Beatrice Heron-Maxwell in *The Adventures of a Lady Pearl-Broker*, a tale in nine chapters which first appeared in the *Harmsworth Magazine* in 1899. Slung observes that Mollie Delamere 'sustains a great deal of physical abuse while thwarting the activities of various burglars and kidnappers' (361). The physical abuse is only one of the distinctions given by Heron-Maxwell to her young widow broker/detective. It is, furthermore, significant that Mollie Delamere first appeared in the *Harmsworth Magazine*, which had already made its mark in presenting female detectives.

One of its earliest tales about a female detective, important to the evolution of Mollie Delamere, is Nora Van Snoop, created by Clarence Henry Rook (1862-1915) in the famous short story *The Stir Outside the Café Royal*, published in the *Harmsworth* in September 1898. The story sets a model for the female detective, albeit several well-known women had preceded its protagonist. In the narrative, Nora Van Snoop tracks down and turns over to the London police one Colonel Mathurin, who had shot her fiancé, bank manager William Stevens, to death in Detroit, Michigan. It is disclosed that Van Snoop had become a member of the New York detective force to track down Mathurin. As soon as she secures his arrest, she resigns from the force.

The reader learns that Mathurin is 'one of the aristocrats of crime' who has constantly 'eluded pursuit' although he was 'the most desperate among criminals' (223). The American woman goes to London to pursue her man. There is a 'certain hardness in the set of [her] mouth' (224) which presages her determination and success. When she enters the Café Royal alone, one of the male loungers in the Café remarks: 'American, you bet . . . They'll go anywhere and do anything' (224), but Van Snoop is oblivious to gendered criticism. 'Many curious glances were directed to the girl who sat at a table alone and pursued her way calmly through the menu' (225). She seats herself at a table for four and refuses to budge, since she has perceived Mathurin entering the Café.

When Mathurin leaves the Café, this lady detective follows him and deliberately steals his cigarette case to bring the police to arrest her and detain Mathurin at the station. Van Snoop is 'perfectly ready to face this or any other situation' (226). When Van Snoop is alone with a female searcher, she hands the woman a letter informing her that Mathurin is wanted all over the world, under his various aliases, for crimes. She tells the police that she saw Mathurin kill Will Stevens before her own eyes. They discover she is right. She is dauntless, stating 'I wanted to arrest him myself' (226). After Mathurin is taken into custody, the narrator concludes:

> Miss Van Snoop sank into a cane-bottomed chair, laid her head upon the table, and cried. She had earned the luxury of hysterics. In half an hour she left the station, and, proceeding to a post-office, cabled her resignation to the head of the detective force in New York. (226)

Clarence Rook sets limits to Van Snoop's transgressive profession and actions, having her revert to female hysteria and resign, lest she be perceived as too unfeminine, even for an American woman. Also important is the fact that Van Snoop undertakes detection for personal, amorous reasons.

Hal Hurst's illustrations show Van Snoop as quite glamorous. One picture even shows Mathurin killing her lover Will Stevens as Van Snoop tries to restrain the murderer. The third picture depicts her primping nonchalantly before a mirror, while the fourth explicitly depicts the female detective in action, following the top-hatted Mathurin outside the Café. Despite her success in tracking down the criminal, she gives up her career. The story is also remarkable for indicating that Americans can be dangerous criminals, a fact noted in the first Sherlock Holmes narrative, *A Study in Scarlet* of 1887, with its Mormon renegades murdering in London.

Michelle Slung notes that the verb 'to snoop' 'comes from the Dutch *snoepen*, which means "to enjoy stealthily"' (83). But the word also seems to suggest that Van Snoop is not a professional, tempering her achievement. Craig and Cadogan see Van Snoop as a variant of the New Woman character:

> The New Woman was a force to be reckoned with, in fiction as well as in fact. Stories of women and girls in challenging situations proliferated, and these usually had career or sporty backgrounds; weekly and monthly papers, as well as books, celebrated the imaginary exploits of lady balloonists and bicyclists, nurses and newshounds. Enterprising authors soon realized that detection provided tougher physical challenges than sports stories and more mental excitement than the usual run of career tales. (23-4)

In her enterprise, Van Snoop indeed retains some of the quality of a New Woman, although Rook's introduction of the erotic motive dilutes her affiliation with the New Woman model. Craig and Cadogan correctly note:

> Women were already forcing their way into the professions and public life, but it seems that male authors, even when admiring their initiative, wished to imply that detection, except as a temporary measure, was basically unfeminine. (25)

The legacy of the story, however, is important to Beatrice Heron-Maxwell, as Van Snoop is courageous and adventurous, daring to travel alone and invade the Café Royal without concern for male restrictions or glances. The marriage plot, however, as *The Adventures of a Lady Pearl-Broker* will indicate, remains in force even for female writers.

Beatrice Heron-Maxwell was 'left a widow with two daughters after her first husband's death' (Kemp et al. 181). Although Mollie Delamere has no children, she also is forced to work after becoming a widow. By the time Heron-Maxwell published *The Adventures of a Lady Pearl-Broker* in the *Harmsworth*, she had already made a name for herself in its pages. In September 1898, she had published the short story *How the Minister's Notes Were Recovered*, which detailed how Lady Anstiss Carlyon had saved the career of an American diplomat, Julius Berend, by recovering 'some important notes' (250) which he had sent to the incorrect party. Heron-Maxwell includes in the story the observation: 'Women move the levers nowadays, though men make 'em' (251) which, as Craig and Cadogan note

(56), sounds feminist, although Lady Anstiss falls into the young diplomat's arms instead of into a career in espionage at the conclusion. Similarly, Heron-Maxwell has Mollie Delamere engage in many daring escapades, although in the end she marries and abandons her career.

Her stories, however, are bizarre and thrilling. She is hired by Mr Leighton, 'the prince of pearl merchants', who informs her that she needs above all 'pluck' (1), that key necessary masculine attribute. Several times he tells her of the 'danger' (2, 3) which she must confront. Having told her that lady pearl-brokers have been tried successfully in Paris, he defines the position: 'There is a certain number of ladies of good position who undertake to be mediums between pearl merchants and their clients. I do not mean to say that you have to solicit orders from your personal friends – not at all' (3), assuring her that her main business is with jewellers.

· However, the very terms 'broker' and 'solicit' suggest that these are indeed dangerous waters for a woman, a hint not lost on Mollie Delamere, who thinks: 'And poor widows are looked upon in society so often as adventuresses' (6). Pluck is decidedly key, since Leighton advises her:

> 'Only remember that you must always be looking out for an attack. If it once gets known – and London thieves learn these things in the most marvellous way – that a woman is in possession of jewellery to any extent, she is marked at once, and sooner or later they have a try for it.' (5)

It takes little imagination to read between the lines here that the woman's body is the 'jewel' which might be assaulted and taken, i.e., raped. This is especially true since Mollie Delamere conceals the jewels around her body: 'I had contrived secret pockets in various unexpected places in my dress . . . It would be impossible for me to lose anything out of them, and quite impossible for anyone to cut out the pockets while I had my senses about me' (9-10).

One of these jewels is a 'pink pearl' (13), which Delamere retains, thinking she might sell it to an Australian millionaire. As the reader will learn when she marries this Australian man, Anderson, she is herself the pink pearl. The correlation between the pearl and the female body is evident. Leighton informs his new pearl-broker:

> 'We find that ladies have an instinct for appraising the values of jewels. We in the trade of course learn how to distinguish between good and bad, but ladies seem to become experts without any training at all.' (4)

According to Leighton, women are almost inherently mercantile. This mercantilism is given an ethical ambiguity by his use of the word 'trade', which evokes the bartering of the body in prostitution. Heron-Maxwell emphasizes that a woman is always an object of exchange, always priced, evaluated, commodified – and brokered.

The scenario of potential rape and rape threat is reinforced in several of the tales in which Mollie Delamere is rendered a prisoner in a locked room, once with a deranged man attacking her. The locked room, while signifying several elements – the unconscious, the past or paranoia, for example – is also for a woman the vagina, certainly here with Heron-Maxwell's discussion of pearls, hiding jewels on the body, brokering and trading.

Mollie Delamere has an opportunity to learn about locked rooms in the first chapter. Asleep in her room at the Howarth Hotel in London, where she has checked the hasp on the window and the lock on the door, she has a dream that she is at the bottom of the sea, surrounded by pearls. Awakening, she is aware of 'a hand . . . stealing gently, stealthily, amongst the folds of the sheet around my neck . . . The stealthy fingers reached my lips . . . I was almost unconscious, when, with a new thrill of horror, I recognised the strong, sharp smell of chloroform' (16-17). When a woman in another room screams out seeing a second man on Delamere's ledge, the thieves flee, never to be found.

Delamere's room number, 13, should have indicated the danger, but the actual attempt to chloroform her, and steal the jewels in her safe, is described as an attempted rape. The story is given a particularly grim twist because Delamere herself had secured the chamber to render it a locked room, which nevertheless two males can invade. She does leave the hotel, moving to a flat at Royal Mansions, Victoria Street. In the next chapter, Leighton advises her that she has learned the 'dangers' (22) of her profession. The fact that the two men are never apprehended means they continue to prey on women.

The second chapter contains another episode involving a locked room. Ali Mahomed Khan tries to abduct Delamere to be a companion to an English woman who had been captured in India and made the wife of a Rajah. To effect the abduction, Delamere is drugged with a sweetmeat laced with cocaine. When her captor goes to the landing of the room for a moment, she flees and jumps sixteen feet to escape. She had noted in the previous chapter: 'I have always hated having things made easy for me – there is then no satisfaction in accomplishing them' (11), and in this episode nothing is made easy.

Although Leighton is worried about Delamere's 'adventurous spirit' (24) nothing shakes her 'resolve' (25). Once her speech is paralysed by the cocaine, she experiences 'powerlessness' (33), wondering: 'Was there no possible outlet through which help might come? . . . Was I, then, to be left absolutely alone with this awful man?' (35, 38). She even acknowledges 'that my only chance was to appear submissive' (37). Adroitly, she saves herself by catering to male gendered preconceptions about women's behaviour.

After her escape, Delamere conceals the truth from her employer Leighton, telling him that the 'interview had been unsuccessful' (41). She records: 'I was anxious to avoid all questions on the subject of my interview with Ali Mahomed Khan' (42). That her fate would have been that of the captured English woman there can be no doubt. As with the previous tale, the evil men are not apprehended. The engagement with the subcontinent evokes the parallel locale of the origin of evil in Conan Doyle's *The Sign of Four* in 1890.

Leighton is not to be put off, however, as he tells her at the beginning of the next episode: 'I confess to having an uneasy feeling about you sometimes, and I hope you will under no circumstances be venturesome. Be discreet' (43). In this tale, Delamere saves a little girl from being killed on the street. The girl's mother takes her to a room, which turns out to be in a thieves' den, that of the Association of Gentlemen Burglars, whose president is the man who had attempted to chloroform her in the first episode.

In the locked room, Mollie Delamere realizes that the pink pearl is missing. Finding a spring next to a mirror, she goes down a long corridor, where the thieves are debating her fate, which consists of two options: either she joins them or is killed. A young man, who is revealed later to be an acquaintance going to the devil, Gerard Beverley, speaks up for the criminal woman, the Countess, who has asked that Delamere's life be spared. With the aid of the little girl and her remorseful mother, Delamere escapes. The pink pearl is later returned.

It is only in the final chapter that Delamere labels herself a 'detective' (154), but her exploits disclose a London and an England rampant with criminality. At the end of this 'third adventure' (58) as she labels it, Delamere reflects:

> I had fancied till then that in London one must be absolutely safe, but there are many hidden tragedies there, submergences that make no ripple on the surface; and although my experience of a very dangerous society was personally a unique one, I believe that this superior Association of Gentlemen Burglars is not by any means the only one, nor the most unscrupulous, that lives and thrives in and near our law-ridden city. (59)

Mollie Delamere is indeed a detective, one whose results, however, become known only in her narrative, these memoirs. What she discovers and detects is pandemic crime which, in the individual cases, is never brought to the authorities in order to protect her identity in her dangerous profession and to save her employer Leighton from risk. But the publication of the book itself makes Delamere a detective in the service of the entire society.

The next adventure shows crime in high places. Delamere attends an engagement party for Nellie Brand and Sir Charles Merivale. At the dinner, Brand's engagement ring is passed around the table to the guests. When it is discovered that it has not been returned, Delamere suggests that the electric lights be shut off to enable the guilty party to place the ring on the table, which in fact occurs.

The guilty party turns out to be Gerard Beverley, the son of an admiral, 'a confounded young fool' who 'throws all his money away on betting, and gets into no end of scrapes' (64) according to Nellie's brother Tom Brand. Tom Brand, furthermore, is willing to dismiss masculine transgression: 'I don't know anything worse of him than that' (64). Delamere, however, does know more, for Beverley is the man who defended her in the thieves' den and thereby saved her life. She advises Tom Brand that Beverley 'wants a very great deal of looking after' (65).

Delamere never informs anyone that Gerard Beverley is a thief. Eventually, he is sent to South Africa as an overseer, with the family's hope that he will reform. Heron-Maxwell reveals that young men are going to damnation in the culture and that other young men, like Tom Brand, condone their antics or refuse to recognize the decline in British masculine behaviour. Delamere might provide a man's one chance of recovery.

In the next story, a Russian dog, Serge, loaned to Delamere for the night by the artist Charles Seton, a fellow dinner guest, saves Delamere when a man breaks into her flat and confronts her with a Derringer. The dog attacks the man and subdues him. Delamere dismisses her two maids, whose loquacity had caused her to be robbed. Again, the motif of the locked room appears:

> A flat always seems so safe and self-contained! When you close your front door you seem to shut yourself up in your castle and pull up a metaphorical drawbridge between yourself and the world, and there is an added sense of security in the knowledge that though enclosed in your own domain you are not really isolated, and there are human beings within call at your desire. (74)

As with her other lodging at the Howarth Hotel, however, this sense of security is false. Does she leave herself open to these depredations? She has 'an uneasy feeling it was time for me to have another adventure of some sort, a vague presentiment of something unpleasant in store for me' (75). Later she has 'an indefinite sense of uneasiness' (79), but she plans to stay the night alone in her room.

When Delamere has the man cornered, she wonders:

> What was I do to about the man? . . . If I raised an alarm I should be obliged to give him in charge, and to state that he had broken open my safe. This would lead, perhaps, to a revelation about the pearls, and in accounting for their presence in the safe my occupation would become known. (86)

Later she resolves: 'I thought it best to tell no one on account of the risk it would add to my business if it became generally known' (90). It appears, however, that risk is something she almost seeks in order to test her resolution and commitment in the male world and to determine the parameters of her independence.

Mollie Delamere's next adventure is a railway tale involving the locked train carriage. A Mrs Westall, the wife of a lawyer, is brutally attacked en route to Bristol. Delamere is on the same train in an adjacent carriage. She hears a woman's scream as the train enters the Box Tunnel. It results that the woman attacked and almost murdered looks like her, wearing the same kind of dress. Delamere, who had been on a business trip, realizes that she was the intended object of the murderous assault in the adjacent carriage. 'I looked at the face, the poor disfigured face – it certainly, except for the accidental alteration of it, might have been very like mine' (101) she acknowledges. Mrs Westall is the victim of a 'chance resemblance' (106) to the pearl-broker.

This increasing awareness emerges in several stages in the narrative. First, a Scottish friend of Delamere, a Miss Burnley, warns her something will happen. Then, after seeing Mrs Westall's beaten body:

> I had a vague indescribable feeling of participation in this mysterious crime as though I were in some way, unknown to myself, involved in its guilt. (103)

This suspicion then becomes a certainty:

> I saw only too plainly that she had been mistaken for someone else, and in my horror at this confirmation of my undefined dread, I nearly betrayed myself. (105)

Mollie Delamere never reveals why the man attacked Mrs Westall:

> I felt that it would be unwise and a mistake, both for my own
> sake and my employer's, that this should be known publicly, and
> as soon as I had finished my commission at Bristol, sold the
> pearls, and ascertained that Mrs Westall's recovery though slow
> was sure, I hurried back to town and told Mr Leighton the whole
> story.
>
> He commended my discretion.
>
> Since the man had escaped, and was still in ignorance as to
> his own mistake, there was no object to be gained in our
> explaining it to the public. (105-6)

She concludes with another declaration:

> Mr Leighton was inclined, for my own safety, to give me my
> dismissal; but I persuaded him at last to reconsider it, and
> promised to be very careful, and to have no more adventures if
> possible. (108)

Still, the reader is left to wonder if business reasons are sufficient for a
woman to conceal the facts of a case from the authorities.

Delamere is a perverse businesswoman and detective, discovering the
truth but concealing it, unwilling to acknowledge that by so doing she
jeopardizes other women. In this respect, she can scarcely be said to
identify with the plight of women. Instead, for her own economic survival,
she camouflages the dangers women might encounter at the hands of men,
who often exercise surveillance over her movements by following her in
order to rob, abduct or even eliminate her.

In her seventh adventure, Mollie Delamere is almost burned alive. She
goes to see a man, Arnold Gervoise, who is confined to a wheelchair from
an accident. He asks her to copy a set of pearl earrings. Gervoise correctly
believes that his wife, Vera, stole them from Mrs Hamilton during a holiday
when they were resident in the house. He plans to restore the originals to
Mrs Hamilton, who is returning from an excursion, and place the duplicates
in his wife's care, so she will not know he suspects her.

When Delamere takes the copies to the husband, Vera Gervoise
surprises them, drops her lamp and sets fire to Delamere's dress. The wife
saves Delamere, who has to remain in their house. While there, Delamere
discovers that Vera Gervoise is a somnambulist and that she took the
earrings without knowing she had done so. In the end, the husband and
wife reconcile.

The interesting dimension of this case is the preamble. Leighton reproves Mollie Delamere for her narrow escape during the Bristol train episode:

> 'You are too confident, Mrs Delamere . . . too reckless. Certainly you manage to escape scathless from danger in the most wonderful manner, but you know in all cases of risk it is only a question of time. Sooner or later I am afraid something bad will happen to you, and then – how should I forgive myself?' (109)

Delamere, however, will not be put off by her employer:

> 'Nonsense, Mr Leighton . . . you are over-cautious and over-sensitive. You are giving me, at my earnest desire, the opportunity to earn a comfortable living in a congenial way. If you take it from me, then I must become a governess, or a companion, or a typist, or something equally arduous, and for an income that will only just clothe me.' (109-10)

There can be no doubt about the economic imperative which drives Delamere to her dangerous work. Strikingly, she rejects the male-defined appropriate occupations for a lady such as governess or typist. Leighton describes her as 'wilful' (110) but yields, and Delamere undertakes the commission to the Gervoise home before he can 'raise any fresh objections' (111). Heron-Maxwell gives particular point to this episode since the Gervoise marriage is contaminated by suspicion. Is Delamere better off being a widow employed in a well-paying if dangerous job?

In the penultimate chapter, the profession proves extremely dangerous when Delamere goes to the isolated estate, The Gables near Brentham, of Philip Magnus, a recluse who turns out to be a madman. When she is alone with Magnus, he locks the chamber and proceeds to assault her with a stiletto, since she reminds him of a woman who had jilted him years ago. Delamere is saved only when her screams drive the housekeeper to get her husband to subdue the madman.

As Delamere approaches the house, she feels 'suddenly cut off from the outer world' (130) as she thinks of Tennyson's Mariana. She notices 'the loneliness and silence of the place' (132) and eventually in the locked room realizes she is 'powerless' and 'a prisoner' (137). Magnus is as diabolical as Grimesby Roylott from the Holmes tale *The Speckled Band*. 'He was a raving madman now, and . . . I was alone in the room with him, with a locked door between me and any possible help' (139). Since the door locks by a pulley device, Heron-Maxwell intends the reader to recall the bell-pull in Doyle's narrative, which also is set in a horrifying locked room.

When Mollie Delamere returns to her employer, she does not tell Leighton the entire story. But she now realizes that men like Magnus are a continuing threat to women:

> I have often thought of my narrow escape, and wondered whether Mr Philip Magnus, of The Gables, near Brentham, will yet succeed in avenging his wrongs, and also whether in such a risky profession as pearl-broking the game was always worth the candle. (143)

As with many other diabolical males in the previous stories, such as the assailant on the Bristol train or the thief with the Derringer, Philip Magnus is never brought to justice, eluding any punishment or treatment. Heron-Maxwell leaves it an open question whether this is the result of male domination of the legal establishment or of a woman's failure to protest such violence.

In the final tale, Delamere establishes that Dick Blount, private secretary to the Australian millionaire Anderson, had the maid at a country house cut the string of Adela Fenton's pearls, so when they scattered he could sell some of them. Delamere is at the estate, Hurst Dene, of George and Fannie Brockhurst in Hampshire for a holiday when these events transpire. Blount also manages to steal the pink pearl, which Delamere has sold the Australian. At the conclusion, Blount is expelled. Adela Fenton's fiancé, the young barrister Harry Duncan, becomes the secretary, a post which permits him to marry Fenton after her father no longer objects to the match.

Delamere recognizes in this final episode that all along she has been and wished to be a detective: 'I had a sort of detective feeling on me, and felt a sudden impulse to do these things' (154). She realizes that some of the pearls on Fenton's necklace have been replaced by imitations after the necklace broke. Furthermore, she sees Blount take the key of Anderson's jewel box.

After the theft of the pearl is discovered, Delamere discerns that the one put in its place is 'an excellent imitation of it' (162). She had devised the means of exposing Blount with 'the sudden certainty of an inspiration' (156). Blount tells her when he is discovered to be a thief: 'If I had known that a lady detective was disguised as a guest of this house, I should have laid my plans better' (163).

Throughout the story, Blount is energetic 'to prevent Mr Anderson's marriage' (148), presumably to retain his influence over the Australian millionaire. Blount's theft of the pearl is really the removal of Delamere from the Australian's presence. That Delamere and the pearl are symbolically linked is made evident in the final paragraph:

> And the pink pearl has again changed hands, for it belongs now to me, and was given to me, as one of my wedding presents on the happy day when I became Mrs Anderson, and gave up the profession of pearl-broking once and for all. (164)

Like other female detective narratives of its time, *The Adventures of a Lady Pearl-Broker* concludes with the satisfying of the marriage plot convention. Yet, in giving this conclusion to the text, Heron-Maxwell complicates it.

Having throughout the text desired to conceal her profession, after marriage Mollie Delamere decides to write and publish her adventures in a memoir. One can speculate that although she is married, she still admires her former existence sufficiently that she must record and publicize the events of her career. This publication of the memoir indicates that her life was meaningful only when she was a pearl-broker and amateur detective, despite her apparent happiness as a married woman. A further motive may be to advise the country about the true state of crime in England. Although Delamere never brings in the police after her discoveries, she does chronicle the crimes she encounters to alert the public about the criminous state of late-Victorian society.

The year 1899 was a particularly important one for the appearance of female detectives: Grant Allen's Lois Cayley and Hilda Wade, Fergus Hume's Hagar Stanley, L. T. Meade and Robert Eustace's Florence Cusack, and Beatrice Heron-Maxwell's Mollie Delamere. At the end of the century, these women peered into the future – of both women and of the culture. Mollie Delamere of *The Adventures of a Lady Pearl-Broker* proves herself a person of 'pluck', detecting for the newly-emerging era by embracing a spirit of adventure. It is undoubtedly in homage to Heron-Maxell's 'lady pearl-broker' that Emmuska Orczy named her famous female detective of 1910 after her in *Lady Molly of Scotland Yard.*

L.T. Meade (1844-1914) and Robert Eustace [Barton] (1868-1943): *The Detections of Miss Cusack* (1899-1900)

Elizabeth Thomasina Meade, born in Ireland, came to London in 1874 to pursue a career as a journalist and writer. Collaborating with male colleagues, she became one of the most important writers of detective fiction in the Victorian and Edwardian eras, producing such key volumes as *Stories from the Diary of a Doctor* (2 series, 1894 and 1896) and a work about one of the most famous female criminals in detection history, *The Sorceress of the Strand* (serialized in the *Strand Magazine* from 1902-1903) about the infamous psychopath Madame Sara. Meade collaborated with Robert Eustace Barton in creating one of the most important female detectives of the nineteenth century, Miss Florence Cusack, in a series of five stories published in the *Harmsworth Magazine*, beginning in April 1899 and concluding in March 1901.

The tales involving Florence Cusack are narrated by a male physician, Dr Lonsdale, who records his impressions of her in the first case, *Mr Bovey's Unexpected Will*, published in the *Harmsworth* in April 1899. His description of her is calculated to convey information and to suggest mystery:

> Amongst all my patients there were none who excited my sense of curiosity like Miss Florence Cusack. I never thought of her without a sense of baffled inquiry taking possession of me, and I visited her without the hope that some day I should get to the bottom of the mystery which surrounded her. (3)

Florence Cusack is a patient, and Lonsdale proceeds to detail her appearance:

> Miss Cusack was a young and handsome woman. She possessed to all appearance superabundant health, her energies were extraordinary, and her life completely out of the common . . . Her beauty, her sprightliness, her wealth, and, above all, her extraordinary life, caused her to be much talked about . . . It was almost impossible to believe that she was a power in the police courts, and highly respected by every detective in Scotland Yard. (3-4)

Lonsdale is asked by a colleague to see her, and he learns that 'strong as she was she was subject to periodical and very acute nervous attacks' (4). Then Florence Cusack tells him: 'I know well that my whole condition is abnormal; but, believe me, I am forced to do what I do . . . You see before you . . . the most acute and, I believe, successful lady detective in the whole of London' (4). When Lonsdale remarks that such a life is 'extraordinary', Cusack responds: 'To me the life is fraught with the very deepest interest . . . In any case, . . . I have no choice; I am under a promise which I must fulfil . . . If the time should ever come, will you give me your assistance?' (4). Through the series, in fact, this 'promise' is never explained. When Lonsdale notes two brazen bulldogs in the home, Cusack comments: 'But for these dogs . . . and the mystery attached to them, I should not be the woman I am, nor would my life be set apart for the performance of duties at once herculean and ghastly' (4). No explanation about the dogs is ever revealed. As Craig and Cadogan observe, however: 'Miss Cusack is unlike many of her sisters in detection in that she is not explicitly out to clear some tarnished male reputation' (31).

The first case Lonsdale records occurs in November 1894. The case involves the will of Henry Bovey, who states that one of three claimants to his estate will inherit the sovereigns in his safe. The sovereigns will go to 'the one whose net bodily weight is nearest to the weight of these sovereigns' (7). The three claimants are Edgar Wimburne, engaged to Cusack's niece Letitia Ransom; Campbell Graham, alias Joshua Linklater, 'one of a gang of coiners, but managed to pass as a gentleman of position' (22); and William Tyndall, Bovey's servant.

At the bizarre weighing of the sovereigns, Wimburne comes closest to their weight and inherits the money as Bovey's legatee. When Wimburne decides to take the gold to the city, there is a highway robbery on the Richmond Road, during which Wimburne is hurt and the money taken. Cusack remembers seeing a notice in the Agony Column under the name Joshua Linklater. When she goes to the pawnbroker Higgins's shop, she does so as a 'domestic servant on her evening out' (16), informing Lonsdale 'I employ many disguises' (15). When there, she overhears Campbell Graham, alias Linklater, discuss his plan to get Bovey's money. Cusack informs the police, and the pawnbroker is arrested, although no gold is found on the premises. Cusack takes the inspector and Lonsdale to the shop, and there, after examining the ashes in the furnace, discovers that the gold had been melted and turned into one of the three golden balls outside the pawn-shop. Cusack concludes: 'The lost gold . . . has been cast as that ball . . . Yes, the lost fortune is hanging outside the house. The gold was melted in the crucible downstairs, and cast as this ball' (21). Graham is arrested on Florence Cusack's testimony.

Of particular interest in *Mr Bovey's Unexpected Will* is that Cusack had suggested the servant Tyndall had 'probably' (13) been in the plot of the robbery, but in fact this is never discussed or proved. Hence, this first case contains not only the mystery of Florence Cusack herself but also leaves at least one of the claimants and his guilt unresolved. Whether this is carelessness on the writers' parts or not, it suggests that even solving a crime leaves issues unexplained. Possibly, therefore, Tyndall may well get another situation and bring criminality into his new master's house. Such a situation raises suspicions about servants, invasion of privacy and criminality in the homes of the wealthy.

Furthermore, other elements of the tale are intriguing. Cusack had informed Lonsdale that not only Wimburne but also Campbell Graham were both lovers of Letitia: she remarks that 'Lettie must be saved' (9).

Proving that Graham is a thief not only saves Edgar Wimburne but also saves Cusack's niece from the unwelcome attentions of a bounder, a man much older than herself. Here her motive as a woman is to save another woman. In addition, the reader learns that Cusack had involved Lonsdale after asking him if he were interested in 'queer mental phases' (6). Of course, Lonsdale is interested. In however basic a form, then, the case suggests the human propensity for eccentric behaviours, giving the word 'unexpected' in the title an additional inflection. Not only is the legacy unexpected by Wimburne, but it also exposes the 'unexpected' dimensions of the human will. While the will itself is not criminal, its bizarre nature leads to crime, giving the cliché about 'worth its weight in gold' a new disturbing valence.

In July 1899 Meade published *The Arrest of Captain Vandaleur*, a narrative concerning two scoundrels in horse-racing. Two men, Vandaleur and Rashleigh, are arrested when Rashleigh's partner Walter Farrell learns their scheming. Cusack saves the life of Farrell's wife Laura, since she had been wilting away because of her husband's gambling on the turf. This case, set in April, begins when Lonsdale visits Cusack's house, now stated to be at Kensington Park Gardens instead of the Kensington Court Gardens of the previous tale. Jack Adrian (109) suspects that such carelessness indicates Meade and Eustace had lost interest in the project, but it is possible that readers would not be disturbed by such an oversight. Farrell's wife has been a friend of Cusack since the young woman's school days, but Cusack particularly wants Lonsdale to save Farrell. 'His disease is more moral than mental, and is certainly not physical' (26) she informs Lonsdale. Lonsdale labels it 'moral insanity' (26). Cusack explains she has been asked to get involved by the C.I.D., but her reason for participating is personal: 'Had it not been for [Farrell being married to her friend] I should have refused to have anything to do with the matter' (27).

Lonsdale visits both Farrell and his wife. He remarks that Laura Farrell is 'more child than woman' and learns that she is 'tired of life' and 'tired of misery' (32), as she falls into 'hysterical' crying. She then explains that Walter Farrell will be 'ruined, body and soul' (33) from his gambling. Of particular interest is the appearance of Walter Farrell when Lonsdale visits him:

> A man was lying back in a deep leather chair, near one of the windows. He was a dark, thin man, with features which in themselves were refined and handsome; but now, with the haggard lines round the mouth, in the deeply set, watchful, and somewhat narrow eyes, and in a sort of recklessness which was characterised by his untidy dress, the very set of his tie, I guessed

> too surely that Miss Cusack had not exaggerated the mental
> condition of Mr Walter Farrell. (33)

Ernest Prater's illustration is calculated to disturb readers about the state of the nation's young manhood, as the demoralized Farrell is slouching in his chair, the newspaper lying on the floor. Lonsdale notices his 'sleepy indifference' (34). Farrell thinks his wife is 'just a bit lazy' (34), not ill, and he states that 'men have troubles and anxieties' (35). Then he describes Cusack and his wife: 'Florence and Laura are a pair of fools, the greatest fools that ever walked the earth. . . They want a man to do the impossible' (36). This is, in terms of late nineteenth-century culture, an amazing statement, showing that men as much as women repudiate or find intolerable the expectations of their gender construction.

Cusack brings in Inspector Marling from the Yard. They proceed to Rashleigh and Farrell's 'Turf Commission Agents' business. Vandaleur places a large bet, guaranteed to ruin the business if the horse comes in. Vandaleur writes his slip at a table at the last possible second. When the tape machine announces the winner, Vandaleur is successful. Cusack however, studies the chimney of the gas-lamp at the table. Vandaleur is arrested by Marling. Cusack explains that from another room, also equipped with a tape machine, the winner's name came in, at which a gentleman's scent, corresponding to the correct horse, was passed via a gas pipe to the table below. Vandaleur 'had only to bend over the chimney to get the scent and write out the name of the horse which it corresponded to' (44) declares Cusack.

By this device, Vandaleur and Farrell's partner Rashleigh were ruining Farrell's business, driving Farrell into depression and his wife into a despairing death. One gang communicated with the other via a notice which linked the horse Sea Foam with Jockey Club. Cusack recognizes that the latter is a reference not to a place but to a scent. Having formed her plan, Cusack is transfigured: 'An extraordinary exaltation seemed to possess her. The pupils of her eyes were largely dilated' (38). She asserts to Lonsdale that she has 'no fear of personal rudeness or violence' (38) when he asks her. Rashleigh, Farrell's corrupt partner, and Vandaleur are punished, and Laura Farrell recovers 'her strength, and also her youth and beauty' (44).

As Jack Adrian notes in his afterword to the edition, the case is one of an 'impossible crime' (109), a sub-genre for which Meade and Eustace were famous. This genre, however, in this story assumes a symbolic dimension. Members of the culture would not believe a husband could so callously cause his wife's demise by his recklessness. Nor would they believe that a young male would express his dissatisfaction at the cultural expectations of men: Farrell's outré behaviour is really a form of revolt against the female conception of the perfect man. If women are forced to accept the model of the Angel in the House, then men suffer as well from the expectations of their respective Angels. The fears of the culture about the racial decline of British males pervade the *The Arrest of Captain Vandaleur*.

That Meade and Eustace are engaging a source of cultural anxiety about young men is confirmed by the presence of the same issue in the next narrative, *A Terrible Railway Ride*, published in July 1900. Lonsdale states in the first sentence that Frank Kaye is 'a young fellow in whom I had long taken a deep interest' (45). Kaye comes to Lonsdale, telling him he is 'feeling rather hipped . . . and the hotel is lonely' (45). He is on his way to Paris that night to bring back the jewels of Lady Southborough, to whose husband he is private secretary. Lonsdale tells him he looks 'seedy' and asks if anything is wrong. 'He had lost flesh considerably since I had seen him last, and his fresh and ruddy complexion had left him' (45).

Frank Kaye informs Lonsdale that he is engaged to Violet Fortescue. In addition, he has lost a lot of money on Rand Diamond shares and is in debt 'to a man in town' (47). While on the train returning from Paris, Frank Kaye is robbed of Lady Scarborough's jewels, having been felled by some narcotic. Violet Fortescue asks Lonsdale to see her fiancé Frank Kaye: 'His face was white, and his whole appearance ghastly . . . He was still under the influence of some narcotic' (49). Having lost the jewels, Kaye believes 'I am a ruined man' (49). As with the Ernest Prater illustration in the previous story, Victor Venner's drawing shows the young man on the sofa, hand to head, as Lonsdale writes a description of the lost jewels. Cusack states, 'It must be our business to clear him . . . I may as well say plainly that I am languishing for something to do' (52). She is eager 'to the point of madness' to work (55).

Suffering young manhood becomes the point of the story. Violet Fortescue labels Frank's problem 'a mind diseased . . . This terrible trouble is weighing on his mind . . . No other woman ought to help Frank but me' (53-4). In contrast to so much representation of gendered roles, here the woman is rescuing the male. The mental prostration of Frank Kaye recalls the similar situation described in Conan Doyle's tale *The Naval Treaty* of October/November 1893, in which a young man, Percy Phelps, becomes embroiled in the theft of an international treaty from the Foreign Office, a situation which prostrates him. Cusack discovers a man, using the name of the Reverend John Wilberforce, has been involved in a series of thefts on the London-Paris train. He uses a false nose to disguise himself.

However, it is Lonsdale who in fact finds the thief. On a train from Bournemouth to Waterloo, Lonsdale observes such a man and follows him to Paddington, booking a ticket on a train to Bristol between two reserved carriages. On the journey, Lonsdale notices his man moving along the footboard to the other reserved carriage. Lonsdale follows him and sees his expression just before the train enters the Box Tunnel. Falling from the train, the man plunges into the darkness. Lonsdale, entering the adjacent carriage, finds a man lying on the floor, stunned by a piece of solid carbon dioxide, which had volatized, filling the carriage with poisonous gas so the thief could rob the unconscious victim. The man's body is found in the Box Tunnel the next day. While the jewels of Lady Scarborough are never recovered, Kaye is vindicated, retains his post as private secretary to Lord Scarborough and eventually marries Violet Fortescue.

In *A Terrible Railway Ride*, as in the Sherlock Holmes tale *The Naval Treaty*, it is a fiancée, here Violet Fortescue, there Annie Harrison, who assists in the vindication of her lover. In the Holmes tale, the implications of the theft are international, while here they are local. But in each instance, the imperilling of young British manhood is cause for alarm. The illustrations by Victor Venner reinforce this hazard. In one, the thief 'Wilberforce' is shown falling from the footboard; in another, the next victim is found by Lonsdale in the compartment. Perhaps most unsettling is the illustration of Lonsdale peering out the train carriage window – an image of terror, as the train provides an extremely vulnerable environment for crime. Lonsdale's gaze suggests that every person must keep constant surveillance to avoid being a victim.

It is remarkable that in this case Cusack, although she provides the clue to the criminal's identity (the false nose), does not herself engage in the final resolution. As in *The Arrest of Captain Vandaleur*, so the emphasis in *A Terrible Railway Ride* is on male mental disease and depression, hence male vulnerability. In contrast to the previous story, however, the rescuer here is another male, the physician Lonsdale. The close parallel between a doctor's diagnostic procedures and a detective's reading of evidence is underscored, not surprising considering Meade's authorship of the two volumes of 'detection' by the young physician Halifax in her volumes of 1894 and 1896. This narrative, with its emphasis on the railway, also suggests the enduring situation of railway crime narratives, represented above all in the work of Victor Whitechurch with his *Investigations of Godfrey Page, Railwayac* of 1903-1904 and *Thrilling Stories of the Railway* of 1912 (discussed in Kestner 2000) or Conan Doyle's Holmes tale *The Bruce-Partington Plans* of December 1908 (discussed in Kestner 1997).

In October 1900, Meade and Eustace continued the Florence Cusack series with *The Outside Ledge: A Cablegram Mystery*, which, as Jack Adrian states, is an 'impossible crime' story with a 'startlingly original solution' (109). Set in November 1892, the story records how the financier Oscar Hamilton, a friend of Miss Cusack, has become 'the victim of a series of frauds' (63). Investing in South African Gold Mines, he finds that his 'private advices' about the 'gold crushings' are not bringing him the expected earnings. He keeps losing investment opportunities to James Gildford. Hamilton's partner is Henry Le Marchant, engaged to Evelyn Dudley, a friend of Miss Cusack, with the marriage imminent the following week. Gildford's office is four doors from the office of Hamilton in Lennox Court, near the Stock Exchange. Cusack learns that Le Marchant is in financial difficulties, 'staving off his crash until he can marry Evelyn Dudley, when he hopes to right himself. If the crash came first, Colonel Dudley would not allow the marriage . . . Evelyn is a dear friend of mine, and if I can prevent it I don't want her to marry a scoundrel' (66-67).

At a dinner party, Lonsdale, being a physician, identifies the scent of valerian on Le Marchant's handkerchief. Florence Cusack rents an office in the same building and solves the crime: a cat goes from Hamilton's office, by which his treacherous partner Le Marchant sends private advice about South African gold to James Gildford via the outside ledge connecting their offices. As Craig and Cadogan comment, Cusack solves the case with 'keen logical deduction' (31).

The cat is lured along the ledge by the valerian. Cusack intercepts the animal and finds the information on a slip of paper in Le Marchant's handwriting around the animal's collar. The previous day, Cusack had visited Le Marchant's office and found a cat nestled on the man's knee. One of the 'sharpest detectives in London' (75) then arrests Henry Le Marchant and James Gildford. After informing Evelyn Dudley of the results of her investigation, Miss Cusack takes the young woman to the south of France for the winter. Lonsdale records that she 'married a man in every respect worthy of her' some time later (75).

The Outside Ledge is justifiably a famous 'impossible crime' narrative. Cusack labels her solution as a result of 'a chain of reasoning' and 'surmises' (74), linking together the detective deployment of both facticity and imagination in the solution of crimes. In typical male form, Lonsdale had labelled Cusack's initial theory as based on 'intuitions' (67); Cusack herself calls it 'reasoning.'

The story demonstrates that Cusack acts to save a woman friend, a situation similar to that in *The Arrest of Captain Vandaleur* in which she saved the gambler's wife Laura Farrell. As with other female detectives, the motive of female friendship spurs the professional engagement. Victor Venner's illustration of the cat sitting on Le Marchant's knee is striking, as cats are traditionally associated with females – the man's cunning, unpredictability and reserve are communicated in the illustration, linking the male with the seemingly docile but deceptive cat. Le Marchant is described as having 'a black, short moustache and very dark eyes' (68), which link him with the animal, giving him in the illustration a possibly Middle Eastern cast evocative of cats and Egyptians.

Of particular significance is the linkage of the erotic and the economic in the story. Le Marchant deceived the Dudleys about his financial situation, seeking to exploit the marriage, and his access to the Dudley money, to save himself. A woman could not be more commodified than is Laura Dudley in this tale. When Miss Cusack cautions Lonsdale to be quiet while she awaits the appearance of the animal, *The Outside Ledge* evokes its famous predecessor about an animal, Conan Doyle's *The Speckled Band* of February 1892, another famous 'impossible crime' of the locked room genre.

The final tale about Miss Cusack is *Mrs Reid's Terror* published in March 1901, a narrative exposing the fissures in a bourgeois marriage. James Reid comes to his friend Lonsdale to discuss his young wife, who is acting strangely, exhibiting a 'loss of control' (78) and going 'all to pieces' (79). When Lonsdale visits Reid's home, Lakewood in Surrey, an announcement informs the group at dinner that one Walter Cardwell is returning from abroad. Mrs Reid then confesses to Lonsdale that she is ' in extreme danger of being arrested. I am a felon' (81). Addicted to 'speculating and gambling' (82), Mrs Reid has forged her husband's name to a bill given to a loan shark, Richley. When Richley discovers the forgery, he blackmails her for more money, which drives her to steal bonds her husband was keeping for Walter Cardwell, who is now returning. The wife describes her life as 'madness' (82), an addiction she cannot surmount. Since her husband James Reid has a heart condition, she cannot tell him lest he suffer an attack.

Cusack has informed Lonsdale that her 'mission in life is do good in my own way' (84), and while she does not approve of Mrs Reid, she decides to intervene for the husband's sake. Even Lonsdale does not think it is a case of 'right' in this instance. Cusack regards a blackmailer as 'the vilest of all vile people' (85). Meeting with George Richley, she draws up a contract to pay Richley 10,000 pounds over ten months, a contract Lonsdale witnesses with great reluctance. Cusack dismisses Mrs Reid with a stern injunction never to gamble again.

Then, in a *coup de théâtre*, Cusack informs Lonsdale that the contract was written in 'sympathetic ink' (89), which will vanish without a trace and render it nothing but a 'blank sheet of paper' (90), totally non-negotiable. When Lonsdale claims this is 'marvellous', Cusack asserts she is only using the 'brains nature has given me' (90). In the final paragraph, Lonsdale recounts that Mrs Reid became quite well and that 'Reid to this day believes that his wife is one of the most innocent and perfectly delightful women who ever lived' (90).

Mrs Reid's Terror conveys well the insidious nature of crime within the bourgeois household. In this instance, the wife engages in forgery and gambling, placing herself in the hands of a blackmailer: the Angel in the House has become a criminal. The manifestations of her crime appear in her body and behaviour, rendering the female body, already a mystery to men, *the* mystery in the text. At one point, Lonsdale, having seen the wife, tells Reid 'I do not like your wife's condition' (79), scarcely grasping the implications of his statement.

All four of the illustrations by Ernest Prater for *Mrs Reid's Terror* show the wife: in the title weeping over a table; then leaving the dinner table at the announcement of Cardwell's return; then lying on a sofa being treated by Lonsdale as she announces she is a felon; and finally seated during the confrontation with Richley at Miss Cusack's house. All these pictures are of domestic surroundings, reinforcing the anxiety revealed in the text about the presence of crime in middle-class homes. In the final illustration, Miss Cusack and Mrs Reid are diagonally opposite one another, juxtaposing the integrity and rationality of Florence Cusack with the ostensibly respectable but actually criminal wife of James Reid.

Craig and Cadogan note that Lonsdale in these narratives is obviously derived from Dr John Watson in the Holmes narratives. There is, however, a difference, as they observe: '[Lonsdale's] admiration for Florence [Cusack] seems avuncular and a little less awe-ridden than Watson's for Holmes' (30). Lonsdale as narrator derives from Clifford Halifax, the doctor, observer and diagnostician of the two volumes Meade and Eustace published in 1894 and 1896, where Halifax is the narrator of his own adventures. To what extent readers were expected to know some of the *Stories from the Diary of a Doctor* is unknown, but the presence of Lonsdale as narrator/physician recalls the situations in the earlier volumes where there are dangerous activities happening in domestic locales.

In the narratives recounted by Clifford Halifax, bizarre events indeed occur within homes. In *The Oak Coffin*, published in the *Strand* in March 1894, Horace Heathcote and his wife stage his burial to secure insurance money to pay off a trust from which he had appropriated funds earlier; their daughter Gabrielle, however, had seen him. In one scene, Gabrielle leads back her supposedly dead father, an episode depicted in one of the illustrations. The girl's mother commits suicide and the dead father actually dies the same night. Halifax in *Without Witnesses*, appearing in the *Strand* in April 1894, establishes from a post-mortem that Arthur Randall had died by falling off a cliff from an attack of vertigo. By this discovery, Halifax frees Randall's friend, Ronald Carleton, from suspicion of having killed Randall, because a woman, Barbara Farnham, had come between them. In *The Ponsonby Diamonds*, published in the *Strand* in June 1894, the diamonds given by Captain Geoffrey Ponsonby, aged 35, to his fiancée Lady Violet Dalrymple, aged 17, are stolen. It evolves that the young woman has herself taken them while suffering from hallucinations. Clearly, Lady Violet had subconsciously feared the marriage with Ponsonby, stealing the diamonds and giving them to her mother to repudiate her commodification as bride to a man twice her age, confirmed when the engagement is broken. These disturbing exposés of domestic life parallel in their implications the threatened homes in the Cusack tales, such as *The Arrest of Captain Vandaleur* and *Mrs Reid's Terror*.

In order to complete the probable contractual obligation of six stories, Meade and Eustace wrote a final one, *The Great Pink Pearl*, published in June 1901 in the *Harmsworth Magazine*. However, it does not include Florence Cusack, albeit it does include Lonsdale. Very striking, however, is that without Florence Cusack, the narrative takes on the bizarre element of the *Stories from the Diary of a Doctor*. The story is set in October 1896, the year of the publication of the second series of Halifax's experiences while a physician. Ella Forrester, the daughter of Lonsdale's patient, the jewel merchant Ralph Forrester, invites Lonsdale to a dinner, where he meets the vulgar man Sutherland and also Cyril Tempest. The latter has returned from the Queensland reefs, where he is a pearl diver and an associate of Ralph Forrester in business. Lonsdale accepted the invitation because 'I felt that in some sort of way I protected her from [her father's] rough and cruel treatment' (92). Again, the domestic situation is disturbing.

Cyril Tempest recounts to Lonsdale an accident which happened while he was diving for pearls. A shark attacked him as he found a great pink pearl. In a tent he was operated on by a young surgeon, Robertson. Local workers attacked the tent to get the pearl. Before dying in the melee, Robertson tries to tell Tempest something, but since he is still under anesthetic, he does not grasp Robertson's words. Lonsdale decides to put Tempest under chloroform to see if he can recall Robertson's words.

In another Meade/Eustace coup, Tempest utters: 'The pearl is safe in the wound. I have put it there for safety. It is your only chance' (105)! Robertson had sewn the pearl into Tempest's wound as the attack commenced. Lonsdale extracts the pearl from Tempest's chest. With the revenue from the pearl, Tempest is able to take Ella Forrester from her abusive father to Queensland, preventing the father from marrying her off to the disgusting Sutherland, whom the young woman had confronted with 'absolute repulsion' (92). There, back in his native Australia, Tempest 'is the happiest man in the world' (105). Lonsdale in this tale assumes some of the nature of Florence Cusack, especially in facilitating the marriage of two deserving people, as Cusack had done with Edgar Wimburne and Letitia Ransom in *Mr Bovey's Unexpected Will* and with Frank Kaye and Violet Fortescue in *A Terrible Railway Ride*.

Jack Adrian correctly notes some of the carelessness which slips into these stories, published over a two-year period: the mistake about the location of Florence Cusack's home and the fact that over the course of the series, Lonsdale moves from balding to having hair. The latter, however, is the concern of the illustrators, an anomaly never recorded in the texts per se. The reader encountering these stories for the first time would probably not notice such inconsistencies. The first narrative, about Mr Bovey's will, is given the dramatic date of November 1894; others are set in 1892 or 1893. However, this is not an inconsistency as Jack Adrian labels it. In fact, Lonsdale in the first story never claims it is his first case with Florence Cusack – it is only the first one recounted. Adrian regards the final story as completely out of the series, since Cusack does not appear at all. He concludes that 'a neat little six-story, six-issue series ended up as a rambling and wholly unsatisfactory saga in which authors and editors simply forgot what had gone before' (109). One could just as easily assert, however, that in the final story Lonsdale demonstrates what he has learned from Florence Cusack, that far from undercutting Florence Cusack's saga, it confirms her ability to teach the physician/narrator Lonsdale about her profession and its similarity to his own. The reader is likely to concur with Jack Adrian's astute final estimation of Meade's significance:

> Meade's place (and her collaborator's) in detective and mystery fiction's pantheon is assured. Certainly no other woman in that post-Holmes, pre-Great War period put into the genre so much creative effort, and surely no other woman from that pre-Golden Age era has left us so entertaining, so wide-ranging, and so brain-racking a legacy. (110)

In exposing the mental, moral and marital crises of the late Victorian period, *The Detections of Miss Cusack* confirms the importance of the female detective narrative for analysing the culture.

Grant Allen: *Hilda Wade* (1900)

Grant Allen had already made a successful attempt at a female detective with the protagonist, Lois Cayley, of *Miss Cayley's Adventures* in 1899. This success explains his desire to continue with another female detective of a different kind. As Craig and Cadogan note, 'Hilda Wade, [Cayley's] successor, is a less lightweight personality, a fact indicated by her choice of profession: she is a nurse' (27). There is little doubt about Grant Allen's following in the tradition established by Arthur Conan Doyle, who was his friend. While the series of tales which became *Hilda Wade* was appearing in the *Strand*, Allen died in 1899. Conan Doyle completed the series for his friend, as he recalled in *Memories and Adventures* in 1924:

> It is a desperately difficult thing to carry on another man's story, and must be a more or less mechanical effort. I had one experience of it when my neighbour at Hindhead, Grant Allen, was on his death-bed. He was much worried because there were two numbers of his serial, *Hilda Wade*, which was running in the *Strand Magazine*, still uncompleted. It was a pleasure for me to do them for him, and so relieve his mind, but it was difficult collar work, and I expect they were pretty bad. (261)

One might dispute Conan Doyle's assessment of the final two instalments, which seem rather in line with some of the experiences of Hilda Wade earlier in the text. However, the series of twelve tales does in effect constitute a novel, for an episode might extend over more than one instalment and the protagonist, the narrator/colleague and the 'villain' remain constant throughout the book. The cases are not self-contained within one instalment. The most direct link to Conan Doyle is the profession of nursing assumed by Hilda Wade and the fact that the narrator and her colleague is a young physician, Hubert Cumberledge, who works with Hilda Wade at St Nathaniel's Hospital in London. At the end of the novel, he marries Hilda Wade, but not before the young couple encounters some harrowing adventures in Britain and in South Africa and Rhodesia.

Thus, not only does Hubert Cumberledge assume the role of a John Watson, but he also is in the same profession. The text of *Hilda Wade* has a distinguished pedigree, therefore, not only in detective fiction but in its sub-genre of the physician-detection narrative. In particular, the work recalls other texts of the 1890s, especially the two volumes written by L. T. Meade, the two series of *Stories from the Diary of a Doctor*, published in 1894 and 1896. Cumberledge and Wade both engage in a kind of detection, with Wade, as her name suggests, leading the way for her companion and lover. However, the use of medical personnel for detection also recalls the series of tales Conan Doyle collected in *Round the Red Lamp* in 1894.

In the history of detective fiction, this focus on medical personnel will prove crucial in the twentieth century, particularly in the works of R. Austin Freeman such as *From a Surgeon's Diary* (1904-1905) and *The Red Thumb Mark* (1907), and the focus on psychologists in Algernon Blackwood's *John Silence, Physician Extraordinary* (1908) and Ernest W. Hornung's *The Crime Doctor* (1914), the latter Conan Doyle's brother-in-law (for which see Kestner 2000). The stories about Hilda Wade appeared in the *Strand* from

March 1899 through February 1900, with the final two written by Doyle, who surely learned from the dying Grant Allen his intentions for the series.

The outline of the text is that Hilda Wade is really Maisie Yorke-Bannerman, the daughter of a physician accused of murdering his uncle, Admiral Scott Prideaux, for his money by administering lethal doses of the experimental drug aconitine. Hilda Wade's purpose is to vindicate her father's reputation, since he died from heart failure while awaiting trial. The other physician who attended Prideaux was one Dr Sebastian, who in fact confesses at the end that it was he, rather than Yorke-Bannerman, who administered the lethal dosages to Prideaux. Sebastian is a brilliant professor/physician at St Nathaniel's Hospital, a hero and idol to his students, including the young Cumberledge, who describes him as a 'fiery-eyed physiologist' (1) who is 'tall, thin, erect, with an ascetic profile not unlike Cardinal Manning's' (2), a cue followed by the illustrator of the series, Gordon Browne. Sebastian experiments with new drugs on both animals and himself, often with Cumberledge as observer and recorder. Cumberledge, like Hilda, is of Welsh descent, and he begins the text by conceiving Sebastian as a hero in the mould of Thomas Carlyle's stellar men.

Cumberledge describes Hilda Wade in conventional terms at first, but this focus soon changes:

> Hilda Wade, when I first saw her, was one of the prettiest, cheeriest, and most graceful girls I have ever met – a dusky blonde, brown-eyed, brown-haired . . . She was in the main a bright, well-educated, sensible, winsome, lawn-tennis-playing English girl [who yet had] undercurrents of depth, of reserve, and of a questioning wistfulness . . . Hilda Wade interested me immensely. I felt drawn . . . She stood out. She was the sort of girl one was constrained to notice. (69-70).

Hilda Wade suspects that Sebastian is the true killer of her father's uncle and contrives at a dinner party for Cumberledge to get her a place at St Nathaniel's Hospital, where she can keep Sebastian under observation.

The key element of the stories about Hilda Wade, however, is to debate the nature of female epistemology, whether women are intuitive or rational. As Mary Wollstonecraft recognized in the previous century in her famous *Vindication of the Rights of Woman* (1792), without rationality an individual could not be considered to have a system of morality, so the issue is decisive. By the time of *Hilda Wade* in 1899, of course, many legal, educational, marital and institutional reforms had liberated women from stifling constraints, and yet Allen uses the medical variant of the detective genre to explore the question of female epistemology. Cumberledge in fact makes the issue explicit early in the first story:

> I did not wonder . . . that Hilda Wade, who herself possessed in so large a measure the deepest feminine gift – intuition – should seek a place under the famous professor [Sebastian] who represented the other side of the same endowment in its masculine embodiment – instinct of diagnosis. (3)

Grant Allen discerns that the parallels between detection and medicine render the medico-detective narrative a particularly apt form for the analysis of different epistemologies. The crucial gendering of epistemology is in fact expressed by Sebastian to Cumberledge in a succeeding passage in the first instalment, when Sebastian informs Cumberledge:

> 'Most women . . . are quick at reading *the passing emotion:* they can judge with astounding correctness from a shadow on one's face, a catch in one's breath, a movement of one's hands, how their words or deeds are affecting us. We cannot conceal our feelings from them. But underlying character they do not judge so well as fleeting expression. Not what Mrs Jones *is* herself, but what Mrs Jones is now thinking and feeling – there lies their great success as psychologists. Most men, on the contrary, guide their life by definite *facts* – by signs, by symptoms, by observed data. Medicine itself is built upon a collection of such reasoned facts. But this woman, Nurse Wade, to a certain extent, stands intermediate mentally between the two sexes. She recognises *temperament* – the fixed form of character and what it is likely to do – in a degree which I have never seen equalled elsewhere.'
> (4-5)

Throughout the novel, the problem of gender and epistemology is a constant focus, along with detection/diagnosis. For instance, Cumberledge observes soon that 'towards Sebastian [Hilda] seemed like a lynx-eyed detective' (6). This ability is threatening to both Sebastian and Cumberledge, however. Amidst all his admiration for Hilda's methods of drawing conclusions, for example, Cumberledge calls Hilda Wade a 'sibyl' (11, 99) or 'witch' (65, 89, 91, 252) or 'Cassandra' (75) or '[Delphic] pythoness' (75), commenting upon her 'sphinx-like smile' (10) or her 'Chaldean smile' (185).

It is Hilda who first detects the malice underlying Sebastian's diagnostic and experimental brilliance, when she tells Cumberledge, who admires the doctor's 'coolness', that to her it is 'cruelty', at which insight the young man is 'aghast' (14). It is difficult for Cumberledge to get beyond his belief that Sebastian is a Carlylean hero. Sebastian, however, has no difficulty discerning the threat Hilda Wade poses him. When Hilda predicts the outcome of an experimental drug, Sebastian tells Cumberledge 'We shall have to suppress her' (11). Cumberledge labels Hilda's observation the result of 'intuition', but Sebastian does not: 'Inference, I call it . . . All woman's so-called intuition is in fact just rapid and half-unconscious inference' (11).

Cumberledge first meets Hilda Wade at a dinner at the home of his friend, Hugo Le Geyt. At the dinner, Hilda tells Cumberledge he is from Wales, which she recollects, by her extraordinary memory, having read in a newspaper. When Cumberledge declares he fails to perceive her 'train of reasoning', Hilda responds:

> 'Fancy asking *a woman* to give you "the train of reasoning" for her intuitions! . . . That shows, Dr Cumberledge, that you are a mere man – a man of science, perhaps, but *not* a psychologist. It also suggests that you are a confirmed bachelor. A married man accepts intuitions, without expecting them to be based on reasoning. . . So there you see you have "the train of reasoning." Women *can* reason – sometimes.' (67-8)

Grant Allen's point is that of course women have and can reason. Cumberledge's response is to think Hilda, again, a 'witch' (69).

Allen accepts that in one instalment after another Hilda Wade must defend her methodology and epistemology, so much so that it is clear the key point of the text is to demonstrate and define woman's epistemology. Hilda defines her method as 'prevision based, not on omens or auguries, but on solid fact – on what I have seen and noticed', correcting Cumberledge's addressing her as a 'prophetess' (76). By the fourth instalment, Cumberledge can note Hilda Wade's 'analytical accuracy' (96) but still stress his 'man's desire for solid fact in place of vague intuition' (97) a page later.

Hilda claims to 'have something of the novelists's gift: I apply the same method to the real life of the people around me. I try to throw myself into the person of others', and she accepts Cumberledge's label of 'psychologist' (114-15). As she clarifies to Cumberledge when they are in the middle of a Matabele uprising in Rhodesia, she joins factuality *with* intuition, which she labels as 'common sense' (224) and a 'knowledge of types' (225) of persons.

It is here that Grant Allen makes one of his most decisive modifications of the legacy of Sherlock Holmes. As in the Holmes tales, the official police are dismissed and even despised in *Hilda Wade*. However, it is a *woman* in *Hilda Wade* who critiques the performance of the police: it is a question not only of epistemology but of gender, as could not be the case in the Holmes texts involving a male detective. Significantly, it is Cumberledge who has learned the lesson:

> The police are no respecters of persons; neither do they pry into the question of motives. They are but poor casuists. A murder is for them a murder, and a murderer a murderer: it is not their habit to divide and distinguish between case and case with Hilda Wade's analytical accuracy. (96)

Hilda speaks of the police 'with a touch of contempt' (107) when she learns they are trying to watch railway stations to apprehend a killer, and in the same narrative she declares: 'The police – well, the police are not [psychologists]; they are at best but bungling materialists. They require a *clue*. What need of a *clue* if you can interpret character?' (115). In the sixth instalment, Cumberledge longs for Hilda's 'infallible instinct' and 'unerring intuition' (172) when he is blocked by masculine modes of thought:

> I realised how feeble and fallacious was my own groping in the dark. Her knowledge of temperament would have revealed to her at once what I was trying to discover, like the police she despised, by the clumsy 'clues' which so roused her sarcasm. (172)

Superficial diagnosis is not sufficient. Necessary are psychology, grasp of motive and empathy. The stories in the text become, therefore, textbook demonstrations of the validity of woman's epistemology, which combines facticity with insight. The narratives, in effect, gauge the degree to which Cumberledge learns from Hilda Wade the validity of this epistemology.

The first two narratives about Hilda, tellingly, involve two different types of women. In the first, *The Patient Who Disappointed Her Doctor*, Hilda rallies Dr Sebastian's patient Isabel Huntley, who has an internal lesion. Cumberledge notes the woman's 'passionate nature' (17) and thinks her 'distinctly hysterical' (18), but he realizes that Hilda Wade 'was strongly drawn towards her. Their souls sympathised' (18). To Sebastian Isabel Huntley is only a tobacco-trimmer, but to Hilda she is 'a lady in fibre' (18). Hilda discerns that if Isabel learns the fate of her lover, Arthur, she will recover. In fact, when Hilda tells Isabel that her lover has returned from the South Seas, she does indeed recuperate. Cumberledge notes that 'a mere man would never have thought of that' (19).

Sebastian, who has recognized that Hilda Wade's remarkable memory and appearance resemble those of his ruined colleague Yorke-Bannerman, finds Hilda's conduct 'unpardonable', as he instructs Cumberledge:

'[Isabel Huntley] *ought* to have died. It was her clear duty. *I said*
she would die, and she should have known better than to fly in
the face of the faculty. Her recovery is an insult to medical
science . . . Nurse Wade should have prevented it.' (28)

Such a diabolical response rejects Hilda's method of psychology and
sympathy, which the doctor describes as '*not* science' (29).

This reaction confirms instead Hilda Wade's analysis of Sebastian as
cruel, a trait hidden by his moustache. Hilda had noted that men's facial hair
permitted them deception: 'Providence . . . gave you moustaches. That was
in order that we women might be spared from always seeing you as you are'
(16). The lesson is not lost on Cumberledge: 'For the first time in my life, I
had a glimmering idea that I distrusted Sebastian. Hilda Wade was right –
the man was cruel. But I had never observed his cruelty before – because
his devotion to science had blinded me to it' (29). Grant Allen's title of this
first episode marks its quality of querying and undermining patriarchal
authority.

A second kind of woman appears in the next tale in the series, *The
Gentleman Who Had Failed for Everything.* Hilda Wade proves that Sissie
Montague, a music hall performer, is deceiving Cecil Holsworthy, the heir
of a Canadian millionaire, pretending to love him to get his money. Hilda
labels Holsworthy as 'just the sort of romantic, impressionable hobbledehoy
such women angle for' (35). Holsworthy is in love with Daphne Tepping,
Cumberledge's cousin, but Hilda discerns that Holsworthy is entangled by
his prior attachment and commitment to the grasping Sissie Montague.
Hilda rescues two persons, Holsworthy from a demeaning engagement and
Daphne Tepping from loneliness. She does so by analysing a photograph
and the handwriting in a letter, which establish that Sissie Montague is
having a dalliance with Reggie Nettlecraft.

Nettlecraft, the titular character of the tale, had been at Charterhouse
with Cumberledge, who declares that Nettlecraft 'belonged to that sub-
species of the human race known as the Chappie' (51). Nettlecraft is 'an
indeterminate young man' (54) who cannot succeed now that there are Civil
Service examinations. Gordon Browne's illustration of Nettlecraft shows
him as a self-dramatizing indulgent dandy. Cumberledge confronts
Nettlecraft after Hilda has observed him. Holsworthy learns 'that one could
have innocent eyes and golden hair and yet be a trickster' (61) like Sissie
Montague. Montague, both men realize, had 'a determination to sell her
charms in the best and highest matrimonial market' (60). Nettlecraft
eventually marries Sissie and joins her on the music hall stage. In addition,
as Browne's illustration shows, Sissie Montague actually smoked! This and
the previous story demonstrate the operation of Hilda's sympathetic

psychology in two erotic situations, which nevertheless end in happiness for the deserving parties. This practise is completely reversed in the next two stories.

The Wife Who Did Her Duty and *The Man Who Would Not Commit Suicide* concern Hugo Le Geyt, a Queen's Counsel known for his outstanding legal skills. In the first tale, Le Geyt murders his second wife, Clara, having been driven to kill her by her unremitting criticism of him and her authoritarian, callous treatment of Le Geyt's two daughters, Maisie and Ettie, from his first marrige. It is at a dinner at the Le Geyt home that Cumberledge and Hilda Wade first meet, during which she asks him to secure for her a place at St Nathaniel's Hospital so she may observe Sebastian's medical methods. Hilda Wade informs Cumberledge that Clara Le Geyt is 'predestined to be murdered' (75) because of her true disposition. Cumberledge tours the wards at St Nathaniel's with the house-surgeon Travers, who confirms Hilda's awareness of 'a type of women who get assaulted . . . *always* get assaulted' (78).

Hilda Wade defines this kind of woman: 'She has no more doubt [about being a model step-mother] than about anything else. Doubts are not in her line . . . Not angry – it is never the way of that temperament to get angry: just calmly, sedately, and insupportably provoking. . . When all is said and done, it is the poor man I pity!' (89, 92). Yet Hilda declares Le Geyt must accept the results of his marriage:

> 'He has married that woman, and he must take the consequences. Does not each of us in life suffer perforce the Nemesis of his own temperament? . . . Women of this temperament [are] born naggers . . . We human beings go straight like sheep to our natural destiny . . . [It is] not fatalism: [it is] insight into temperament . . . I only believe that in this jostling world your life is mostly determined by your own character, in its interaction with the characters of those who surround you. Temperament works itself out. It is your own acts and deeds that make up Fate for you.' (82-3)

In the end, Le Geyt stabs his wife with a Norwegian dagger. Here particularly the illustrations reinforce the tale in a disturbing way. In one (81), Browne shows a nagging lower-class woman haranguing a seated but angry man. In the final illustration, Clara Le Geyt is shown dead on a chaise longue. Both illustrations render strong advice to women to keep silent. This tale is disorienting given the nature of the first two tales, which defend women's rights. Hilda Wade virtually condones violence and murder as justifiable recourses for unhappy husbands. It is not clear from his other works that Allen endorses such a belief.

Hilda Wade may think she is recording facts, not taking a political position, but the ideology of the tale indicts the women, the victims, as being responsible for their destruction. The title of the tale, *The Wife Who Did Her Duty*, refers to the murdered woman. Does it mean that in thinking to do her duty she destroyed herself? Or, might it mean she did the best thing by getting herself murdered? In the same tale, Sebastian indicts Wade for 'thinking' (84). The narrative shows the disturbance female initiative causes in the social field of Victorian society.

The next tale, *The Man Who Would Not Commit Suicide*, concerns Hugo Le Geyt, about whom Hilda Wade had prophesied that he would commit suicide rather than ever be apprehended and executed for his wife's murder. Hilda Wade does not deny that Le Geyt must endure retribution for his crime. This narrative provides some moderating effect to the previous tale, but readers had to wait an entire month with the bizarre impression of the history of the Le Geyt marriage. In this tale, Hilda recounts the lives of several members of the Le Geyt ancestral family who committed suicide without necessarily making it overt: a general killed in the Indian Mutiny, a constable who brutally assailed Chartist rioters. Each died, one at the head of his troops, the other off Waterloo Bridge, but in each case by his own volition, not by accident. Gordon Browne's illustrations (98, 101) show these deaths, which reveal the Le Geyt family's 'luck in their suicides' (101) according to Hilda.

Cumberledge follows Hilda's suggestion that despondent persons return to their place of origin. Tracking Le Geyt to the coast, Cumberledge observes him bathing. Le Geyt admits to Cumberledge he killed his wife but will not commit suicide, for the sake of his children. Instead, he takes a boat out to sea during a storm, leaving it to God to determine his fate. Le Geyt's body is found ashore the next morning, a scene depicted by Browne (126). Le Geyt's demise is ruled 'Death by misadventure' (127), which saves his family from disgrace. His children will not be known as a murderer's daughters, which is the stigma under which Hilda Wade herself lives among the few who remember her father. In the next tale, Cumberledge will label Le Geyt one of the group of 'accidental murderers' (156).

The Needle That Did Not Match is the next story. Its focus is on the antagonists Hilda Wade and Sebastian. In this tale, it is established that Hilda Wade is in fact Maisie Yorke-Bannerman, whose father was thought to have murdered his uncle. Hilda Wade tells Cumberledge of her 'Plan' (133) to vindicate her father's name. In demonstrating a blood test for students, Sebastian changes needles in a ward so he can prick Wade's finger with a different needle, which turns out to be tainted with the bacillus of blood poisoning. Cumberledge recognizes the truth of her processes of 'diagnosis' (132) and 'detection' (149). Hilda decides, however, not to expose Sebastian's attack upon her, realizing that in the male worlds of medicine and jurisprudence, she would not be believed: 'Everybody would say I was malicious or hysterical. Hysteria is always an easy stone to fling at an injured woman who asks for justice' (152).

When Cumberledge asserts his love for her, Hilda leaves the hospital and writes him a letter reinforcing her 'Purpose' (155) to clear her father's name, although she admits she loves Cumberledge. Before his attempt on Hilda's life, Sebastian had called her 'dangerous' (141), even if intelligent. 'We must get rid of that woman' (145) he tells Cumberledge. Sebastian advises Cumberledge that Hilda 'was getting too great a hold on you' (156). He then recounts the truth about Hilda's parentage, noting 'she is passing under a false name, and she comes of a tainted stock' (156). Cumberledge, however, defends Hilda, noting that the doctor tried to poison Hilda, declaring that Sebastian rather than Yorke-Bannerman might have murdered Prideaux. Repudiating his mentor, hero and surrogate father Dr Sebastian, Cumberledge leaves St Nathaniel's Hospital.

In the next story, *The Letter with the Basingstoke Postmark*, Cumberledge consults Horace Mayfield, who had been Yorke-Bannerman's counsel, to learn about the death of Admiral Scott Prideaux. Mayfield, however, while stating that Sebastian as well as Yorke-Bannerman attended the dying Admiral, still believes that Hilda's father was guilty. In the interview, Cumberledge learns that Hilda has inherited the same gifts of 'diagnosis', 'astounding memory' and 'power of recalling facts' (164) as her father possessed. The narrator finally knows her identity as Maisie Yorke-Bannerman. Cumberledge acknowledges 'how great a gulf separated the clumsy male intelligence from the immediate and almost unerring intuitions of a clever woman' (161).

Surmising that Hilda may have left for South Africa, Cumberledge goes to Cape Town. After being handed a letter from Hilda, Cumberledge follows her to Salisbury in Rhodesia. Accidentally, he meets her on the veldt while she is bicycling! Hilda Wade reiterates that although she loves Hubert, she will not marry him until she has cleared her father's name. For the reader's sake, however, Browne does get in one illustration of the two lovers embracing on the veldt.

After the rather extensive coincidences of the previous story, Grant Allen renders the entire narrative again horrific and disturbing. In *The Stone That Looked About It*, Cumberledge takes up residence on the farm of Jan Willem Klaas to learn farming in Rhodesia. When he goes to Salisbury for business, he returns to find the entire family killed during a Matabele uprising which Sebastian had instigated to assure Hilda's death at the farm. Instead, Hilda lay like the rock signified in the title and saved herself and a female infant of the Klaas family from the 'bloodthirsty savages' (201).

Klaas's wife's body is 'pierced through by innumerable thrusts, which I somehow instinctively recognised as assegai wounds', while Klaas is killed by a bullet which 'pierced his left temple: his body was also riddled through with assegai thrusts' (201). The latter is depicted in an illustration (202).

Hilda and Cumberledge gather supplies and make a run for Salisbury. Hilda at first rides her bicycle but then exchanges with Cumberledge and rides his horse: 'Hilda rode like a man, astride – her short bicycling skirt . . . made this easily possible' (211-12). Browne illustrates this daring riding position (214). Undoubtedly, Grant Allen has taken his lovers to South Africa to capitalize on the Boer War then occurring.

Hilda had told her lover when he arrived: 'You have betrayed my whereabouts to Sebastian . . . You are a man, you see . . . I was afraid from the first you would wreck all by following me' (191-92). Sebastian has pursued Cumberledge to Africa. Hilda informs her lover: 'The Matabele are his pawns. He wanted to aim a blow at *me*' (218). Cumberledge observes Sebastian spying on them in the refuge of Salisbury, recognizing that it was only by 'mere accident' (219) that he failed. Hilda has proved decisively that 'in works of necessity a woman . . . should flinch at nothing' (207), but the brutal context of her vindication is disturbing.

This turmoil appears in the succeeding tale, *The European with the Kaffir Heart*. The title refers to Sebastian and his alliance with the natives. The story opens with Cumberledge's assessment of the English in Africa:

> I am a man of peace . . . Still, there *are* times which turn even the most peaceful of us perforce into fighters . . . and at moments like that no man can doubt what is his plain duty. The Matabele revolt was one such moment. In a conflict of race we *must* back our own colour. I do not know whether the natives were justified in rising or not; most likely, yes; for we had stolen their country: but when once they rose, when the security of white women depended upon repelling them, I felt I had no alternative. For Hilda's sake, for the sake of every woman and child in Salisbury and in all Rhodesia, I was bound to bear my part in restoring order. (220)

Hubert Cumberledge joins other men, including two American scouts, to defend Salisbury, although Hilda tells him to take Sebastian alive. If not, she cannot marry him, as without a credible witness she could not clear her father's reputation.

There is one fierce battle with the Matabele, after which the men pursue Sebastian, who manages to escape. Browne's illustrations of white men scouting or fighting (230, 233, 235, 238, 242) are like battle artists' records of the Boer War. The Matabele appear as if they 'sprang up from the ground by magic' (239); 'the black bodies could crawl unperceived through the tall dry herbage' (229) in 'serpentine curves . . . trailing their snake-like way' (237). In the next tale, Cumberledge is more nonchalant about the revolt:

> People seemed to believe in Rhodesia none the less firmly because of this slight disturbance. They treated massacres as necessary incidents in the early history of a colony with a future. And I do not deny that native risings add picturesqueness. But I prefer to take them in a literary form. (248)

Allen's attempt to align his narrative with current events is intriguing. Without clarifying issues of imperialism, the two stories set in South Africa and Rhodesia provide an alignment with national debates that broadens the scope of *Hilda Wade*.

The next two tales, *The Lady Who Was Very Exclusive* and *The Guide Who Knew the Country*, involve Sir Ivor Meadowcraft, a nouveau riche manufacturer of steel, and his pretentious, nervous wife Emma, the woman alluded to in the first title. Hilda Wade and Cumberledge leave Africa for India, and on ship they encounter the Meadowcrafts. Hilda regards Emma Meadowcraft as a 'sham great lady' (255) marked by 'inanity' (259). When Emma Meadowcraft learns of plague and fever in India, she begs Hilda and her lover to accompany her to India in case she needs medical assistance. Calling Cumberledge her 'knight-errant' (259), Hilda agrees to this arrangement. The social satire in this chapter is undistinguished and perfunctory, and the only reason for the story is to contrast a woman with no purpose, like Emma Meadowcraft, and a woman with one, like Hilda Wade.

The succeeding tale involves a treacherous guide, one Ram Das, who leads the party on a tour of monasteries in Nepal but, bribed by Sebastian, allows the party to cross into Tibet. At first the group is threatened with death by the monks, but the intrepid Hilda and Cumberledge use photographs, a form of zoetrope, and gin and soda to deceive the Buddhist monks, who believe they are converts to the religion. However, the people, thinking these white persons are saints, wish to kill them so they will remain in the territory. Warned, the group manages to flee and return to Nepal. The depiction of Tibetan life offers opportunities for Gordon Browne to do some exotic illustrations, but the chapter comes too close to Rudyard Kipling's *The Man Who Would be King* (1888) to be convincing. Although demonstrating Hilda Wade's resourcefulness once again, this and the preceding chapter constitute filler in the narrative, an indication of Grant Allen's weakening health and impending death.

The final two tales in *Hilda Wade* were written by Conan Doyle, presumably following Allen's instructions. In *The Officer Who Understood Perfectly*, Cumberledge nurses Sebastian back from fever in the hills of the Himalayas. In the process, Sebastian admits he tried to kill his former student and his former nurse. Cumberledge now defends Hilda to his former mentor:

> 'You can't bear a woman, whose life you have attempted . . . to have a hand in nursing you . . . But, remember, you have attempted *my* life too; you have twice done your best to get me murdered . . . You are a man . . . and she is a woman. That is all the difference.' (319)

Even Sebastian admires her 'tenacity of purpose' (320) and her 'intellect' (321). Cumberledge discovers on which ship Sebastian is returning to England by bribing the shipping clerk for the passenger list, telling the clerk 'I am a private detective' (324), a statement he now regards as 'perfectly true in essence' (325). When the ship reaches the Channel, it founders because the first officer is flirting with a woman instead of navigating, a responsibility he acknowledges, as the title suggests. The most interesting part of this tale occurs when Hilda Wade defends Ibsen to a fellow passenger, stating that Ibsen 'is leavening England' (335). This discussion occurs just before the crash of the ship, so there is a clear suggestion that women rather than men might best navigate England. In the next and final story, one learns that Hilda Wade, Cumberledge and Sebastian were tossed about on a raft on the Atlantic for three days before being rescued. Hilda is determined to keep Sebastian alive so he can prove her father innocent of murder.

The Dead Man Who Spoke, the final story, describes how Sebastian is finally compelled to confess the truth about Hilda Wade's father before witnesses, including Yorke-Bannerman's counsel Mayfield, who had doubted his innocence. Sebastian admits on his death-bed that he administered too much aconitine to the Admiral as a scientific experiment to determine if the drug could cure the Admiral of a tropical disease he had contracted on the Malabar Coast during his service. The dying Sebastian allows that Hilda 'has conquered' (351) and that 'for firmness and tenacity, this lady is my equal' (353). Sebastian admits before dying that 'a woman only has had the wit to see that a gross injustice has been done' (355). After Sebastian has died, Hilda declares: 'He was a great man, after all, Hubert. Not good, but great.' Hubert Cumberledge responds to Hilda: 'You are a great woman' (360). Having cleared her father's reputation, Hilda asserts that 'Actual life comes next' (360).

Craig and Cadogan correctly observe about Grant Allen's female detective: 'Hilda brings a touch of religious fervour to her nursing and detective work; she is not one of those mundane mystery-solvers given to peering at small objects through a spyglass' (27). Grant Allen brought the British female detective into the twentieth century by his adroit combination of medical precision with adventurous incident. *Hilda Wade* with its intelligent, professional, independent and brave protagonist set a standard for female detectives in the new century. Her chronicler Hubert Cumberledge revealed that a new century demanded that males master a new epistemology.

M. McDonnell Bodkin (1850-1933): *Dora Myrl, The Lady Detective* (1900)

Among the most engaging of the female detectives appearing at the end of the nineteenth century in England was Dora Myrl, the focus of twelve stories serialized in two sets of six in *Pearson's Weekly* from 27 May 1899 through 26 August 1899, published in book form in 1900 (for serial dates, see Locke 18-19). *Pearson's Weekly* published a wide range of literature. In 1897, for example, H. G. Wells's *The Invisible Man* had appeared in its pages. A particularly important writer, Victor L. Whitechurch, who was to make railway crime the focus of his stories, had already published such key tales as *Lost on the Line* (September 1896) and *The Mystery of the Corridor Express* (April 1899) in its pages, and the first significant 'railway detective' was to appear in *Pearson's* with Whitechurch's *The Investigations of Godfrey Page, Railwayac* during 1903-4 (see Kestner 2000). An anonymous article *Scotland Yard in 1897*, about the Yard in the future, had appeared in February 1897.

The record of *Pearson's* in dealing with crime literature was a strong one when M. McDonnell Bodkin, a Queen's Counsel born in Ireland, published his narratives as *Dora Myrl, The Lady Detective*. The book publication contained all 12 of the original stories, although not in the order in which they had originally appeared in the magazine. The sixth tale, for example, was in fact the final tale of the second series.

In the first story, *The False Heir and the True*, Bodkin introduces Dora Myrl through the eyes of Roderick Alymer, who sees 'a dainty little lady leaping from [a bicycle]' and wonders that 'that schoolgirl [is] a Cambridge wrangler and a Doctor of Medicine!' (1). While these tales have no first person observer/narrator in the manner of Watson, the third-person narrator comments: 'There was certainly nothing of the New Woman, or for that matter of the old, about the winsome figure . . . The short skirt of her tailor-made dress twitched by the light wind showed slim ankles and neat feet cased in tan cycling-shoes' (1-2). As Kathleen Gregory Klein notes, however, Dora Myrl is a New Woman: 'In appearance, education, occupation, and recreation, Dora Myrl corresponds perfectly with the Girton girl whose independence so challenged her countrymen . . . The protagonists's background is not unusual for a detective but markedly different than most women's in her time' (58). Bodkin appears to deny Myrl is a New Woman only to confirm the fact.

This background is made explicit when Dora Myrl tells Alice Aylmer about herself:

> 'My father was an old-fashioned Cambridge don who married late in life. My mother . . . I never saw. She gave her life for mine. My father grieved at first that I was not a boy. Afterwards, I think, he liked me better as I was. It was his whole ambition that I should be a lady and a scholar. He waited in this world three months beyond his time, so the doctors said, to see me a Cambridge Wrangler; then he died content, leaving me alone at the age of eighteen with two hundred pounds and my wranglership for a fortune. I had no taste for the humdrum life of school-teaching, so I spent the little money I had in making myself a doctor.' (5-6)

A number of important elements emerge here, especially that Myrl is a university graduate and even a physician because of her father's encouragement. The absence of the mother, of course, at least since the time of Jane Austen's fiction, is a sign that the young woman must define herself in a patriarchal world without the mother present as a stifling paradigm.

Like the protagonist of Grant Allen's series concerning Lois Cayley, Dora Myrl rejects school-teaching as a profession. Since she becomes a physician, the parallel between detection and medicine is indicated in these narratives, as it is in Grant Allen's narratives about the nurse Hilda Wade, although not so insistently as in Allen's series. For example, Myrl discovers the disturbance in her first client, Alice Aylmer 'like a skilled physician searching a patient's body with a stethescope when he finds the lurking disease at last' (7) the reader is informed.

At the same time, the prejudice against female doctors is clear in her subsequent discussion of her background: 'But practice didn't come, and I couldn't and wouldn't wait for it. Within the last year I have been a telegraph girl, a telephone girl, a lady journalist. I liked the last best. But I have not found my vocation yet' (6). Bodkin's advantage with this strategy is to show Myrl rejecting various 'female' occupations while still leaving open for the reader's curiosity the choice of profession for his Cambridge woman. Sylvia Mellecent, a friend of the young detective in a later story, describes Dora as 'the brilliant leader of the school, alike in the playground and in the study' and as 'the head girl' (23). There is little doubt of her distinction, energy, determination or originality.

These are all confirmed in the first story, *The False Heir and the True*, which concerns Roderick Aylmer and his wife Alice. Alice Aylmer had thought her baby was exchanged at birth with the son of Mrs Caruth, who had been the maid, since Alice Aylmer's son was sickly and likely to die, and she herself was dangerously ill after the birth. Instead, the Irish nurse to Alice Aylmer, Kitty Sullivan, had placed a Roman Catholic medal around the baby's neck, which had been preserved. The children had not in fact been swapped, although the corrupt Mrs Caruth kept trying to get money for 'her' baby's care for years.

The story shows the mother, Alice Aylmer, in great emotional turmoil, since she loves the child who has been with her. She feels she has robbed 'the rightful heir of Dunscombe . . . of his rights. I have been miserable ever since. I feel I am an unnatural hearted mother, but I could not and I cannot give up the boy I love for my own that I do not love' (13). Since the boy with Mrs Caruth has now been sent to prison for thieving, the former maid threatens to expose all to Roderick Aylmer if she is not given money to save the young man.

Dora discovers the truth, telling Alice Aylmer that Mrs Caruth 'kept her own child, which she doubtless loved after her own fashion. But she deceived you into the belief that it was yours' (17). After Caruth confesses, Dora draws an important personal conclusion: 'I have found my vocation. I am about to send this card to the engraver at once . . . : MISS DORA MYRL *Lady Detective*' (18-19). From this point on, Myrl pursues this profession as a private investigator, whose business becomes known from newspaper accounts and who works amiably with detectives from Scotland Yard, unlike her famous predecessor Holmes.

In *The Hidden Violin*, Dora Myrl discovers the location of a stolen Stradivarius belonging to the Italian young prodigy Nicolo Amati, a friend of Dora's school friend Sylvia Mellecent. As Dora discovers, a French violinist, M. Gallasseau, has stolen the instrument, hiding it on his back in his rooms, in which all the mirrors have been turned to the walls. Dora is modest about her accomplishments at this point, telling her friend that 'they call me a detective . . . when they want to flatter me' (20).

While the story is itself undistinguished, it is important as an indicator of European influences in Victorian culture. Dora herself loves music, and Nicolo Amati would appear to be the ideal performer: 'His beauty would have in itself compelled attention apart form the subtle rumours of his genius. He had the figure of a Greek god, black eyes full of light and fire, and a face perfect in curve and colour' (26). He sounds in fact like the embodiment of the Spanish violinist Pablo de Sarasate, who had been painted by James McNeill Whistler in 1884. Bodkin may also be evoking the famous Italian artists' models of Victorian England, such as Angelo Colorosi, who had modelled for Frederic Leighton, President of the Royal Academy and who became himself an artist.

In the third tale in the series, the anthologized *How He Cut His Stick*, Bodkin resorts to the railway detective story for which *Pearson's Weekly* was already known through the work of Victor Whitechurch. In this story, a young man, Jim Pollock, is asked by Sir Gregory Grant, owner of a banking house, to be a courier on the train for some of the bank's gold deposits. During the journey, Pollock is chloroformed by a thief who has hidden underneath the seat in the locked train carriage. This thief, one McCrowder, then swung out from the carriage by means of a notched, crooked stick, by which he grasped some wires of the telegraph. Dora Myrl gets Pollock released from prison long enough to assist her in capturing McCrowder, which she does by pursuing him in a rather furious bicycle chase. When she arrests him, she does so with a revolver. She had told Pollock 'I'm not too bad a shot' (50). When she confronts the thief, she is firm of purpose: '[McCrowder] looked again. The sunlight glinted on the barrel of a revolver, pointed straight at his head, with a steady hand' (54).

How He Cut His Stick merits its fame. The brief account of the robbery in the locked carriage is thrilling: '[Jim Pollock] saw nothing and felt nothing till he felt two murderous hands clutching at his throat and a knee crushing his chest in . . . He was down on his back on the carriage floor with a handkerchief soaked in chloroform jammed close to his mouth and nostrils' (42).

The local police of course have it all wrong, and this is the first case in which Myrl subverts the official establishment. Sir Gregory, however, does not believe the police account and encourages Myrl to investigate. She tells him: 'I never talk of the fee till the case is over' (46). Dora Myrl discovers the solution to the theft, which is intriguing for being both an 'impossible crime' (escaping from the carriage at sixty miles per hour) and a 'locked room' mystery (given that the carriage is locked, with no through corridor). In this story, Bodkin writes as strong a railway mystery as does Victor Whitechurch. It may well be that the magazine encouraged Bodkin to mine this vein, since another tale in the series again focuses on the railway.

In the fourth story, *The Palmist*, a physician, Dr Phillimore, kills his angry wife by putting arsenic in her chocolate. He blames it on the old nurse, Honor Maguire, of his ward, Eveline Norris, one of Dora Myrl's friends. Myrl disguises herself as a palmist, and when Phillimore comes to the parlour, Myrl has him arrested.

While the story presumes that Phillimore could not see through Myrl's disguise, it has one key agenda to which Bodkin will return in a later narrative, that of the male sexual predator. Not only has Phillimore poisoned his wife, but he has also made unwelcome advances toward Eveline Norris's companion, Mabel Graham. Myrl, speaking in the guise of the palmist, tells the killer: 'You took your pleasures freely without regard to [your wife's] jealousy. Your ward's governess, Miss Graham, inspired you with a fierce, devouring passion! . . . You proposed to Mabel Graham to become your mistress, and she refused indignantly and left the house the same day . . . You resolved to get rid of your wife without danger to yourself, and make an Irishwoman, Honor Maguire, the scapegoat' (77).

Phillimore had been introduced as an atheist, which he amends to agnostic:

> 'Nobody does really believe nowadays except a very few fanatics, though most people think it respectable to make belief to believe. The priests of all sects of course try to keep up the delusion and to frighten people into faith, as they call it . . . I don't believe in God and I don't disbelieve. I simply don't know. But I, Dr Phillimore, don't expect any existence after death except, of course, the chemical existence of the elements of my body, in which I am not particularly interested. I mean to get all the enjoyment I can out of this life while I have it. A life in the hand, Miss Myrl, is worth two in the bush.' (69)

This detail delineates a strong dimension of late-Victorian speculation. Bodkin appears to suggest that agnostics might be more prone to crime. Dora Myrl remarks: 'This theory of yours . . . would relieve the world from all moral restraint' (70). Phillimore does not accept this idea:

> 'Moral restraint; yes – if there were such a thing. But the fear of detection and punishment remains. It is fear that prevents crime, believe me. We could all go just where we want to if we could be sure of hiding our footsteps.' (70)

Phillimore tells Myrl: 'I believe in anything and everything that is proved to me' (70). Bodkin makes the murder an experiment by this physician to test the man's philosophical/ethical theories.

Furthermore, Phillimore has bemused contempt for lady detectives, laughing when Eveline proposes bringing Dora Myrl to dinner: 'Oh, the lady detective; bring her by all means' (67). He informs Dora when he meets her: 'Still, you must confess it is a somewhat incongruous – I won't say comical – profession for a charming young lady' (72). This dismissal is followed by a veiled threat: 'You, of course, are the exception, Miss Myrl. But do you think that women can fairly pit themselves in mind and body against cunning and strong men, and the so-called criminal classes as a rule are both?' (73). Dora retorts: 'Women are clever and men are confident; their confidence betrays them' (73). In the end, Dora vindicates her position when the handcuffs are placed on the killer: 'This is your answer' (80). Dora not only justifies her professional identity in the story but also removes from society a male sexual predator of the most vile kind.

Bodkin works in a different sub-genre of detective fiction in *The Last Shall Be First*, that of the horse-racing crime story. As Peter Haining has discussed, the anonymously published *Richmond; or, Scenes in the Life of a Bow Street Runner*, published in 1827, was 'the very earliest volume to contain a crime story of the turf' (44). Dora Myrl proves that Sir Warner Hernshaw had an electric current jolt the lead horse in a race as it went over a black bullfinch hedge. In this case, she has the horse of Lord Wellmount, Goneaway, held back by his jockey Ned Carruthers, so that Sir Warner's horse, Jumping Frog ridden by Sam Roper, goes over the barrier first, becoming stunned by the current and losing the race.

The case is brought to Dora by Archie Grant, the son of the banker in *How He Cut His Stick*. When Archie thinks Dora Myrl is 'a dear innocent little thing' (82), his father corrects him: 'Your dear innocent little girl is Miss Dora Myrl, the famous Cambridge wrangler and Lady Detective' (83). When Archie cannot come to the point, Dora rebukes him: 'Tell your story right out, can't you?' (84), which shocks Grant into recognition that Dora is a professional. Archie Grant is friend and cousin to Wellmount, who is losing a lot of money to the corrupt Sir Warner. When Dora confronts Sir Warner, she tells him: 'There's no use making a fuss. You've got to pay up or own up, whichever you choose' (99).

At the conclusion, 'Sir Warner paid up' (99), but there is the suggestion that he will continue his wastrel ways. Bodkin follows the challenge set for Victorian detectives by the example of Holmes in the famous *Silver Blaze* published in the *Strand* in December 1892, creating an ingenious case for his female detective to show she can fully compete with Sherlock Holmes.

The story *The Clue* involves another Phillimore, in this instance Sir Charles Phillimore, who has a letter sent him by Eveline Morris, Myrl's friend from *The Palmist*, although there seems to be no connection between the two men. Sir Charles threatens to send the letter to Morris's fiancé, Jem Trevor, the day she marries him. In the end, Dora Myrl burns the letter after finding it. The narrative echoes the situation presented in Edgar Allan Poe's *The Purloined Letter* of 1845.

Sir Charles is another male sexual predator. When Dora remarks that he has 'threatened' to send the letter to Jem Trevor, Sir Charles corrects her by telling her that 'promise' is the issue (106). The man is a suave deceiver: 'He was most courteous to Dora – a very good parody of the old-fashioned courtesy, with gallantry peeping out through the assumption of homage, but she felt at once that entreaties could not move him' (107). She recognizes him as an 'irresistible lady-killer' (107). He mocks her; 'You are famous as an unraveller of mysteries – a finder out of secrets. It would be crime to rob you of your triumph by tame surrender' (107).

Dora Myrl discovers the location of the letter by putting a thread in Phillimore's morning jacket, which leads her to its location. In this respect, Bodkin evokes the myth of Ariadne and Theseus and the Minotaur, but there is no Theseus here, as Dora is the Ariadne who can operate without male assistance to get at the Minotaur, Sir Charles. She finds the letter behind a photograph of Phillimore, significantly costumed as the libertine seducer Don Juan. When Phillimore confronts her with the photograph and letter, he threatens her with 'a gentle force, a tender violence' (117). She evades him by striking a match and burning the letter in front of him. He is never reported to the police, however, and Bodkin indicates that such men simply move on to other prey to seduce and blackmail. Conan Doyle's infamous male blackmailer appeared in *Charles Augustus Milverton* in April 1904 in the *Strand*.

A completely psychopathic male sexual predator appears in *A Railway Race*. Dora Myrl saves the night mail train from crashing on a barrier erected by the diabolical male sexual predator Richard Dulcimer. He wanted to kill the family of Lord Mordor, his uncle, as they were coming to meet his cousin Tom Mordor, slated to marry the actress Nina Lovell, whom Dulcimer also wanted to possess. When Dora goes to the theatre to see her friend portray Ophelia, she catches Dulcimer's face in a mirror, 'a fiend's as Dante might conceive it' (122), that of 'handsome debonnaire Dick Dulcimer, the most light-hearted and popular man in all London' (122).

Nina Lovell tells Myrl that Dick Dulcimer 'gets on my nerves' (125). As Bodkin demonstrates, this phrase is merely the expression the patriarchy mandates a woman use. Later, the actress admits that she 'hates' Dulcimer (127) and fears him: 'I cannot get myself to trust him. He makes love to me; half joke, whole earnest' (128). When she tells Dulcimer she is marrying Tom Mordor, there is this reaction: 'All at once the smile fell from his lips and eyes as I've seen a mask fall off . . . He looked at me hungrily, as if he'd like to snatch me up in his arms' (129). Nina then informs Myrl that several family members have nearly lost their lives recently, all 'accidents' contrived by Dulcimer. Dora does not conceal that 'it's a very bad case' (131).

Dora disguises herself as a telegraph messenger boy and learns of Dulcimer's plan to wreck the night mail train on which the Mordor family is travelling. She succeeds in getting a train to race to the scene and warn with a red search light. Dulcimer is killed by his confederate, the desperado Filox Cranshaw, who then kills himself. Myrl assembles the torn pieces of a cypher message Dulcimer had thrown into the street, so Bodkin amalgamates two sub-genres here, the cypher tale and the railway narrative. The villain's odd name of Dulcimer evokes Coleridge's Kubla Khan, the imperious tyrant, which Dulcimer proves to be. In disguising herself as a messenger, Dora recalls the male disguise used by Irene Adler in the Holmes tale *A Scandal in Bohemia* from the *Strand* of 1891, another story where a transvestite disguise assures a woman's success.

Dora Myrl employs another male disguise in *The Pauper's Legacy*, where she assumes the role of M. Duval, a French detective, to get valuable blue stamps from Mauritius, which had been stolen by the actress Carrie Vivian. Vivian had taken them from Dora Myrl's friend Margaret Norris, who has been reduced to poverty and making silhouettes after the financial crash and death of her father: 'One week she was a petted and pampered heiress, the only daughter of a reputed millionaire; the next a great commercial crisis carried off fortune and father together, and left her a penniless orphan' (150). The stamps, worth £7,000, enable Norris to start again. She marries her cousin, the physician Frederick Norris. Margaret Norris said she 'would never change my name' (169) if she married, and in fact she does not have to violate her belief.

Margaret Norris relates that the newspapers are 'full of that story of the fiddle' (152), the case recorded earlier in *The Hidden Violin*. Bodkin thus informs the reader about the circulation of Myrl's professional reputation. When Norris notes that a detective must search for the motive in a criminal investigation, Myrl corrects her that '"Cherchez la femme" is the true reading' (153). Bodkin makes it clear that a woman can especially detect criminal behaviour in another woman. The use of the male disguise recalls *A Scandal in Bohemia*, but the device is given a twist by being used against an actress, who is unable to detect the impersonation.

Another insidious family member appears in *Was It a Forgery?*, which concerns Albert Lovel, who alters the will of his uncle, Sir Randal Lovel, to deprive his cousin Annie Lovel of the money. Myrl proves that the will is forged by crushing glass into the ink, which unknowingly Lovel uses to alter the will. Albert Lovel is described as a dangerous man by Sir Gregory Grant:

> 'From his boyhood he was a bad lot, not wild but vicious . . . He got leave to retire from the army, and there was a story of cheating at cards . . . He has been twice co-respondent in the divorce courts. A girl committed suicide the other day whom — but I need not go into those scandals. You may take it from me

> that Albert Lovel – Albert the Good, as he is generally called – is the gayest, brightest, handsomest, most accomplished, and most utterly heartless and conscienceless young reprobate in the three kingdoms.' (171-2)

As with Dick Dulcimer in *A Railway Race*, here is another young man who is utterly ruthless but touted in London society as one of its leading young men. At one point, Sir Randal is shot, though not fatally, presumably by his nephew Lovel.

Lovel is extremely alluring – and dangerous, as Myrl discovers:

> He was an altogether charming Apollo in a perfectly fitting cycling suit. His lips wore a gay smile; his dark eyes sparkled with merriment; his voice was musical as a flute. Yet withal he was a manly man; the kind of man that captures girls wholesale . . . His manner to Dora was that of frank comradeship. Withal he was so pleasant to look at and talk to that she had to keep her memory fixed on what he really was to save herself from the peril of liking and trusting him. (178-9, 181)

Dora Myrl photographs the will, fortunately so because Lovel contests it. Her evidence proves he used the ink with the crushed glass to alter the legatee's name. But it is not merely the money which Dora Myrl saves for Annie Lovel. Myrl had learned that the woman 'feared her handsome cousin as the devout Christian of the Middle Ages feared the devil, not without admiration in her terror' (176). As in several of the Sherlock Holmes tales, such as *The Speckled Band* (1892) or *A Case of Identity* (1891) or *The Copper Beeches* (1892), a family member preys on a defenceless young woman to obtain her money.

Hide and Seek concerns the art dealer, Jacob Gildmirk, who conceals the latest and greatest painting by Godfrey Morland behind a battle painting that Goldmirk has just purchased. Suspicion is thrown on Morland's friend and fellow artist, Ernest Beauchamp. Both men are in love with the model Alice Lyle, who suggests that Dora Myrl be brought into the case because she loves Morland. Lyle labels Dora 'a very clever woman – a lady detective' (206).

The public is not interested in Morland's battle piece, but his canvas of two lovers is a sensation. Gildmirk makes it appear the canvas was lowered from the studio window, with a button from Beauchamp's studio jacket appearing to indicate he is the thief. Inspector Worral of Scotland Yard appears, with a voice 'civil, almost deferential' (210) when Myrl appears, though he is not 'too well pleased at her sudden appearance' (210). At the conclusion, Goldmirk disappears. In all the stories involving Myrl she never acts out of a romantic attachment, although here she saves a friend's lover, the artist Morland, from being deceived by an unscrupulous art dealer.

Weighed and Found Wanting concerns the jewel dealer Solomons, who has a magnet under his counter to make the scales give false weight by using steel beads to depress the scales. The case is brought to Dora Myrl by Dr Stewart, who has removed what he thought was a bullet from the arm of Alan Collingswood. The bullet in fact turned out to be a diamond, which had been entrusted to the young man by his uncle, Major-General Sir Anthony Collingswood when they were in India. To get the diamond out of India, Alan Collingswood had persuaded the army surgeon to insert the jewel in his arm muscle. Bodkin refers to Wilkie Collins's *The Moonstone* of 1868 as an obvious model for the tale (220).

When the young man takes the diamond to be weighed, Solomons declares it is 49 carats, although the uncle declares it was 65 carats. He believes his nephew is deceiving him by substituting another stone, and a rift is caused between them. Dora Myrl proves the existence of the steel beads and the magnet by placing an item of her dress, some jet beads, close to the scales 'just as the weighed dish came slowly down' (233), causing the steel beads to roll across the counter, thereby exposing the fraud. Dora Myrl is able to solve the case by using a woman's dress accessory, which only she could do. The story contrasts with the use of male costume by Myrl in other stories such as *The Pauper's Legacy* and *A Railway Race*.

The final narrative in the book version of *Dora Myrl* is *The Wings of a Bird*. The inventor Ernest Fairleigh, whom Myrl had known at Cambridge, has plans for human flight, which he has not yet patented. A specification is stolen from his office while he is distracted on the landing of his office building. The culprit is the old family confidential clerk, Joe Bradley, who had the plan removed by carrier pigeon to his rural home. Fairleigh had thought his office was protected by iron bars on doors and windows, so the story is a variant of the 'locked room' sub-genre. Again, another inspector, this time one Adam Warner, appears from Scotland Yard, but it is Myrl who solves the case.

It is important that Fairleigh secure his invention, for he is marked as being opposed to war: 'It is a universal rule that the great science of slaughter – which they call war – almost monopolises invention' (241). Hence, when Myrl saves the invention, she contributes to the use of science for good rather than evil intentions. Bodkin also has Fairleigh and his detective be comrades from Cambridge for two important reasons: first, to demonstrate that men and women are equal in their knowledge and ability; and second, to affirm that detection is a form of science.

In the fourth tale in the volume, *The Palmist*, the physician Phillimore had asked Myrl: 'How could a charming young lady, like yourself, for example, arrest a powerful desperado who had not the least respect for her sex or her beauty?' Myrl replies: 'Oh! I'd manage it somehow' (73). Phillimore then threatens her: 'Let us suppose for a moment that I was your criminal. I never go a step without a loaded revolver, and I'm a dead shot. But I would not need that. I could crush the life out of you with my naked hand' (73). The result of this challenge is that Dora Myrl triumphs over this evil man. Especially in *The Palmist*, *A Railway Race* and *The Clue*, Bodkin is not afraid to have his female detective challenge diabolical male sexual predators. While in a subsequent volume, *The Capture of Paul Beck* of 1909, Bodkin will have Dora Myrl marry the detective Paul Beck, in this series she never operates out of romantic self-interest.

With this first appearance of his female detective, Bodkin eschews the marriage plot. In this respect, he is more unconventional than Grant Allen, who has his female detectives marry in *Lois Cayley* and *Hilda Wade*, published near the same time. Instead, Dora Myrl proves loyal to other women, as in *The False Heir and the True* or *The Pauper's Legacy*. She can use a revolver and a bicycle, as in *How He Cut His Stick*. She is a university graduate and a physician. The publication of the collected stories in 1900 revealed that for at least one male writer, women could do anything and need never marry. Hence, Dora Myrl is not afraid to invade male territory, such as the turf – in the fortuitously and symbolically named *The Last Shall Be First*.

In little over a decade after the appearance of Sherlock Holmes in 1887, male and female writers constructed a range of women detectives who were 'Sherlock's sisters.' Married or widowed or single, university educated or not, working alone like Dora Myrl or with an agency like Loveday Brooke, motivated by private motives like Hilda Wade or disinterested professionalism like Mollie Delamere, an aristocrat like Sibyl Penrith or a free spirit like Hagar Stanley, operating in England like Dorcas Dene or abroad like Miriam Lea, these female detectives demonstrated a bravery, rationality and professionalism at the end of the nineteenth century which rivalled the similar qualities of their distinguished predecessor, Sherlock Holmes.

4 The Edwardian Female Detective to 1913

The year 1901 witnessed the death of Queen Victoria and the accession of King Edward VII. From the appearance of the tales collected as *The Memoirs of Sherlock Holmes* until the first instalment of *The Hound of the Baskervilles* in the *Strand* in August 1901, there were no new appearances of Sherlock Holmes in print. *The Hound of the Baskervilles* was subtitled 'Another Adventure of Sherlock Holmes' to indicate that this was not a revival or resurrection of Holmes but rather an event which occurred before his demise at the Reichenbach Falls recorded in *The Final Problem*.

Doyle's narrative, however, was being read in a world different from that of the first appearance of Holmes in the 1880s. If the Edwardian era, whether defined as ending in 1910 with the accession of George V or in 1914 with the beginning of the Great War, is considered by historians as a 'golden age' or 'twilight', it can only be so because the war years, 1914 to 1918, were so much more dismal. The Edwardian era itself fell 'between an economic depression at the end of the long Victorian age and the carnage of the First World War . . . Behind the glamorous, glittering veneer that marked the style of high society lurked a mean, poverty-stricken "submerged" stratum . . . Behind the apparent prosperity there was anxiety in the economy about industrial retardation and foreign competition' (McKellar, 1980, 2-3).

'The first ten years of the century had the highest murder rate of any decade before 1970' (McKellar, 1980, 26). This incidence of crime was related to other social anxieties. For example, 'race degeneracy' was a recurring topic of discussion. The Report of the Physical Deterioration Committee in 1903 included figures from the Army Medical Corps which established that 34.6 per cent of recruits had to be rejected as 'medically unfit' (McKellar 26) for service. The founding of the Boy Scout movement in 1907 by Robert Baden-Powell can be construed as an attempt to apply the tactics of patrolling the Empire to the reinvigoration of males in the early twentieth century.

Physical degeneracy and crime also contributed to the undermining of England's position on the international stage. The competition Britain confronted by 1900 was coming from two sources, the United States and

Germany. The consanguinity between the royal family and Germany, epitomized by the fact that Kaiser Wilhelm II was the nephew of Edward VII, provoked tense responses between the two countries. Invasion scare literature, such as Erskine Childers's *The Riddle of the Sands* (1903), was a manifestation of this disturbing relationship between Britain and Germany. As the Edwardian era drew to a close, strikes became pandemic: there were miners' strikes in 1910 and 1912, and a strike by railwaymen in 1911. This disturbance in the economic situation gradually became destabilizing. Finally, the unpopular Boer War of 1899-1902 undermined British global prestige.

An additional element of cultural tension relevant to the fictional female detective involved the female suffrage movement. The Women's Social and Political Union was founded in Manchester in 1903, and the activities of the suffragettes were in some instances to become militant during the early years of the twentieth century. The National Federation of Women Workers was created in 1906 and the Women's Freedom League in 1907. By 1908, women were marching with banners of Joan of Arc and of Boadicea; in marches of 1909 a banner of Diana and her hounds appeared. By 1912, window smashing in London by suffragettes brought about the arrest of 200 persons, while the suicidal death of Emily Davison at the Derby in 1913 was an occasion for national mourning and protest.

The phenomenal success of *The Hound of the Baskervilles* in 1902 led Conan Doyle to resurrect Holmes in the stories, all published in the *Strand*, which became *The Return of Sherlock Holmes* in 1905. The female detective continued to be a figure of interest to writers. One might cite the example of a short story by Florence Warden (actually Florence James, 1857-1929), who published *The House by the Vaults* in the *Strand* in June 1905, the same year of the collection *The Return of Sherlock Holmes*. This important short tale has a young woman who is forced by the odd circumstances of her marriage to become a sleuth.

Susie Beech is married to Rothley Beech when she is visited by his aunt, Eleanor Beech. The young wife informs the aunt that her husband, a writer, cannot be disturbed, but the aunt, after peering through the keyhole, asserts he is not in his study at all. When Susie herself peeps into the keyhole later, the husband does emerge 'with a look of terror and dismay . . . thin, pale, even sickly-looking' (641). When the man who loved her, George Merridew, comes to see her, Susie decides to peer through the window of the study to see if her husband is present. In fact, 'there was no sign of her husband' (643). Finding a hole in the floor, Susie Beech goes through a trapdoor into the vaults, coming up into another room, poorly furnished and shabby, in the home of a Mrs Greening. It is discovered that Rothley has been eking out a living writing begging letters to organizations, an impostor asking for charitable money. When a detective arrives with a warrant for his arrest for deserting his first wife and their child, Rothley flees to the United States, where he is arrested as a swindler. The aunt secures a decree of nullity of the marriage, leaving Susie free to marry George Merridew.

The interest of this story of amateur detection is two-fold. In its brief compass, it contains two female detectives, the wronged wife Susie Beech and the aunt Eleanor Beech. Each woman contributes to the exposure of the rogue husband. It is also the older woman who manages to enable the young wife to shed her husband and marry the man who originally loved her. Thus, the two women work in tandem and reveal how a male can use the institution of marriage as a screen for his criminality.

The other intriguing element of the story is supplied through its illustrations by Gordon Browne, one of the great artists for the *Strand* who had already illustrated Grant Allen's *Lois Cayley* and *Hilda Wade* in its pages. The dynamics of female empowerment can be observed in the series of illustrations for *The House by the Vaults*. In the first, Susie Beech is caught kneeling outside his study door by her husband Rothley Beech, who is standing above her. Evidently, she is in his power. In the second picture, however, everything changes. Susie Beech is shown standing on a ladder against the house wall peering into the husband's room through the Venetian blind. Here, she has assumed control of the gaze from the male. Finding the window open, she invades the room. In the third illustration, the wife is shown emerging from the trapdoor to the vaults into the secret shabby room where her husband has been writing his begging letters to charities. The final illustration shows Rothley Beech, seated, confronted by his fierce aunt, who is standing above him. Gordon Browne sharply perceives the feminist, female-empowering ideological drift of Warden's tale. These depictions of the amateur female sleuth convey the idea of her legitimacy in undertaking such a mission. The story demonstrates that women cannot trust husbands and must take action to rectify abuses.

The three narratives examined in this chapter reflect the validity of the woman undertaking detection. In Emmuska Orczy's *Lady Molly of Scotland Yard*, the lady detective confronts female killers in several of the stories, as well as women engaging in blackmailing and forgery. The protagonist of Richard Marsh's *Judith Lee* confronts secret societies, killers, evil women and revolutionaries. Marie Belloc Lowndes deploys her landlady sleuth Ellen Bunting in *The Lodger* to reveal that a woman is capable of detecting a male serial killer, starkly exposing the failure of men to solve the Ripper case. If the Ripper case was one of the reasons for the renascence of the female detective in 1888 and after, Lowndes demonstrates that women should be officially engaged in law enforcement and detection to rectify the incompetence of males who failed to save women from being victims in that notorious instance of serial murders.

These Edwardian female detectives operate in a culture on the brink of the disastrous events which would lead to the Great War. *Lady Molly of Scotland Yard* (1910), *Judith Lee* (1912), and *The Lodger* (1913) continue the adroit tradition of detection established by their predecessors in the nineteenth century. In *Lady Molly*, a female narrator/admirer is employed; in *Judith Lee*, the detective narrates her own exploits; in *The Lodger*, Lowndes brilliantly deploys the third-person restricted form of narration, confining the narrative consciousness to the landlady. At the same time, these protagonists anticipate the achievements of their twentieth-century successors, such as Frederic Kummer's Elinor Vance (1924), Edgar Jepson and Robert Eustace's Ruth Kelstern (1925), Agatha Christie's Jane Marple (1930) and Gilbert Frankau's Kyra Sokratescu (1931). By the time of the publication of Ellery Queen's *The Great Women Detectives and Criminals* in 1943, the fictional female detective had been established as a major tradition of the detectival genre. More importantly, because of these fictions, the female detective was in fact no longer a fiction.

Emmuska Orczy (1865-1947): *Lady Molly of Scotland Yard* (1910)

After issuing her collection of detective stories *The Old Man in the Corner* (Orczy, 1980) in 1909, a compilation of tales first published between 1901 and 1905, Emmuska Orczy turned her attention to creating a female detective, part of a tradition extending back to the 1860s and including such famous exemplars as Loveday Brooke created by Catherine Louisa Pirkis in 1894 and Dora Myrl, created by M. McDonnell Bodkin in 1900. In the instance of Orczy, the creation of Lady Molly Robertson-Kirk, of the Female Department of Scotland Yard, it is clear that this character was formulated to react against the passive Polly Burton, the lady journalist to whom the Man in the Corner narrates his theories about crimes. In *Lady Molly of Scotland Yard*, Orczy (1910) created an active, energetic, insightful detective to contrast with the more reactive Polly Burton of the previous compilation. The stories, 12 in all, were first published in 1910 with illustrations by Cyrus Cuneo.

The tales are chronicled by Lady Molly's female Watson, Mary Granard, who began as 'maid to Lady Molly Robertson-Kirk at the time' (1904) (298), 'once her maid, now her devoted friend' (310). She is adept at taking shorthand, which she does both for Lady Molly and at the Female Department of the Yard: 'I made excellent shorthand notes of the conflicting stories I heard' (239); 'Lady Molly was at work with the chief over some reports, whilst I was taking shorthand notes at a side desk' (270-

71). Mary Granard is 'determined to obey like a soldier, blindly and unquestioningly' (160), observing Lady Molly's commands 'like a soldier . . . to the letter' (163). She and Lady Molly have a residence at Maida Vale. As time passes, her situation changes: 'It was about this time that I severed my official connection with the Yard. Lady Molly now employed me as her private secretary' (57). Mary Granard is marked by her devotion to her 'dear lady', as she constantly denominates Lady Molly. Like Watson, she can be obtuse and imperceptive (118, 128), but in sharing a flat with Lady Molly, in recording her exploits, and in being an associate in her investigations, she is like the famous doctor.

The history of Lady Molly Robertson-Kirk emerges through the series of 12 tales. In the first tale, *The Ninescore Mystery*, Mary Granard records as follows:

> Well, you know, some say she is the daughter of a duke, others that she was born in the gutter, and that the handle has been soldered on to her name in order to give her style and influence.
>
> I could say a lot, of course, but 'my lips are sealed', as the poets say. All through her successful career at the Yard she honoured me with her friendship and confidence . . .
>
> Yes, we always called her 'my lady', from the moment that she was put at the head of our section; and the chief called her 'Lady Molly' in our presence. We of the Female Department are dreadfully snubbed by the men, though don't tell me that women have not ten times as much intuition as the blundering and sterner sex; my firm belief is that we shouldn't have half so many undetected crimes if some of the so-called mysteries were put to the test of feminine investigation. (1-2)

When Lady Molly goes out into society, 'none of these people knew that she had anything to do with the Yard' (47). Molly is 'my own dear lady, the woman for whom I would have gone through fire and water with a cheerful smile . . . my own dearest friend, dearer than any child could be to its mother' (75), 'the woman I loved best in the world' (78). If Holmes and Watson are patterns of male comradeship, Lady Molly and Mary Granard are no less so female friends.

Lady Molly, however, has a history that is only gradually revealed as the stories progress. In the penultimate tale, *Sir Jeremiah's Will*, Mary Granard announces:

> Many people have asked me whether I knew when, and in what circumstances, Lady Molly joined the detective staff at Scotland Yard, who she was, and how she managed to keep her position

> in Society – as she undoubtedly did – whilst exercising a profession which usually does not make for high social standing. (292)

Sir Jeremiah Baddock lives at Appledore Castle in Cumberland, being a shipowner in Liverpool. The history of Lady Molly is revealed. Sir Jeremiah Baddock leaves his fortune by a will of 1902 to Captain Hubert de Mazareen, his grandson. Sir Jeremiah had married a 'pretty French actress, Mlle Adèle Desty' (293) who eventually 'ran away with the Earl of Flintshire' (293). From this second marriage, Sir Jeremiah has a son, Philip Baddock. As it evolves, the Earl of Flintshire's daughter by Adèle Desty is Lady Molly Robertson-Kirk, with whom Captain de Mazareen falls 'desperately in love' (293). Although Sir Jermiah establishes, supposedly in a later will which remains unsigned, that Captain Hubert loses all his money if he marries anyone connected with the Flintshire clan, he and Lady Molly defy his wishes and marry in 1904.

It evolves that Alexander Steadman, solicitor for Sir Jeremiah, is found murdered at Appledore. De Mazareen, despite his heroic service in the Boer War, is arrested the day following his marriage to Lady Molly, convicted, and sentenced to imprisonment at Dartmoor for 20 years. Lady Molly, interestingly, asks him to marry her knowing that he will be arrested immediately. As Mary Granard notes, it is the 'ancient, yet ever new, story of Capelletti and Montecchi over again' (294). After the arrest of her new husband, Lady Molly

> applied for, and obtained, a small post on the detective staff of the police. From that small post she has worked her way upwards, analysing and studying, exercising her powers of intuition and deduction, until at the present moment, she is considered, by chiefs and men alike, the greatest authority among them on criminal investigation. (309)

Throughout the tales, Lady Molly's 'intuition' (101, 119, 257, 302, 307, 320) is constantly stressed, which both sets the female detective apart but also reinforces standard gendered stereotyping about male and female sexual differences, men being rational, women intuitive.

Thus, the agenda of a female tec like Lady Molly is a conflicted one: on the one hand she is independent, has a career, and takes risks; on the other, she is married and intuitive more than rational. As Slung notes, 'the lady detectives were forced to trade on natural deductive abilities, on what might be termed a practical application of their never-to-be-doubted "women's intuition", this quality eliciting alternate scorn and admiration from colleagues, clients, and criminals alike' (17). When her husband briefly escapes in 1906, Lady Molly is the one who turns him in to the police, since 'I am of the police, you know. I had to do my duty' (318); then she determines to prove Hubert de Mazareen's innocence.

In the final story of the series, entitled *The End*, Lady Molly carries on flirtations with Philip Baddock and his associate Felkin, a male nurse and associate in league with Baddock. Mary Granard disapproves of this behaviour by Lady Molly (322, 328, 334), not knowing she intends to set the men against each other to discover the killer of Sir Jeremiah's solicitor Steadman. Felkin eventually reveals that he impersonated the old man, dictating a will to Steadman in a darkened room in 1904, who never grasped the deception. Philip Baddock killed Alexander Steadman, but not before having signed a letter enlisting Felkin as an accomplice (338). In a fire at Appledore Castle, set by Baddock to destroy the proofs of his guilt, Lady Molly snatches the key documents when Felkin hurls them from above during the conflagration, giving them to Inspector Etty and thus proving her husband's innocence. Philip Baddock shoots himself, and Captain Hubert de Mazareen obtains 'His Majesty's gracious pardon after five years of martyrdom which he had borne with heroic fortitude' (343-4). As a result:

> [Lady Molly] has given up her connection with the police. The reason for it has gone with the return of her happiness, over which I – her ever faithful Mary Granard – will, with your permission, draw a veil. (344)

When her husband is freed, Lady Molly of Scotland Yard ceases to be a professional detective. Thus her career engages Edwardian gendered conceptions in an ambivalent manner: she is independent enough to have a career, yet abandons it when her marriage can be pursued without difficulty, a situation reflecting the conflicted attitude about female independence during the Edwardian years and just before the outbreak of militant suffragism.

Orczy creates in *Lady Molly* a series of tales of intense interest to the study of Edwardian gendered mores. For example, the men at the Yard are called 'our fellows' by Mary Granard (212, 243, 244, 278) and 'our own men' (259) in a spirit of equality. Throughout the tales, a series of male associates appears, certain men reappearing: Townson, the medical officer (260-61), Detective-Inspector Etty (176, 318) 'the chief' (45, 260), Danvers (200, 254) Detective-Inspector Saunders (240, 242, 260), Elliot and Pegram (23), and Detective-Inspector Hankin (37). Danvers's wife Fanny is 'one of our female searchers at the Yard' (254).

In one of Orczy's most renowned of the Lady Molly tales, *The Woman in the Big Hat*, the role of woman at the Yard is particularly stressed. A man, Mark Culledon, is murdered at the Mathis Tea Room in Regent Street by a woman wearing a large hat. Saunders addresses Lady Molly: 'The chief suggested sending for you . . . There's a woman in this case, and we shall rely on you a good deal' (260). After Katherine Harris, the parlour-maid at Lorbury House makes a statement, the chief questions whether it is helpful, retorting to Lady Molly's remarks 'somewhat testily'. When she comments with an 'enigmatical statement' she 'effectually silenced the chief' (270).

A former lover of Culloden's, the Austrian singer Elizabeth Löwenthal, comes to the Yard and informs the detectives that she was to have married Culloden but, to gain money from his rich aunt Mrs Steinberg, who would have disapproved, he married Lady Irene, the daughter of the Earl of Athyville, of a family 'as penniless as it was aristocratic' (264). Culloden himself 'possessed neither ancestors nor high connections' (264). Although Lady Molly is sure Löwenthal is innocent, the chief has her arrested; after an inquiry, Löwenthal is discharged for lack of evidence. Lady Molly disagreed with this arrest: 'the prosecution had been instituted in defiance of Lady Molly's express advice' (281). When the public mocks the police force for its ineptitude, the chief is compelled to give Lady Molly a 'free hand' (282). When Lady Molly confronts Lady Irene, she sets a plan with the servants which drives Lady Irene to confess she killed her husband. She then commits suicide by poison, but the public never knows the truth.

Lady Molly figures the woman in the big hat could not have been Löwenthal, who is tall, but instead a petite woman, since there was dispute about the size of the hat:

> 'The wearer must have been *petite*, hence the reason that under a wide brim only the chin would be visible. I at once sought for a *small* woman. Our fellows did not think of that, because they are men.' (291)

Orczy cleverly makes Lady Molly's gender indispensable to the solution of the case. In no other story is Lady Molly so confrontational with 'the chief.'

The redefinition of gendered concepts during the Edwardian period is reflected in other dimensions of the story. Lady Irene knew of her husband's relationship with Löwenthal, but she 'had not thought fit to make him accountable for the past' (280). Lady Irene thereby endorses the sexual double standard as well as exhibits her greed for the aunt's money. She also wanted to avoid a scandal. At the same time, although Löwenthal threatens Culloden with a breach of promise suit to 'punish him by making a scandal' (274), she does not pursue it. It is possible that Lady Irene did resent her husband's past, but she also feared the breach of promise suit would lose her husband the aunt's money, which would be hers on his decease. *The Woman in the Big Hat* is striking in two dimensions: its willingness to confront women's sexuality (the singer admits the relationship in a forthright manner) and the focus on woman as killer. Lady Irene Culloden demonstrates Orczy's intention to concentrate in these stories on female transgressive behaviour, whether it be Lady Molly's having a career or women fearlessly committing crimes. The stories in *Lady Molly of Scotland Yard* often focus on female criminals, which makes the omission of the series from a study such as Klein's *The Woman Detective* (1995) particularly unusual.

In addition to *The Woman in the Big Hat*, three other stories focus on female killers. In *The Fordwych Castle Mystery*, Joan Duplessis makes false claims to the Alboukirk title and estates, asserting she is the legitimate heir. She murders her half-caste companion Roonah, who after converting to Roman Catholicism refused to swear to the documents faked by Joan Duplessis to get the estate from her sister Henriette Marie. Joan claims her father was still legally married to a half-caste woman when he married her mother and had Henriette. Joan claims she is thus the only legitimate heir, since her father remarried her mother before her own birth, 'a second form of marriage' (98). The fact that Joan was born in Pondicherry, in India, evokes the background of Conan Doyle's Sherlock Holmes tale *The Sign of Four*.

In a similar manner, the complications and consequences of a colonial past return to Britain. Lady Molly, after breaking the locks of Joan Duplessis's dressing-case, finds the false documents. Lady Molly admits that 'of course I had no right to do that' and that if she was wrong 'I would probably be dismissed the force for irregularity' (107). Joan Duplessis kills herself by jumping from a window. Lady Molly concludes: 'I know my own sex pretty well' (108). In other words, Lady Molly does not accept the stereotype of The Angel in the House. Rather, she believes women quite capable of committing murder.

Another female killer appears in *A Christmas Tragedy*. Annie Haggett, the wife of the half-witted gardener Haggett at Clevere Hall, the estate of Major Ceely, murders the Major early on Christmas morning after the Major dismissed her husband from service. Arrested for the murder is Laurence Smethick, a suitor of the Major's daughter Margaret Ceely who, however, has recently transferred her affections to a Captain Glynne, who himself had just inherited an estate. Smethick is arrested after a ring is found in the mud at the murder site. Smethick's attorney Grayson reveals that that night Margaret had had a rendezvous with Smethick and dismissed him in favour of Glynne, hurling the ring in the mud.

Smethick, to save her reputation, would not reveal the encounter, and Margaret would not reveal the meeting to save Smethick. Haggett found the ring, and his wife decided to use that to lead to Smethick's arrest. Although she wanted Haggett to kill the Major, when he fled she did the deed herself, a woman with a 'coarse and elemental personality' (200). Lady Molly's view of Smethick is strange. Mary Granard writes she is convinced of his innocence, 'but in her the professional woman always fought hard battles against the sentimentalist' (192). She declined to act because of the man's silence, the weight of circumstantial evidence, and the 'conviction of her superiors' (192), deciding that 'it were in vain to cling to optimistic beliefs in that same man's innocence' (192). After an interview with Grayson, she decides to act.

Women in this story are dangerous and callous. Not only is Annie Haggett a murderess, angered when 'with rough, cruel words [the Major] suddenly turned her husband adrift' (200). She may well be expressing a bitter form of class resentment. Equally disturbing is the behaviour of Margaret Ceely, 'an outrageous flirt [who] openly encouraged more than one of her crowd of adorers' (174). Grayson notes: 'Miss Ceely was playing a double game . . . for she had transferred her volatile affections to Captain Glynne' (189). Mary Granard records:

> Margaret Ceely alone could have saved [Smethick], but with brutal indifference she preferred the sacrifice of an innocent man's life and honour to that of her own chances of a brilliant marriage. There are such women in the world; thank God I have never met any but that one! (190)

Whether of the lower classes, such as Annie Haggett, or an heiress, such as Margaret Ceely, women in *A Christmas Tragedy* are revealed as treacherous across class lines.

In *The Bag of Sand*, another murderess appears in the figure of Miss Cruikshank, who murders her employer Mrs Dunstan, by bashing her on the head with a bag of sand and then asphyxiating her by turning on the gas, to get money Mrs Dunstan said she would leave her in her will.

Mrs Dunstan's niece Violet Frostwicke is engaged to one David Athol, who turns out to be a collaborator with Miss Cruikshank, who impersonates a charwoman Mrs Thomas to get her blamed for the murder, though Mrs Thomas never exists. Lady Molly then herself impersonates the non-existent Mrs Thomas and compels Miss Cruikshank to confess. Despite her aristocratic background, Lady Molly demonstrates her professional acumen by being able to cross class lines and disguise herself as the charwoman:

> The clothes of the charwoman who had so mysteriously
> disappeared had been found by Lady Molly at the back of the
> coal cellar, and she was still dressed in them at the present
> moment . . . No wonder I had not recognized my own dainty
> lady in the grimy woman who had so successfully played the part
> of a blackmailer on the murderess of Mrs Dunstan. (226)

Lady Molly informs Mary Granard: 'The charwoman was also a bag of sand
which was literally thrown in the eyes of the police' (227), that is, in the eyes
of men. Lady Molly in *The Bag of Sand* transgresses both class and gender
boundaries and thereby solves the case. The result of the impersonation and
transgression is interesting:

> Miss Cruikshank did make a full confession. She was
> recommended to mercy on account of her sex, but she was
> plucky enough not to implicate David Athol in the recital of her
> crime . . . He has since emigrated to Western Canada. (228)

The woman pays; the man escapes.

In addition to the murders, women in these tales also aspire to being
blackmailers. In the first tale in the series, *The Ninescore Mystery*, the body of
a woman is found in a pond. It turns out to be that of Susan Nicholls, a
woman who blackmailed Lord Edbrooke of Ash Court, who had fathered a
girl by Susan's sister Mary Nicholls. Lady Molly tricks Mary Nicholls into
admitting the truth about the child after placing a false story in a paper that
the infant was dying. Praising Lady Molly, Mary Grandard observes:

> The veil of mystery had been torn asunder owing to the insight,
> the marvellous intuition, of a woman who, in my opinion, is the
> most wonderful psychologist of her time. (27)

In *The Woman in the Big Hat*, Mary had twice noted she herself was no
psychologist (276-7). Lady Molly's abilities may not be marked so much by
intuition as by a new science of 'psychological' detection. Mary Nicholls is
fickle, as she is also seeing Lord Edbrooke's brother Lionel Lydgate,
described as 'good-looking, very athletic' (17), a 'pleasing specimen of
English cricket-, golf- and football-loving manhood' (18). In the second
part of the story Orczy uses a favourite motif of hers, that of the inquest.
Lord Edbrooke throws himself in front of an express train before he can be
arrested for the murder. Lady Molly triumphs over her male associates:
'Our fellows at the Yard . . . took their lead from Lady Molly' (27):

> Don't tell me that a man would have thought of that bogus paragraph, or of the taunt which stung the motherly pride of the village girl to the quick, and thus wrung from [Mary Nicholls] an admission which no amount of male ingenuity would ever had obtained. (28)

The independent Lady Molly knows how to deceive a young mother of an illegitimate child. At the same time, Lady Molly appears to attack the double standard and to punish the errant brothers Lord Edbrooke and Lionel Lydgate for their sexual behaviour. If the male escapes punishment in *The Bag of Sand*, in *The Ninescore Mystery* the philandering Lord Edbrooke is driven to murder and then suicide.

In *A Day's Folly*, Lady Muriel Wolfe-Strongham, daughter of the Duke of Weston, marries the German Grand Duke of Starkburg-Nauheim in a 'morganatic' union (120), a marriage opposed by the Duke's mother and sister. Visiting Folkestone 'for the benefit of her little boy's health' (121), the Countess meets 'an old acquaintance of her father's, a Mr Rumboldt, a man whose recent divorce 'brought his name into unenviable notoriety' (121). While with Rumboldt, the Countess is photographed by Jane Turner, who proceeds to blackmail her, in a device clearly anticipated by Conan Doyle's *A Scandal in Bohemia*. The Countess admits:

> 'My husband would never forgive me . . . Promise me that my name won't be dragged into this case . . . You won't do anything that will cause a scandal! Promise me – promise me! I believe I should commit suicide rather than face it.' (125-6, 127)

It becomes a case 'which at the chief's desire [Lady Molly] had now taken entirely in hand' (119). Lady Molly impersonates the Duke's mother and confronts Jane Turner, who admits the photograph never existed but kept up the blackmailing. In a statement recording her own sense of class distinctions, Mary Granard observes that Jane Turner represents 'the British middle-class want of respect for social superiority' (131). Turner tries to hang herself.

The matter is 'hushed up' and 'the public will never know' (137), at which Lady Molly is 'a little regretful' (137). Lady Molly vindicates the chief's opinion:

> No doubt he began to feel that here, too, was a case where feminine tact and my lady's own marvellous intuition might prove more useful than the more approved methods of the sterner sex. (114)

Indeed, as Lady Molly avers, 'there is a woman in the case' (114). The focus on the marriage of Lady Muriel to a German Duke exploits the intense anxiety about Germany during the Edwardian period. Jane Turner uses the 'Agony Column' to send notices to Lady Muriel, a device used by Conan Doyle in the Holmes tales. As in *The Ninescore Mystery*, so in *A Day's Folly* Mary Granard praises Lady Molly's 'intuition', which in fact is the detective's shrewd and calculating ability to impersonate across class lines (*The Bag of Sand*) or nationality, as in this text.

Women can engage in other forms of criminality. In *The Frewin Miniatures*, Mrs Frewin, the wife of an art dealer and collector, has a wastrel son, Lionel, heavily in debt. She copies Frewin's valuable Engleheart miniatures and sells them to the art museum in Budapest, deceiving her dying husband.

When he gives all his money to his nephew James Hyam, she fears in probate the copied miniatures will be discovered and stages a theft of the 'miniatures', really the copies. After pretending she purchased two of the originals from Budapest, Lady Molly confronts Mrs Frewin and compels her confession, although Lady Molly advises her to admit the truth to Hyam and the matter is never formally prosecuted. Mary Granard notes about Lady Molly: 'She could do anything she liked with the men [of the Department], and I, of course, was her slave' (54).

The motif of protecting wastrel or dishonest sons reappears in *A Castle in Brittany*. Since Orczy uses this motif several times, one wonders if she is querying the degree to which women, especially mothers, are willing to protect patriarchal privileges even in the face of criminality. In this tale, Miss Angela de Genneville, old and wealthy, is living at Porhoët, Brittany, in France. She enlists Lady Molly's help to foil her greedy sister Madame la Marquise de Terhoven and her son, Amédé, from getting her money. The son is in debt in Paris, but the mother will do anything to save him: 'too indulgent! but an only son!' (141). The nephew has forged his aunt's signature and is forced to sign a confession. The old woman claims the will is hidden in a clock, and Lady Molly goes along with it to confute the Marquise and Amédé, having advised the woman to leave the will with her solicitor.

In the end, the poor of the town inherit all the woman's wealth. The Terhovens get the nephew's confession back and receive an annuity. Lady Molly compels Mary Granard to attend the opening of the clock, knowing the will is not there, much to Mary's chagrin. Lady Molly is nevertheless 'the woman I loved best in all the world' (154). The case is interesting because it is 'a non-professional experience' (167). In both *The Frewin Miniatures* and *A Castle in Brittany*, mothers support the wastrel behaviour of their sons and manage to avoid public exposure in the end. Despite her own independence, Lady Molly appears to endorse this allegiance to errant sons. John Gore notes that 'to be found out was still social suicide' (21) during the Edwardian era, a situation which would apply to sexual and to familial transgressions represented in several of the Lady Molly narratives.

If one excludes the two stories, *Sir Jeremiah's Will* and *The End*, dealing with Lady Molly's own history, it is only in two of the remaining ten cases that males are the major criminals. In both these stories, Orczy deals with events or topics of strong interest to the Edwardian reader. In *The Irish-Tweed Coat*, her focus is on secret societies, Italy, and especially 'the ever-growing tyranny of the Mafia' (55). Andrew Carrthwaite, an Englishman, is murdered at Palermo in Sicily where he does business, since he refuses to deal with the Mafia. His English overseer Cecil Shuttleworth is arrested. His father Jeremiah Shuttleworth in England, requests Lady Molly's aid. Lady Molly eventually takes Cecil's Irish tweed coat (a fragment of which was in the dead man's hand), his watch and chain to one Colonel Grassi, chief of the Italian police at Cividale, Cecil Shuttleworth's uncle, who through his exertions is 'acquitted of the charge of murder' (81). The killer of Carrthwaite had worn Cecil Shuttleworth's coat to deceive the Italian police. His father had discovered two men, the Piattis, associated with the Mafia, had brought this evidence to London and had buried it behind a lodging house owned by a Mrs Tadworth, evidence which the father had unearthed and taken, for which he substituted a similar coat.

Throughout the story, the contrast between England and Italy, North and South, is emphasized:

> Mind you – according to English ideas – the preliminary investigations in that mysterious crime were hurried through in a manner which we should think unfair to the accused. It seemed from the first as if the Sicilian police had wilfully made up their minds that Shuttleworth was guilty. For instance, although so many people were prepared to swear that the young English overseer had often worn a coat of which the piece found in the murdered man's hand was undoubtedly a torn fragment, yet the coat itself was not found among his effects, neither were his late master's watch and chain. (56-7)

Addressing Lady Molly, Jeremiah Shuttleworth declares:

> 'You see, you do not know Sicily, and I do. You do not know its many clubs and bands of assassins, beside whom the so-called Russian Nihilists are simple, blundering children. The Mafia, which is the parent of all such murderous organisations, has members and agents in every town, village, and hamlet in Italy,

in every post-office and barracks, in every trade and profession
from the highest to the lowest in the land. The Sicilian police
force is infested with it, so are the Italian customs.' (62)

Mary Granard records that the consequences of the Mafia reach from
England to Sicily:

> I may as well tell you here that neither Piatti nor his son, nor any
> of that gang, were arrested for the crime. The proofs of their
> guilt – the Irish-tweed coat and the murdered man's watch and
> chain – were most mysteriously suppressed . . . Such is the
> Sicilain police. (81)

In its focus on the Mafia, *The Irish-Tweed Coat* may well have influenced
Arthur Conan Doyle when he wrote his story about the Mafia, *The Red
Circle*, in 1911. To increase Edwardian angst about international terrorism
and secret societies, the Piattis are never arrested.

Issues of gender are central to *The Man in the Inverness Cape*. Leonard
Marvell, with his wife (alias the maid Rosie Campbell) commits robberies in
London, one of the actress Lulu Fay, who had entrusted him with both her
money and her diamonds. Lady Molly goes as the slatternly ex-lady of
means, a Mrs Marcus Stein, to a lodging house and tricks 'Rosie Campbell'
who is staying there into a trap. Lady Molly with this contrivance catches
Leonard Marvell dressed as a woman, his 'sister' Olive Marvell. Marvell thus
dresses as two women, his 'sister' and even when required the maid 'Rosie
Campbell', the part usually played by his wife:

> [Lady Molly] had from the first suspected that the trio who
> lodged at the Scotia Hotel were really only a duo – namely,
> Leonard Marvell and his wife. The latter impersonated a maid
> most of the time; but among these two clever people the three
> characters were interchangeable. Of course, there was no Miss
> Marvell at all. Leonard was alternately dressed up as man or
> woman, according to the requirements of his villainies . . . 'As
> soon as I heard that Miss Marvell was very tall and bony . . . I
> [Lady Molly] thought that there might be a possibility of her
> being merely a man in disguise . . . You see the game of criss-
> cross, don't you? This interchanging of characters was bound to
> baffle everyone. Many clever scoundrels have assumed disguises,
> sometimes personating members of the opposite sex to their
> own.' (255, 256)

In this tale, transvestism becomes symbolic of a larger mode of
transgressive behaviour, criminality. That the last name is that of Andrew

Marvell, one of the greatest poets in the English language, adds an irony to the narrative.

So skilled is Marvell that he appears able to deceive Lulu Fay, whom he had known as a man and even perhaps Lady Molly herself during their joint interview (233-9). Lulu Fay is herself an actress, although described as a prostitute:

> There sat beside her an over-dressed, much behatted, peroxided young woman, who bore the stamp of *the* profession all over her pretty, painted face. (234)

That a man could so counterfeit his gender suggests a cultural marker, the blurring of gender distinctions, which has interested Orczy throughout the *Lady Molly* narratives. Lulu Fay plays 'principal boy' at the Grand Theatre (236), which suggests that all gender roles are merely that, scripts requiring role-playing. This impersonation crosses class lines when Lady Molly impersonates the slovenly Mrs Stein, 'her part' (249).

Lady Molly of Scotland Yard constitutes a key compendium of Edwardian thought. With its focus on gender definitions in the *Inverness Cape*, secret societies in *The Irish-Tweed Coat*, and female criminals in a range of stories, the book reveals its linkage with Edwardian culture. A number of the texts cover the ramifications of class, including the resentment at her husband's dismissal by Annie Haggett in *A Christmas Tragedy*. There are several snobbish observations about servants in such tales as *The Bag of Sand*:

> Mrs Dunstan's servants, mind you, all knew of the engagement between the young people, and with the characteristic sentimentality of their class, connived at these secret meetings and helped to hoodwink the irascible old aunt. (205)

Mary Granard criticizes two waitresses interrogated in *The Woman in the Big Hat* for 'that vagueness which is a usual and highly irritating characteristic of their class' (279). Mary Granard's rise from lady's maid to employee of the Yard to Lady Molly's personal amanuensis also reflects a fluidity in class structures of considerable interest.

By the time Orczy published *Lady Molly of Scotland Yard* in 1910, Arthur Conan Doyle had published six of the nine volumes devoted to his detective Sherlock Holmes. The similarities between the two detectives are conspicuous: each has a narrator-companion, both engage similar crimes such as blackmail and murder. Yet it is clear that Orczy seeks to differentiate her protagonist from that of Conan Doyle. In addition to creating a female detective, Orczy makes her official, that is, connected with

Scotland Yard, in contrast to the unofficial status of Sherlock Holmes. While Holmes and Watson are of similar social status, Mary Granard and Lady Molly are not. It is possible to construe this to mean that, because women are marginalized, they possess a freedom, less available to males, to cross class lines in their friendships. A final point of contrast is that Orczy proportionately focuses much more on female criminals than does Conan Doyle.

The cases investigated by Lady Molly are striking for their focus on female transgressive behaviours. One form of female transgression explored by Orczy is female criminal behaviour. Unlike Conan Doyle in the Holmes narratives, Orczy stresses cases evoking the cases of accused murderesses such as Constance Kent (1860), Florence Bravo (1876), Adelaide Bartlett (1886), and Florence Maybrick (1894). In *The Woman in the Big Hat*, for example, it is revealed that a woman killed her husband. The text confronts the sexual double standard as well as greed. In *The Fordwych Castle Mystery*, Joan Duplessis commits murder to secure an estate. In *A Christmas Tragedy*, a woman murders the employer of her husband after the husband is dismissed. Another female killer appears in *The Bag of Sand*, where a woman murders her employer. Women are also blackmailers in these narratives. In *The Ninescore Mystery*, a female blackmailer is murdered by a titled male, who is driven to suicide to avoid exposure. A woman proceeds to blackmail another woman in *A Day's Folly*. In *The Frewin Miniatures*, a woman forges miniatures to pay the debts of her wastrel son.

Such transgression reflects Edwardian ambivalence about female nature, particularly striking if one compares the stories in *Lady Molly of Scotland Yard* with those in the Holmes canon, where of the 60 narratives fewer than ten recount instances of women committing murder or suspected of it. Orczy certainly knew tales such as *The Musgrave Ritual* (1893) or *Charles Augustus Milverton* (1904), but as Virginia Morris notes, 'Doyle's violent heroines are not threats to the social order but avengers of misuse' (151). In the *Lady Molly* narratives, women are determinedly criminal. Unlike Conan Doyle, Orczy is not inclined to invoke extenuating circumstances when depicting female criminal behaviour. Of the criminals depicted in the stories, women constitute the majority.

The other major transgression investigated in these narratives is that of Lady Molly Robertson-Kirk herself. The fact that she has a career through her association with Scotland Yard makes her transgressive, a circumstance Orczy reconciles with cultural prescriptions by giving Lady Molly a strong personal motive for her career, to vindicate her wrongly-arrested husband Hubert de Mazareen. Still, some of the methods employed by Lady Molly are transgressive, particularly her impersonations of women and especially of those from other social classes. Such impersonation is unavoidably associated with deception, however legitimate its objective. *Lady Molly of Scotland Yard* thus presents a conflicted but powerful presentation of issues involving femininity at the beginning of the twentieth century. The text thus engages central questions of female empowerment and transgression.

In particular, the transition of women during the Edwardian era is remarkable if one considers the progression from Polly Burton, the passive listener to the Man in the Corner and his narratives, to the active, energetic Lady Molly Robertson-Kirk of the *Lady Molly* texts. In most of these tales, Lady Molly triumphs over her male associates at the Yard, doing so often at their own request. As Mary Granard discusses:

> Although, mind you, Lady Molly's methods in connection with the Ninescore mystery were not altogether approved of at the yard, nevertheless, her shrewdness and ingenuity in the matter were so undoubted that they earned for her a reputation, then and there, which placed her in the foremost rank of the force. (29)

Lady Molly of Scotland Yard of 1910 remains a key document regarding Edwardian thinking, above all about gender and class, during the early twentieth century. On the basis of Orczy's reputation and the intriguing nature of its protagonist, one may apply to the entire volume *Lady Molly of Scotland Yard* the observation of Mary Granard about *The Fordwych Castle Mystery*: 'From the very first, mind you, the public took more than usually keen interest in this mysterious occurrence' (88).

Richard Marsh (1857-1915): *Judith Lee, Some Pages from Her Life* (1912)

The name of Richard Marsh will be forever associated with that masterpiece of Victorian horror novels, *The Beetle*, published in 1897, the same year in which Bram Stoker's *Dracula* made its appearance. As William Baker notes in his introduction to that novel, Marsh was born Richard Bernard Heldmann in 1857 at St John's Wood, London. He was a swimmer and sailor, and in 1886 he ascended Mont Blanc. During the 1880s, he published a number of books about school life, but in 1892 in the *Strand* he published *A Vision of the Night* under the name Richard Marsh, Marsh having been his mother's maiden name.

In his selection *Victorian Villainies*, Hugh Greene comments that Marsh 'seems to have been a man haunted by demons' (9) and that 'some mystery hung around his death' (10) in August 1915, an assertion more a surmise than a certainty. Baker states that there 'is no evidence to suggest that [Marsh] attended either Eton or Oxford' (vii) as Hugh Greene declares.

However, as Baker discusses, Marsh did make one great contribution to the tradition of the female detective in English literature, *Judith Lee, Some Pages from Her Life*, serialized in the *Strand* from August 1911 through August 1912. Michelle Slung describes this female sleuth Judith Lee well: 'She is a teacher of the deaf-and-dumb and is an adept at lip-reading' (362). In addition, Baker is correct to note her 'brilliant intellect' (ix). Marsh has given Judith Lee many traits to differentiate her from Sherlock Holmes as well as from other female detectives.

For example, in addition to Judith Lee's profession of teaching and the extraordinary skill it enables her to exercise, she is distinguished by never being involved in any personal romance, nor does Marsh end the series with a satisfying marriage to compel Judith Lee to be under the control of a man. Furthermore, Lee does not work with any detective agency, although on occasion she will call in a member from Scotland Yard to assist in an arrest.

In the first tale in the series, the stunningly-titled *The Man Who Cut Off My Hair*, Lee witnesses a robbery as a young girl. One of the thieves cuts off her hair, which is clearly a symbolic rape, providing a strong sexual subtext to the narrative. Lee records her investigations in her own memoir, and she defines the background which led to her amazing expertise:

> I teach [my students] by what is called the oral system – that is, the lip-reading system . . . In my case the gift, or knack, or whatever it is, is hereditary. My father was a teacher of the deaf and dumb – a very successful one. His father was, I believe, one of the originators of the oral system. My mother, when she was first married, had an impediment in her speech which practically made her dumb; though she was tone deaf, she became so expert at lip-reading that she could not only tell what others were saying, but she could speak herself – audibly, although she could not hear her own voice . . . So, you see, I have lived in the atmosphere of lip-reading all my life. (1)

Lee is forthright when she remarks that her profession and expertise have 'been the cause of many really extraordinary adventures' (2). This ability means that her epistemology is synaesthetic, that is, combines two senses, those of sight and sound. The results are such sentences as the following which appear throughout the text: 'I only saw the fag-end of the sentence' (2) or 'I could see what he said' (3).   At the age of twelve or thirteen, Lee notices that two men are planning to rob Myrtle Cottage, where a Mr Colegate has a vast collection of antique silver. Lee goes to the cottage and is apprehended by one of the thieves. She is tied up, and then:

> Just as I made sure he was going to cut my throat he caught hold
> of my hair, which, of course, was hanging down my back, and
> with that dreadful knife sawed the whole of it from my head. . .
> And to think that this man could have robbed me of it in so
> hideous a way! I do believe that at the moment I could have
> killed him. (6-7)

Lee is left in a locked room all night, only to be freed by Colegate when he returns to Myrtle Cottage. Remembering what the men said about Victoria Station, Lee and some detectives go to the station and find a bag full of feminine clothing and jewels, the latter belonging to the Duchess of Datchet. She then directs the police to a shop where the thieves who deal in stolen jewels are apprehended and sent to prison and penal servitude. Lee is never called to testify, since the men had committed many more horrible crimes, so far as the police are concerned.

But not so far as Judith Lee is concerned. She reflects about the theft of her hair, which really is a rape. The detective treats the cutting of her hair as a joke:

> The big man laughed. He seemed to find me amusing; I do not
> know why. If he had only understood my feeling on the subject
> of my hair, and how I yearned to be even with the man who had
> wrought me what seemed to me such an irreparable injury . . . I
> do not think it was a question of vengeance only; I wanted
> justice. (15)

Even the police do not acknowledge the outrage:

> It was his cutting my hair that did it. Had he not done that I
> have little doubt that I should have been too conscious of the
> pains caused me by my bonds . . . to pay such close attention to
> their proceedings as I did under the spur of anger . . . It was the
> outrage to my locks which caused me to strain every faculty of
> observation I had. (18)

The symbolic rape is evident in her final summation about this experience:

> I endeavoured to console myself . . . that, owing to the gift
> which was mine, I had been able to cry something like quits with
> the man who in a moment of mere wanton savagery had
> deprived me of what ought to be the glory of a woman. (19)

She retains 'something of that old rage . . . which had been during that first moment in my heart, and I felt – what I felt when I was tied to that chair in

Myrtle Cottage' (19). Judith Lee does have a motivation beyond her professional skill for her acute sensitivity to criminous persons in this nightmarish assault on her liberty and her body when she was a young girl. No memory has haunted a fictional character so strongly since the nightmare of 'pieces of eight' strafed the dreams of Jim Hawkins in Stevenson's *Treasure Island* (1883).

In the next episode, *Eavesdropping at Interlaken*, Lee is in Switzerland with her friends the Travers at the age of seventeen. Two individuals, a Mr Reginald Sterndale and his sister, are guests at the hotel. These two rob everyone in the hotel and blame it on Judith Lee while the Travers are on an excursion. In the end, Lee unmasks them, and the Sterndales, not brother and sister as they had announced, turn out to be professional jewel thieves. Among the losses are a diamond pendant belonging to a very unpleasant woman, Miss Goodridge; a set of diamonds belong to a Mrs Anstruther; and a set of pearls belonging to a Mrs Newball. When Judith Lee attempts to return the pendant to Miss Goodridge, she is labelled a thief and accused of the other robberies as well.

The narrative is a disturbing one because it records the distress of the wrongfully-accused person in such clear terms:

> I was all alone; I had never thought that anyone could feel so utterly alone as I did in that crowded lounge . . . The feeling [was] that I was so entirely alone, and that there was not a soul within miles and miles to whom I could turn for help . . . These things were hard enough to bear; but they seemed to be as nothing compared to that man and woman's [the Sterndales'] treachery. (27, 30)

Judith Lee, however, fortified by the evidence she has gained from lip-reading, braves her accusers in front of the hotel guests. When Mr Travers returns, he supports her. The jewels are discovered, as Lee detects, partly concealed in the clothing on the bodies of the Sterndales, the professional thieves, who are in fact not brother and sister. Although they are released once the owners have regained their property, they are apprehended the following night for another theft at a different location.

Judith Lee's next adventure, entitled *Conscience*, is one of the greatest railway crime stories. It is unique in that it concerns a serial killer of women and spans more than two years. Its purpose is indisputably to express female if not feminist outrage. Judith Lee keeps re-encountering John Tung, a man with a Mongolian appearance, who had been murdering women on trains for years. In the end, he is driven to suicide by letters Judith Lee sends him, informing him that someone knows of his criminality. She is at

Brighton when she first reads/hears the description of a designated victim: 'Mauve dress, big black velvet hat, ostrich plume; four-thirty train' (47). Lee is at Brighton for a rest, 'because I had nearly broken down in my work' (50), whether as teacher or more likely as investigator. The next day, Lee reads in the *Sussex Daily News* that such a woman was found lying on the line, as if she had fallen out of a train. On a later occasion, Lee learns of the imminent death of a woman in a white dress, and sure enough a woman's body is found in the courtyard of the Embankment Hotel. Another woman is killed on the Great Western Line near Exeter station. Although she warns Tung his crimes are known, the police fail to capture him.

After an interval, Tung reappears:

> The sight of him inspired me with a feeling of actual rage. That such a dreadful creature as I was convinced he was should go through life like some beast of prey, seeking for helpless victims whom it would be safe to destroy – the sight of him made me positively furious. (65)

At yet another railway station, Lee sends him a note to prepare for the end. At the same time, two plainclothesmen begin to approach him. At this point, John Tung shoots his brains out.

That this story is a scarcely veiled discussion of the Ripper case is not in doubt. In Tung's flat the police find considerable evidence:

> There were feminine belongings of all sorts and kinds. Some of them were traced to their former owners, and in each case the owner was found to have died in circumstances which had never been adequately explained. This man seemed to have been carrying on for years, with perfect impunity, a hideous traffic in robbery and murder – and the victim was always a woman. His true name was never ascertained . . . He seemed to have been a solitary creature – a savage beast alone in its lair. (67)

Lee even encounters a woman whose life she saved, and she is spurned by that very woman. 'Even when I do [good], for the most part it's done by stealth, and not known to fame; and sometimes, even, it's not recognized as good at all' (68). Marsh's rewriting the Ripper text from a female point of view suggests the much more extensive practise of Marie Belloc Lowndes when she writes *The Lodger* in its short story form in 1911 and its novelized version in 1913.

In the next story, *Matched*, Marsh takes the opposite line from the previous narrative. In this tale, Marianne Tracy is a serial wife, who marries men and then takes all their money and the wedding gifts, fooling men. She does not, however, deceive Judith Lee. The story begins at Charing Cross Station, when Everard Brookes is about to being his honeymoon excursion when his wife, Clare, runs from the train, contending she had left something behind. Instead, she vanishes with all his money and his goods. Lee notes: 'The thing was very well done; Mr Brookes found that he had been robbed in almost every direction in which he could have been robbed' (75).

Marianne Tracy's deceptions of men are unending and global. Later, on a cruise near Gibraltar, Tracy has Judith Lee removed from the ship and cast off in a small boat, suspecting that the private detective had discovered her stratagem. Lee is 'consumed with rage' (78). Later, an American, Alexander King, succumbs to Tracy's wiles. Judith Lee concludes that men are besotted about women: 'Where women are concerned, men are the most amazing things. What all those men, of different ages, different tastes, different altogether, saw in her was beyond my comprehension. . . What absolute idiots [are] all sorts and conditions of men, old and young, . . . over a woman' (88, 91). Marianne Tracy, about to marry a Russian merchant, writes Judith Lee, telling her she is 'famous' and recognizing the good that Lee does in the world! Lee thinks: 'The audacity of the woman in writing to me at all! (92). Lee perceives that her 'gift . . . of entering into people's confidence, even against their will' (70) can have distressing consequences.

The next episode, *The Miracle*, is the first to be described by Lee as a 'case' (93). In this story, the American businessman Fred Curtis gives money to enable Margery Stainer and Cecil Armitage to marry and avoid blackmail by a man, Clarke, who has a forged bill of acceptance from Armitage. Judith Lee also pays off the blackmailing Morgan. Cecil had planned to marry the old governess Elizabeth Drawbridge for her money to save himself. All these results are because of Judith Lee's intervention.

The Miracle has one revolutionary focus – the commodification of men. Cecil Armitage is forced to marry Drawbridge, he tells Clarke, experiencing what was so often a female situation of commodification:

> 'I'm going to marry the woman I'm going to marry because I'm a thief, and because I'm such a cur that I shrink from paying the penalty. She's a wretched old fool who comes all to pieces . . . [B]ut she's got money, and she's willing to give me money, enough to be rid of you and save myself from the treadmill . . . If you only knew how I hate the woman . . . Heaven knows how far it will go by the time we're married. I shouldn't wonder if I were to murder her on our wedding night.' (97)

Lee discerns the truth from her lip-reading:

It was no business of mine, this affair of the old maid and the young bachelor . . . But it was no use my talking to myself like that. I could not allow a person of my own sex to enter into what I knew would be such a hideous marriage without making some attempt to lay before her the facts. (100)

Miss Drawbridge, however, does not wish to be rescued:

'That sort of thing is quite common with a man – you must take a man at his own valuation, my dear. We should never get one at all if we took them at ours . . . You don't think I'm very much to look at, do you? I'm not; I never was. Time has not improved me, either outside or in. When I was young I was very poor. For seven years I was governess . . . I couldn't expect to get married on that, could I? And no one wanted me anyhow, though I wanted to marry very badly . . . I wonder how many women would make it if they told the truth.' (103-4)

Then Miss Drawbridge gets down to the individual case of Cecil Armitage:

'Don't suppose that my desire to marry grew less as my years grew more; that's a silly notion which some young girls seem to have. If I have to advertise for a husband, I'm going to have one before I die . . . I'm quite aware that he isn't at all fond of me. But he's so young . . . Of course, I shall have to pay for him – you needn't tell me that; my experience is that one always has to pay for anything that's worth having – and generally through the nose. I expect to have to pay through the nose for him . . . I don't suppose for a moment that he isn't what I've seen described as "shop soiled". . . I've grown out of all my illusions . . . It's all a question of making it worth their while . . . How many really honest men do you suppose there are, if the truth were known?' (105-6)

Lee can only reflect: 'I had never supposed that there were such women as she existing in the world' (106).

When a young woman, Margery Stainer, arrives at the resort at Dieppe and falls into Cecil's arms, Judith Lee perceives the genuine lovers. The wealthy American couple, Fred and Elinor Curtis, give Judith Lee the money enabling Margery and Cecil Armitage to marry and emigrate to America. Meanwhile, Lee purchases back the forged bill from Clarke and dissolves the engagement between Armitage and Drawbridge. The old woman does not mind, as she has found an even worse bounder than Armitage to marry. In America, Cecil Armitage becomes a successful businessman. The real focus of the text is on the commodification of males, a subject not that frequently dealt with in female detective literature, a true innovation by Richard Marsh in the genre.

The next case revolves around the ballad in its title, *'Auld Lang Syne'*, and terrorists acting in London. The tale echoes the agenda of Joseph Conrad's classic 1907 story of terrorism *The Secret Agent*. Judith Lee leads the Scotland Yard men, Inspector Davis and Mr Ellis, to the room of the German/Polish terrorist Stepan Grilovitch. Grilovitch had killed members of the London police earlier. Judith Lee reads the lips of his girlfriend, since Lee had been in Germany at Posen to start an institution for the deaf; there she had perfected her German. Grilovitch has been shot and is dying of gangrene.

Stepan's brother has been blackmailed by some man who theatens to turn in Stepan to the police. Grilovitch has a bomb by his bed in a glass ball ready to go off if the proper signal – the song – is not sung by someone entering. The story engages issues of terrorism in London, and Judith Lee takes on the disguise of the girlfriend in order to effect an entrance to Grilovitch's flat.

The Edwardian fear of terrorism resulting from globalization is marked from the beginning of the text: 'There was . . . an epidemic of shooting in that part of London in which the inhabitants, for the most part, are certainly not natives of the great city' (121). Again, through her expertise, Judith Lee is 'in possession of information for which, figuratively, all London was groping' (123). By her daring, Lee saves the situation, although the blackmailed brother disappears. In its focus on revolutionaries living in London, the narrative recalls such Sherlock Holmes tales as *The Golden Pince-Nez* of 1904 with its Russian anarchists.

Another bizarre dimension of London life appears in *Isolda*, which concerns George Ratton. Ratton gets the palmist Isolda to blackmail Lucille Godwin into marrying him. Judith Lee tells Lucille Godwin what Isolda is going to say about her future. To save his professional identity after Godwin discovers he is a fraud, Isolda drugs her with morphine, kidnaps her and holds her for several days. She is released due to Judith Lee's intervention. There is a strong suggestion that Isolda has done this to other women, maybe raping them and then blackmailing them.

Isolda is never caught or convicted, going on with his depredations. Judith Lee saves the charming but foolish Lucille, who marries her lover Jack Upcott. However, it is Lucille's sister May, who is so engaging that Lee admits 'I fell in love with her at sight' (152), who gives Lee the information necessary to intervene.

Judith Lee tracks Isolda and his henchman Ratton to Isolda's studio in Bond Street, confronting them:

> 'I, Mr Ratton, am Nemesis. Mr Isolda, if I may add what seems
> to be an unaccustomed prefix, is a worker of wonders; I
> represent that power which brings those wonders to naught,
> proving them to be the poor antics of a clumsy charlatan.' (167)

Furthermore, when Isolda's thug Brayshaw tries to remove her from the
premises, Lee actually knocks him on the floor. Even though Lee brings
this particular case to a happy conclusion for the Godwins, Isolda is never
apprehended, causing Lee to speculate: 'He probably still practises on
feminine credulity elsewhere' (174).

Was It By Chance Only? begins with a speculation about whether or not
Providence exists or takes a hand in events:

> It is not easy to determine what part accident plays in the affairs
> of daily life. I have not been able to decide where, so far as I was
> concerned, it began, and where it ended, in what was known to
> the public as the Fulham Mystery. Who can say, for instance,
> that it was not by design – the design of a force beyond our ken?
> (175)

In the narrative, Judith Lee restores to Annie, Mrs George Ryder, the
money Ryder's aunt, Mrs Dawson, had intended to leave him. Mrs
Dawson's companion, Lily Lisle, had her red-headed lover Dan murder
Ryder. Then, she married the other nephew, Athelstan Ward, getting the
money but cutting out her lover Dan. Mrs. George Ryder has been reduced
to selling flowers. Lisle all along had been secretly engaged to Ward. She
originally had Ryder hit by a car, but when this failed she had her lover
bludgeon him with a candlestick after Ryder survived this first attempt.

The case is protracted. Judith Lee learns at Boscombe that Mrs Ryder
had become a nursery governess under an assumed name, as she is still
suspected after two years of being the killer of her husband. After another
two years, Annie Ryder is even more reduced, to selling flowers at
Eastbourne. Lee wonders: 'Was it by accident, or design, that I was
stumbling on these things?' (191). When Dan confronts Lily Lisle, now Mrs
Ward, she drives him to commit suicide by jumping from a cliff.

When Inspector Ellis arrives from Scotland Yard at Judith Lee's
request, Athelstan Ward signs over the money he obtained by the villainy of
his wife to George Ryder's widow Annie. The evil couple leaves for South
America, forbidden to return to England. In this tale, Judith Lee saves a
young woman from a fiendish member of her own sex.

Lee's next escapade, *Uncle Jack*, begins with the question: 'Why are
some men so silly – so many men – nearly all of them?' (205). Judith Lee
saves Jack Finlayson, the uncle of one of her pupils, Netta Hastings, from

being fleeced of his money in a poker game by conniving Americans, Colonel Frederick 'Chicago Charlie' Stewart and Arthur Poyntz, and their female associates, Mrs Hammond and Miss Baby Parsons. Finlayson, a stupid man, had imagined Judith Lee was in love with him. He is a man 'with a good opinion both of himself and of his money' (207). When he asks Judith Lee to marry him, assuming she will, she replies:

> 'I, at an early age, made up my mind to live and die an old maid, and if anything could strengthen my resolution it is the fact that there are in the world such funny little men as you, and that some women, poor souls! have to have them as husbands.'
> (211-12)

In disguise, Lee tracks the criminals to a gambling establishment at a remote house called 'The Wilderness' in an obscure location. The Colonel is truly evil: 'I set him down as that homicidal type of criminal who holds human life of no account at all; who, indeed, in the gratification of his own lusts, holds nothing of any account' (219). The arrival of the police saves Finlayson, but Lee still wonders: 'Why are some men so silly?' (237).

Mandragora begins with the same speculation as *Was It By Chance Only?*, the eighth tale: 'So many things come about by what seems accident, a caprice of chance' (238). This rumination occurs because Lee goes to Easthampton, since she 'had been threatened by one of those nervous collapses which do come to me when I have been overworked' (243). So, does her own illness lead her to help someone else?

In this story, Michael Hutton's son Frank embezzles securities from the firm owned by his father and Thomas Walker. Walker drives young Frank Hutton to suicide by supplying him with poison. Walker blames the theft on George Young, a managing clerk in a firm of solicitors, who is sent to prison for fourteen years. Judith Lee gets a confession from the older Hutton. She subsequently confronts Walker, who attacks her, then takes poison intended for his conscience-stricken partner Michael Hutton.

Lee learns of the case involving George Young when she stays in the cottage of a woman pretending to be a widow, one Mrs Vinton. Lee, 'resolved to force her confidence' (245), learns about the fate of her husband George Young. Lee had seen/heard the elder Hutton and Walker speaking, and she wonders: 'Had they been sent to that particular table, and had I been directed to watch them, by what almost seemed to be a special Providence?' (251).

Judith Lee corners Michael Hutton, announcing that she is 'the voice of an avenging angel' (258), and gets him to sign a complete confession. When Lee confronts Walker, she is moved 'to sudden rage' (261), feeling Walker is 'one of those unspeakable creatures who are dangers to whom ever they are brought in contact with' (262). Lee declares: 'You seem to be all evil . . . My knowledge is of God. He has given me the power to put to confusion such men as you' (264). When Walker assaults her, Lee practises jiu-jitsu on him: 'I am a woman, but I am no weakling' she notes (266). George Young is pardoned. While Lee seems to believe that God had led her to avenge George Young, the question is not thoroughly answered. What is clear is that it takes a woman to rectify the injustices wrought by men on men through the male-administered 'justice' system.

'*8 Elm Grove – Back Entrance*' is the address where the next action occurs. Judith Lee prevents the robbery of the house owned by her friends, the Arnolds, where Jane Stamp, the maid, is a convict just released from Wandsworth Prison. The young woman had been seduced by a man, George, who compels her to assist in his crimes. Judith Lee learns the story of the seduction from the young woman's mother. Lee infers that 'it was his set purpose to use her for his own horrible ends, to ruin her body and soul, and then to cast her aside' (286). At the end, the maid refuses to drug the Arnolds and open the house to thieves. George, her lover and murderer, is hung. It is discovered that these men are part of a global, cosmopolitan mob of thieves.

Given the sexual double standard, Lee concludes it might be just as well that the young woman was killed:

> She probably never spoke a word after his bullet struck her. For her it was perhaps as well. It is easy to be optimistic, and even sentimental, if you have no actual experience of the hard facts of life; if you have, it is difficult to see what promise of happiness life could have held for a woman who had begun as she had done. Beyond the faintest shadow of a doubt she was more sinned against than sinning; but in such matters the world has a standard of its own, and, even if it seems to forgive, when a woman has at the back of her what she had it never forgets. (288)

The lover, George, is executed. Lee states: 'The first time I ever appeared in a witness-box was to give evidence against him' (289). If men embrace a sexual double standard, Lee makes the patriarchal justice system work for her own feminist judicial ends.

Arthur Conan Doyle had published his story about the Mafia, *The Red Circle*, in the *Strand* during March and April 1911. Hence, it is perhaps not surprising that the final story in *Judith Lee* is *The Restaurant Napolitain*. Judith Lee goes to an Italian dance. After it, she finds an assassin, Gaspare, has killed a young waiter, Emilio, who had loved a woman, Lucrezia, who is being forced to marry the Mafia restauranteur and villain Alessandro, with her own mother's connivance. Alessandro gets Judith Lee in his establishment, which is actually the headquarters for the Mafia in London. Judith Lee telephones Mr Ellis at Scotland Yard. She and Lucrezia fight Gaspare and Alessandro in the restaurant. Lee is saved from a ferocious knife fight by Ellis, who arrives late. Judith Lee has three scars on her chest as a permanent reminder of this horror.

Lee had been to Italy to help found an institute for the instruction of deaf-and-dumb pupils, so she can lip-read Italian. At several points in this story, Lee experiences outright 'rage' (294, 299, 303) at the events: 'I do get into great furies sometimes. It seems to me that horrible wickedness forces one to be furious' (295). Lee escapes from a locked room by using a poker and later smashes Gaspare with it. This locked room recalls the one in which she was confined as a young girl in *The Man Who Cut Off My Hair*.

The residents of London, Lucrezia informs Lee, are unaware of what crime occurs in their city:

> 'Strange things have happened in London – they happen still, though the people of London do not think it; what do they know of their own city, the people of London? This house could tell them tales – to which they would not listen. The police – they guess – but without proof – what can the police do without proof in London? And they have never had any proof at all, only what they guess.' (309)

Lucrezia concludes: 'For my part, I have no faith in the police, they always come a little too late – I know' (311). Is this a commentary that when foreigners are involved, the police hesitate?

When Lee is assaulted by Gaspare in the final attack, she begins to agree with Lucrezia:

> As Lucrezia had put it – would they be too late – for her, as well as for me? Those men [Gaspare, Alessandro] were like two wild beasts – if they could kill us first they would care nothing for what might happen to themselves afterwards. (316)

The illustration by J. R. Skelton is shocking, showing the murderous Gaspare grabbing Lee's skirt as she tries to drive him off with the poker. The violence depicted in the illustration is a revelation about the wrath a woman might encounter in Edwardian London. Lee declares: 'I was a reek of blood' (317). The pricks of Gaspare's knife are sexual in connotation, suggesting the rape scenario of the first story in the series, *The Man Who Cut Off My Hair*.

Marsh evolves an intricate strategy by which his female detective narrative *Judith Lee* is intertextual with his famous horror novel of 1897, *The Beetle*. In that novel, legislator Paul Lessingham has had a terrible experience while travelling as a young man in Cairo twenty years before the novel begins. Lessingham had been held captive for two months by female devotees of the cult of Isis, during which time he had been subjected to myriad brutalities (including sexual ones) and had witnessed the human sacrifice of many English women before escaping. Twenty years later, a cult member dressed as an Arab comes to London to destroy Lessingham's career and kidnap for human sacrifice Lessingham's fiancée, Marjorie Lindon. At the end of the novel, the abducted Lindon is saved after a harrowing railway chase and wreck, but it requires three years for her to recover from the physical and mental trauma she experienced. It is never learned if she was raped by her transgendering captor, but it is likely given parallel accounts of other women who suffered this abduction.

The affiliation of *The Beetle* to *Judith Lee* is significant. *The Beetle* is narrated in four parts, the third of which is given to Marjorie Lindon in an autodiegetic form, anticipating the mode of narration by the female detective in *Judith Lee*. The fourth and final part of the novel is narrated by a private inquiry agent, Augustus Champnell, rendering *The Beetle* a detective text as well as a horror novel. Marjorie Lindon is granted the power to narrate, like Judith Lee, but unlike the traumatized Lindon, Lee triumphs over circumstances. By 1912, Marsh makes the woman a genuine investigator and narrator of the total text. She does not share the narrating act with anyone else, male or female. Marsh strategizes the female detective novel of 1912 to represent an empowered woman, supplementing the account of an independent woman who is nevertheless destroyed by men in the earlier *The Beetle*.

The various males in *The Beetle* have a low opinion of women in general. Lindon's father feels he is entitled to thwart her marriage plans. Marjorie observes of her father: 'It is papa's misfortune that he can only see one side of a question, – and that's his own' (15). At one point, like Polonius, the father conceals himself behind a screen to overhear his daughter's confidential discussion with Sydney Atherton, a friend who has long loved her and is a rival to Lessingham. When Marjorie suffers mental trauma from her experiences, she does become an Ophelia, but Marsh makes it clear that it is males who cause this mental breakdown. When Marjorie Lindon discovers Atherton allowed her father to conceal himself, she feels betrayed by Atherton:

> 'Am I to understand, Mr Atherton, that this has been done with your cognisance? That while you suffered me to pour out my

heart to you unchecked, you were aware, all the time, that there was a listener behind the screen?' (125)

When Atherton asks her if she can keep her presence of mind during a dangerous excursion, she records: 'The mere question ruffled my plumes' (173). Even Atherton is forced to concede in his part of the narration: 'This is the age of feminine advancement' (87). The presumed male friend is in effect a tormentor.

The shape-shifting androgynous presence of The Beetle throughout the novel bears a strong connotation of sexual defilement of both men and women. Lessingham recalls to the investigator Augustus Champnell:

> 'I was in that horrible den more than two months, – two unspeakable months . . . If my memory is in the least degree trustworthy, [the rites] were orgies of nameless horrors.' (197)

Marsh signals the brutal sexuality of the text by three references to 'six inches' (7, 59, 225) of openings (windows, doors) in the text. With six inches being the average size of an erection, part of every male's slang, Marsh engrafts sexuality onto the text. Little is left in doubt when Marjorie feels the terrifying male and/or female presence of The Beetle:

> It began to find its way inside, – to creep between the sheets; the wonder is I did not die! I felt it coming nearer and nearer, inch by inch; I knew that it was upon me, that escape there was none; I felt something touch my hair. (162)

Marjorie had informed Atherton: 'I felt it bumping against the coverlet . . . It got into the bed . . . I heard it crawl along the sheets, till it found a way between them, and then it crawled towards me. And I felt it – against my face. – And it's there now' (123). The reference to woman's hair anticipates its significance in the episode *The Man Who Cut Off My Hair* in *Judith Lee*, where it is an obvious trope for rape. A woman's severed hair becomes an important part of the narrative of *The Beetle*, for the entrapped Marjorie has her hair cut off and is forced to wear male attire by her persecutor.

When men try to exclude Marjorie Lindon from investigating the premises of a terrifying house, she asserts: 'I did not mean to be left in the lurch' (175). Throughout *The Beetle*, Marjorie Lindon behaves like a female detective. She remarks at one point in her narration: 'It was for me to learn the why and the wherefore; to ascertain what connection there was between this lifeless creature and Paul Lessingham' (153). Marjorie Lindon's independent behaviour, reliance on her own judgement, confrontations with men as equals and action as an investigator all anticipate the female detective Marsh will create with *Judith Lee* in 1912.

Richard Marsh has created one of the most unusual and most powerful of female detectives in *Judith Lee*. Lee is memorable because of her profession, her specific expertise at lip-reading, her adventurous travelling, her willingness to engage in physical self-defence, her quickness to perceive female criminality and her absolute independence. Marsh never resorts to deploying the 'marriage plot' about Judith Lee. The fact that she leaves her accounts as a memoir testifies to her self-sufficiency.

Throughout her investigations, Lee never needs any Watson or any male or female companion. Lee wonders at several points in these stories: 'I have almost wished that the power which nature gave me, and which years of practise have made perfect, was not mine at all' (20). Is it destiny? 'This gift of mine of entering into people's confidence, even against their will, has occasionally placed me in the most uncomfortable situations' (70).

Yet, it is a gift which enables her to save both men and women from their own natures or from the malevolence of their associates. Murderers like the serial killer John Tung in *Conscience* are not uncommon in Judith Lee's world. Evil women like Lily Lisle in *Was It By Chance Only?* threaten both men and women. A criminal organization such as the Mafia in *The Restaurant Napolitain* terrorizes the globe. Men and women use sex to commodify each other, as in *The Miracle*. Revolutionaries in their cells make a mockery of the song in *'Auld Lang Syne'*. As an analysis of crime in the early twentieth century, *Judith Lee* is a formidable document. To Marsh's mind, the horror of *The Beetle* is not confined to the world of horror. One wonders about those other 'pages' from her life which Judith Lee left unrecorded.

Marie Belloc Lowndes (1868-1947): *The Lodger* (1913)

One of the greatest of unsolved crimes from the Victorian period remains the case of the serial killer known as Jack the Ripper, who between 31 August and 9 November 1888 killed five women, all prostitutes, in Whitechapel, East London, a poor district adjacent to the City (or financial district). After killing his victims, the Ripper eviscerated and mutilated the bodies. The area was replete with 'casual' houses, cheap lodging places full of transient occupants. In the *Pall Mall Gazette* in September 1888, William T. Stead, the renowned journalist who was to die in 1912 on the *Titanic*, wrote an article 'Murder and More to Follow' about the Ripper, and indeed there was 'more to follow' after that date. W. T. Stead was one of the earliest employers of Marie Belloc Lowndes, as she began to work for him on the *Review of Reviews* he started in 1890. This knowledge of the significance of the Ripper case proved decisive in the creation of her most famous work, *The Lodger*, first published in January 1911 as a short story (Lowndes, 1989) and then as a novel in 1913 (Lowndes 1996).

The case had multiple consequences. The East End had a population of 900,000, much of which was composed of immigrants, first the Irish and more recently Jews escaping the problems of the 1880s in Europe. Journalists likened the killer to the protagonist of Robert Louis Stevenson's *Dr Jekyll and Mr Hyde* of 1886. Stead claimed the murderer was a savage of the slums 'bathing his hands in blood as any Sioux who ever scalped a foe'; 'a plebian Marquis de Sade' at large in Whitechapel (cited in Walkowitz, 1992, 206). In 1886 there had appeared Richard von Krafft-Ebing's *Psychopathia Sexualis*, giving voice to the pervert and discussing instances of erotomania.

This element was of particular interest when it was discovered that the victims of the Ripper showed evisceration of the pelvis, and bladder, with parts of the vagina and uterus removed. Such details revealed that the female body was 'lesser' than the man's in the view of the murderer. But it also disclosed that the killer was interested in female sexuality and its functioning *per se*. In the next edition of *Psychopathia Sexualis* the Ripper case was included. There was great anxiety about the spread of venereal disease, since Salvarsan as a treatment for syphilis was not available until 1909.

The victims were Polly Nicholls, 31 August; Annie Chapman, 8 September; Catherine Eddowes and Elizabeth Stride (the 'double event'), 30 September; and Mary Jane Kelly, 9 November. These killings created multiple fears about the threat of the prostitute to public morality and domestic ideology, the presence of immigrants in the city, the terrifying nature of London itself, racial degeneration or regression; and the efficiency of the agencies of the law. In the Ripper case, two discourses confronted one another: that of the law, with its stress on individual responsibility and free will; and that of medicine, with its focus on nature, determinism and irresponsibility.

The spectre of the notorious William Burke and William Hare, who had murdered destitute persons to sell their bodies for dissection in 1827, was resurrected. Concerns about 'body-snatching' reappeared. 'Male patrols' to police Whitechapel manifested male surveillance and potential vigilantism. At the same time, men threatening women used the expression 'I'll Whitechapel you' as a threat of violence. After the 'double event' about 5,000 women signed a petition to the Queen to compel the full force of laws to be put into effect. The Queen 'forced Lord Salisbury [the Prime Minister] to hold a cabinet meeting on a Saturday to consider the question of a reward' (Walkowitz, 1992, 223).

The Lodger is the response of one woman to the cultural issues raised by the Jack the Ripper case, which remains officially unsolved. Marie Belloc Lowndes creates a fictional series of killings in the foggy streets of London, confining the reactions to the killings to Ellen Bunting, a poverty-stricken lower middle-class woman who with her husband Robert lets some untenanted rooms to a man known as Mr Sleuth [the Avenger] at their house off the Marylebone Road. The entire novel is recounted in indirect discourse through Ellen Bunting's mind. As ex-servants, the Buntings are desperate for the respectability and for the money the Lodger can provide:

> But appearances were not only deceitful, they were more than usually deceitful with regard to these unfortunate people. In spite of their good furniture – that substantial outward sign of respectability which is the last thing which wise folk who fall into trouble try to dispose of – they were almost at the end of their tether. Already they had learnt to go hungry, and they were beginning to go cold . . . They were now very near the soundless depths which divide those who dwell on the safe tableland of security – those, that is, who are sure of making a respectable, if not a happy, living – and the submerged multitude [who] struggle rudderless till they die in workhouse, hospital, or prison. (Lowndes, 1996, 4)

The Buntings are near 'that deep pit which divides the secure from the insecure . . . [the] dread edge' (6). 'If Mr Sleuth stayed on with them . . . it meant respectability, and, above all, security' (104).

The origins of the novel had stressed this class-conscious desperation for 'respectability', as Marie Belloc Lowndes recorded in her diary 9 March 1923:

> The story of *The Lodger* is curious and may be worth putting down, if only because it may encourage some fellow author long after I am dead. *The Lodger* was written by me as a short story after I heard a man telling a woman at a dinner party that his mother had had a butler and a cook who married and kept lodgers. They were convinced that Jack the Ripper had spent a night under their roof. When W. L. Courtney, the then literary editor of *The Daily Telegraph* . . . commissioned a novel from me (I then never having written a novel for serial publication) I remembered *The Lodger*. I sent him the story and he agreed that it should be expanded . . . As soon as the serial began appearing – it was I believe the first serial story published by *The Daily Telegraph* – I began receiving letters from all parts of the world,

from people who kept lodgings or had kept lodgings. (Cited in Lowndes, 1996, xi)

Robert and Ellen Bunting in the novel became the former butler and lady's maid of the anecdote.

The buttress of the Bunting's respectability comes from the fact that the lodger appears to be and probably is a 'gentleman', a factor of enormous significance to Ellen Bunting:

> On the top of the three steps which led up to the door, there stood the long, lanky figure of a man, clad in an Inverness cape and an old-fashioned top hat . . . Mrs Bunting's trained perception told her at once that this man, odd as he looked, was a gentleman, belonging by birth to the class with whom her former employment had brought her in contact . . . It seemed too good to be true, this sudden coming of a possible lodger, and of a lodger who spoke in the pleasant, courteous way and voice which recalled to the poor woman her happy, far-off days of youth and of security. (13)

The man is marked by a 'dark, sensitive, hatchet-shaped face', 'long, thin hands', and 'high bare forehead' (16), 'undoubtedly a scholar' (17) and an admitted 'man of science' (16). 'I hope I know a gentleman when I see one' she tells him (19), and she announces to Bunting: 'He's quite the gentleman!' (22). When Bunting comments that 'he's a queer-looking cove – not like any gentlemen *I* ever had to do with', Ellen Bunting replies: 'He *is* a gentleman' in a 'fierce' retort. (23). As time passes, she still maintains 'he was such a nice, gentle gentleman' (158) despite his peculiarities, and her stepdaughter Daisy wonders if the killer named by the press The Avenger might turn out to be a 'gentleman' (81), betraying the reluctance of anyone to believe that the murderer might be a respectable, middle-class or upper-class man. References to the 'gentleman' status of the lodger (74, 85, 95, 99, 186) continue as the narrative unfolds. The culture is more than willing to identify such killing with a lower-class immigrant man in Whitechapel.

Throughout the novel, however, it also becomes apparent to Ellen Bunting that the lodger is 'eccentric' (17, 22, 33, 34, 45, 57, 201), 'peculiar' (41) or 'odd' (73), although Ellen Bunting decides that such traits accompany people who are 'clever' (22). Some of these eccentricities are a bit disturbing. For instance, in the front room of the lodgings there 'hung a series of eight engravings, portraits of early Victorian belles, clad in lace and tarletan ball dresses, clipped from an old Book of Beauty', a series of which Ellen Bunting is 'very fond', believing they give the drawing-room 'a note of elegance and refinement' (15). She makes a discovery soon after the lodger moves in:

> The new lodger had turned all those nice framed engravings of the early Victorian beauties, of which Mrs Bunting had been so proud, with their faces to the wall! . . . Mr Sleuth . . . said awkwardly . . . 'I felt as I sat here that these women's eyes followed me about. It was a most unpleasant sensation, and give me quite an eerie feeling.' (24)

This attempt to control the female gaze (only males are allowed to exercise surveillance) is one of the lodger's oddities. Another strange element is that the lodger reads aloud from the Bible, such passages as the following, which Ellen Bunting hears:

> 'A strange woman is a narrow gate. She also lieth in wait as for a prey, and increaseth the transgressors among men.' (26)

> 'Her house is the way to hell, going down to the chambers of death.' (26)

> 'She saith to him stolen waters are sweet, and bread eaten secret is pleasant. But he knoweth not that the dead are there, and that her guests are in the depths of hell.' (116)

> 'She has cast down many wounded from her; yea, many strong men have been slain by her.' (116)

Overhearing such readings, from her own copy of the Bible which she has loaned Mr Sleuth, gives Ellen Bunting 'a feeling of keen distress, of spiritual oppression' (116):

> It hadn't taken the landlady very long to find out that her lodger had a queer kind of fear and dislike of women. When she was doing the staircase and landings she would often hear Mr Sleuth reading aloud to himself passages in the Bible that were very uncomplimentary to her sex. But Mrs Bunting had no very great opinion of her sister woman, so that didn't put her out. Besides, where one's lodger is concerned, a dislike of women is better than – well, than the other thing. (33-4)

One of Mr Sleuth's quoted texts is 'The spirit is willing, but the flesh – the flesh is weak' (94). One newspaper opines that the killings must be 'the work of some woman-hating teetotal fanatic' (48).

The details of the killings begin to intersect with certain elements, traits, or possessions which distinguish Mr Sleuth himself, as Ellen Bunting slowly realizes as the text evolves. These include such details as the red ink on the killer's notes appended to the bodies (4, 74, 96); the grey paper (24, 30, 37, 96, 112) which matches his 'grey eyes' (57); strange smells (109); the leather bag (13, 32, 38, 96); his vegetarian tendencies (35); the Inverness cape (13, 96, 191); his nocturnal habits (34–5); and the rubber soles of his shoes (125, 126, 162). Lowndes brilliantly scatters these allusions throughout the novel, often brought to Ellen Bunting's attention through a newspaper account, as with the grey paper (112). The lodger's peculiar attitude toward women is especially recorded when Ellen Bunting announces his name to Robert, who replies: 'Sleuth . . . what a queer name! How d' you spell it – S-l-u-t-h?' (24), the word *slut* slipping out as part of the lodger's identity. The lodger's animus, as was the case with the Ripper, is against women and especially against prostitutes.

It is Ellen Bunting who in effect becomes the detective in *The Lodger*, not only because she begins to amass an array of clues coinciding with the practises of her lodger. One of Lowndes's purposes in the text is to show the increasing identification between the woman Mrs Bunting and the killer Mr Sleuth on the basis of the fact that both women and criminals are marginalized in the culture, in effect both being outsiders. In the case of Ellen Bunting, this feeling of being 'outside' exists in her origins, for she was a foundling:

> She herself had been trained at the Foundling [Hospital 1739], for Mrs Bunting as a little child had known no other home, no other family, than those provided by the good Captain [Thomas] Coram. (31)

The fact that Mrs Bunting, raised as Ellen Green, was a bastard stresses this feeling of being an outsider. In the text, this link between the woman and the criminal as outsiders is enhanced by the increasing sympathy Ellen Bunting feels between herself and the lodger, as in her repeated defence of him as a 'gentleman.'

This symbiosis is often expressed because the lodger's room is directly above hers: as he takes possession of the room, he takes increasing possession of her mind:

> Mrs Bunting had heard Mr Sleuth moving about overhead, restlessly walking up and down his sitting-room . . . Had he stirred his landlady was bound to have heard him, for his bed was, as we know, just above hers. (89, 90)

> At first she heard nothing, but gradually there stole her listening ears the sound of someone moving softly about in the room just overhead, that is, in Mr Sleuth's bedroom. (103)

> She heard the sound she had half unconsciously been expecting to hear, that of the lodger's stealthy footsteps coming down the stairs just outside her room. (47)

Part of this sympathetic understanding of the lodger is expressed in Mrs Bunting's revolt against the authority and scrutiny of Mr Bunting, which begins when she lies to Bunting's friend and Daisy's fiancé, Joe Chandler, about the lodger:

> She didn't want the lodger upstairs to hear what young Chandler might be going to say.
> 'Don't talk so loud . . . The lodger is not very well today. He's had a cold . . . and during the last two or three days he hasn't been able to go out.'
> She wondered at her temerity, her – her hypocrisy, and that moment, those few words, marked an epoch in Ellen Bunting's life. It was the first time she had told a bold and deliberate lie. She was one of those women . . . to whom there is a whole world of difference between the suppression of the truth and the utterance of an untruth. (58)

> She felt ashamed, deeply ashamed, of deceiving so kind a husband. And yet, what could she do? (133)

When Bunting and Chandler speculate the killer might be mad and she asks then if he is not responsible, the two men claim he is responsible enough to hang, to which she replies:

> 'Not if he's not responsible', said his wife sharply. 'I never heard of anything so cruel – that I never did! If the man's a madman, he ought to be in an asylum – that's where he ought to be.' (84)

Joe Chandler claims that anyone should be willing to turn in someone for a reward: 'You'd only be doing what it's the plain duty of everyone – everyone, that is , who's a good citizen' (83). Mrs Bunting is driven to feel she cannot bear the knowledge of which she is increasingly aware, but:

> The one way in which she could have ended her misery never occurred to Mrs Bunting [to inform the police].

> In the long history of crime it has very, very seldom happened that a woman has betrayed one who has taken refuge with her . . . In fact, it may almost be said that such betrayal has never taken place unless the betrayer has been actuated by love of gain, or by a longing for revenge. So far, perhaps because she is subject rather than citizen, her duty as a component part of civilized society weighs but lightly on woman's shoulders. (98)

Lacking the vote means women do not have a complete stake in society or its laws and protocols. 'She had made up her mind, here and now, never to say anything' (101).

It is with such passages that *The Lodger* undertakes a critique of patriarchal power and authority. At another point, Mrs Bunting becomes defensive about her home:

> To her sharpened, suffering senses her house had become a citadel which must be defended; aye, even if the besiegers were a might horde *with right on their side*. And she was always expecting that first single spy who would herald the battalion against whom her only weapon would be her woman's wit and cunning. (77)

Unbeknown to her husband, Ellen Bunting attends the inquest, at which a juryman cites the newspaper to verify what a witness, Lizzie Cole said, at which the woman declares: 'I never said so . . . I was made to say all those things by the young man what came to me from the *Evening Sun*. Just put in what 'e liked in 'is paper, 'e did' (143). And Ellen thinks later that 'she had, in a sort of way, a kind of right to lie to her husband' (152):

> When with Bunting she was pursued by a sick feeling of guilt, of shame. She was the man's wedded wife . . . and yet she was keeping from him something he certainly had a right to know . . . Not for worlds, however, would she have told Bunting of her dreadful suspicion – nay, of her almost certainty . . . She welcomed anything that took her husband out of the house. (115)

The lodger comes to admire this quality in Mrs Bunting: 'He had acquired a great liking and respect for this well-balanced, taciturn woman' (117). This remark is especially important since it is the first of only a few passages recording the thoughts of the lodger himself.

When Bunting remarks that he would not want his daughter Daisy 'mixed up' (174) with the lodger, the gendering of the marital relationship in terms of silence is evident:

> But though she was suprised and a little irritated by the tone in which Bunting had spoken, no glimmer of truth illumined her mind. So accustomed had she become to bearing alone the burden of her awful secret, that it would have required far more than a cross word or two, far more than the fact that Bunting looked ill and tired, for her to have come to suspect that her secret was now shared by another, and that other her husband.
>
> Again and again the poor soul had agonized and trembled at the thought of her house being invaded by the police, but that was only because she had always credited the police with supernatural powers of detection. That they should come to know the awful fact she kept hidden in her breast would have seemed to her, on the whole, a natural thing, but that Bunting should even dimly suspect it appeared beyond the range of possibility. (175)

Eventually, Bunting surmises the truth, avoiding his acquaintances:

> He feared, with a great fear, that they would talk to him of a subject which, because it filled his mind to the exclusion of all else, might make him betray the knowledge – no, not knowledge, rather the – the suspicion – that dwelt within him . . . As they stared at each other in exasperated silence, each now knew the other knew. (189)

Bunting on his own finally reaches the inevitable conclusion. Writing of Dickens's *Oliver Twist*, D. A. Miller (1988) notes the discipline in the family that parallels the discipline in the culture, equally applicable to *The Lodger*:

> A technology of discipline constitutes this happy family as a field of power relations . . . conjoining those who work the police apparatus and those whom it works over . . . The family itself is 'one of the family' of disciplinary institutions. (10)

This is especially the case from the presence of Joe Chandler, the police detective who is the fiancé of Ellen Bunting's stepdaughter Daisy.

The presence of the law in the Bunting household is complicated by several elements. Bunting's, at best, lower middle-class background makes him suspicious of the law itself:

> He told himself again and again . . . that the most awful thing about it all was that *he wasn't sure*. If only he could have been *sure*, he might have made up his mind exactly what it was he ought to do.

> But when telling himself this he was deceiving himself, and
> he was vaguely conscious of the fact; for, from Bunting's point
> of view, almost any alternative would have been preferable to
> that which to some, nay, perhaps to most, house-holders would
> have seemed the only thing to do, namely, to go to the police.
> But Londoners of Bunting's class have an uneasy fear of the law.
> To his mind it would be ruin for him and for his Ellen to be
> mixed up publicly in such a terrible affair. No one concerned in
> the business would give them and their future a thought, but it
> would track them to their dying day, and, above all, it would
> make it quite impossible for them ever to get again into a good
> joint situation. (182)

Robert Bunting realizes that for persons of his class, the law would be
unevenly and unfairly applied. When Joe Chandler, the detective and
Daisy's fiancé and Bunting's friend, speaks with him, Bunting reacts with
this same awareness of his socially-inferior status:

> Bunting braced himself to hear the awful words – the accusation
> of having sheltered a murderer, the monster whom all the world
> was seeking, under his roof. And then he remembered a phrase,
> a horrible legal phrase – 'Accessory after the fact.' Yes, he had
> been that, there wasn't any doubt about it! (183)

Joe Chandler first became known to Bunting because of Bunting's past
service:

> This was a young fellow named Chandler, under whose
> grandfather Bunting had been footman years and years ago. Joe
> Chandler had never gone into service; he was attached to the
> police; in fact, not to put too fine a point upon it, young
> Chandler was a detective. (5)

Although Daisy's fiancé, Joe Chandler is a disconcerting individual because
he has never been in service and is with the police. Bunting borrows money
from him on occasion (9, 29), and although Chandler has a 'fair, good-
natured face' (29), he resorts to such detective practises as disguise (119,
168). In fact, Joe and Bunting have a shared interest in detective literature
and in crimes:

> He, Bunting, had always had a mild pleasure in such things. In
> his time he had been a great reader of detective tales, and even
> now he thought there was no pleasanter reading. It was that
> which had first drawn him to Joe Chandler, and made him

> welcome the young chap as cordially as he had done when they
> first came to London.
>   But though Ellen had tolerated, she had never encouraged,
> that sort of talk between the two men. More than once she had
> exclaimed reproachfully: 'To hear you two, one would think
> there was no nice, respectable, quiet people left in the world.'
> (125-6)

Chandler is weary of his job, since his friends constantly discuss 'the
remissness of the police' (82) in the case. At one point Ellen Bunting thinks
of easing her mind by reading one of Bunting's detective novels (159). She
compares Joe Chandler with fictional detectives:

> What a good thing it was, after all, that he wasn't like some of
> those detective chaps that are written about in stories – the sort
> of chaps that know everything, see everything, guess
> everything – even when there isn't anything to see, or know, or
> guess! (91)

But even this thought is not completely consoling:

> She felt queerly afraid of Chandler. After all, he was a detective –
> it was his job to be always nosing about, trying to find out
> things. (96)

Robert Bunting is suspicious of the law from the perspective of class. Ellen
Bunting is suspicious on these grounds but also by virtue of her sex, since
the detective's male gaze becomes a mode not only of policing but of
surveillance.

    Because Marie Belloc Lowndes was fictionalizing a case which never
was solved, she has the perfect occasion for critiquing the justice system.
Throughout the narrative, doubts are expressed about the efficiency of the
police, as was the case with the Ripper murders themselves. Joe Chandler is
weary with being taunted for the 'remissness of the police' (82), and rallies
are held in Victoria Park against the agents of enforcement. The Avenger,
as he is known in the papers, 'comprises in his own person the peculiarities
of Jekyll and Hyde' (80). One letter writer to the newspaper believes that
the Avenger 'should be sought for in the West and not in the East End of
London' (80). Such a comment reflects an awareness of the class bias in the
investigation, which assumed that the poor or immigrants of the East End
'must' be guilty. The newspapers fan the anger at the police inefficiency:

> The police have reluctantly to admit that they have no clue to
> the perpetrators of these horrible crimes . . . There is even talk
> of an indignation mass meeting . . . The detection of crime in
> London now resembles a game of blind man's buff, in which the
> detective has his hands tied and his eyes bandaged. Thus is he
> turned loose to hunt the murderer through the slums of a great
> city. (46)

This inability to see the truth and clearly perceive the circumstances is
reflected in the motif of fog, which Lowndes uses strategically throughout
the novel.

In the fifth paragraph of the book 'the red damask curtains . . . shut out
the fog-laden drizzling atmosphere of the Marylebone Road' (3), and this
motif recurs:

> A yellow pall of fog had suddenly descended on London. (94)

> 'Why, the fog's awful; you can't see a yard ahead of you!' (97)

> He described exactly what had happened to him on that cold,
> foggy morning ten days ago. (141)

> 'Yes – yes, it is a foggy night, a night fit for the commission of
> dark and salutary deeds.' (148)

The geography of London becomes part of the befogged investigation, as
the Avenger moves from the East End to the West:

> 'The Avenger's moving West – that's what he's doing. Last time
> 'twas King's Cross – now 'tis the Edgware Road. I said he'd
> come our way, and he *has* come our way!' (111)

The press is more specific:

> Once more the murder fiend who chooses to call himself The
> Avenger has escaped detection. While the whole attention of the
> police, and of the great army of amateur detectives . . . were
> concentrating their attention round the East End and King's
> Cross, he moved swiftly and silently Westward. (111)

The climate conspires as well: 'The winter sun, a scarlet ball, [was] hanging
in the smoky sky . . . and threw blood-red gleams' (118). In the short story
version of *The Lodger*, in 1911 this had read: 'The winter sun, a yellow ball
[was] hanging in the smoky sky . . . and lent blood-red gleams' (81).

The law is perceived as dubious. Joe Chandler and Bunting have this disturbing conversation in the novel:

> 'I suppose a good many murderers get off?' . . .
> 'I should think they did! . . . There's no such thing as justice here in England. 'Tis odds on the murderer every time . . .
> 'I don't believe he'll ever be caught.' (69-70)

After one killing, Joe Chandler admits that 'there was a policeman there, within a few yards' (30), as Bunting paraphrases it. Things become so bad that the Commissioner of Police is forced to resign (120). 'Then the five thousand constables weren't no use?' (53) asks Ellen Bunting. An easy way to exonerate the police, society, the public, and the culture is to claim the Avenger is mad (70, 194) or a lunatic (148) or 'an escaped lunatic' (186, 195).

All of these agendas – feminist, classist, reformist, sensational – coalesce in the final confrontation between the lodger and Ellen Bunting during the tour of Madame Tussaud's, the collection which opened in London in 1802 and was moved to a museum – on Baker Street – in 1833. As the Buntings tour the Chamber of Horrors, Mr Sleuth appears, 'discomposed, livid with rage and terror' (195) and hisses to his landlady:

> 'A last word with you, Mrs Bunting . . . Do not think to escape the consequences of your hideous treachery. I trusted you, Mrs Bunting, and you betrayed me! But I am protected by a higher power, for I still have much to do . . . Your end will be bitter as wormwood and sharp as a two-edged sword. Your feet shall go down to death, and your steps take hold on hell.' (196)

Mr Sleuth feels Ellen Bunting has betrayed him to Sir John Burney, the new Commissioner of Police:

> He had remembered his landlady. How could the woman whom he had treated so generously have betrayed him to his arch-enemy? – to the official, that is, who had entered into a conspiracy years ago to have him confined – him, an absolutely sane man with a great avenging work to do in the world – in a lunatic asylum. (197)

Ellen Bunting thinks she would not have 'sheltered him – kept his awful secret' had she known he was mad (198). He was 'a madman, a homicidal maniac' (199). She tells Bunting:

'So you see . . . that 'twas me that was right after all. The lodger
was never responsible for his actions. I never thought he was,
for my part . . . He was a lunatic,' she said fiercely . . . 'A religious
maniac – that's what he called him.' (200)

Ellen Bunting finds her voice and preserves her integrity.

In a sense, there are two endings to the novel. The conventional one,
the resolution of the marriage plot, records Daisy's engagement to Joe
Chandler (202). The radical ending records Ellen Bunting's responses, as
she 'left off listening for the click of the lock which she at once hoped and
feared would herald her lodger's return' (202). She sends the money left
behind by the lodger to the Governors of the Thomas Coram Foundling
Hospital. When Daisy's old aunt hears of her engagement, she remarks 'that
if gentle folks leave a house in charge of the police a burglary is pretty sure
to follow' (203). This statement makes Joe Chandler the thief taking Daisy
Bunting as the prize: in other words, the detective is a kind of thief and
marriage is a crime. At the end of *The Lodger* Lowndes conflates the public
and private spheres, linking them by their criminous bases: men in marriage
take possession as much as do thieves. Crime is pandemic and endemic: the
murders placed throughout the text (29, 36, 40, 49 [the double murder])
reflect this belief.

It is interesting to compare the short story version of *The Lodger*, 1911,
with its novelistic counterpart of 1913. In the main, the short story contains
most of the elements expanded in the novel: the bag, the fog, the women's
pictures on the wall, the Foundling Hospital history, the gynephobia of the
lodger, the rubber shoes, the double murder, the tour through the Chamber
of Horrors at Madame Tussaud's, the confrontation between Ellen Bunting
and Mr Sleuth, and his escape. However in the novel version of the tale, Mr
Sleuth simply disappears. In the short story version, he is found drowned in
Regent's Canal. Also, in the short story there is no detective Joe Chandler.
For the novel *The Lodger*, Lowndes added both the detective and the
disappearance of the lodger, indicative of her simultaneous affirmation of
and doubt about the law and its agents.

The Lodger sold a million copies in 20 years, making it one of the all-
time best-sellers of the Edwardian/early Georgian era. On the issues it
engages – women, crime, urbanization, enforcement, justice, detection,
respectability, gentility, criminality – it remains a peerless index to the
Edwardian state of mind.

Conclusion

From the earliest female detectives examined in this study until the last, the landlady in Marie Belloc Lowndes's *The Lodger*, one quality above all distinguishes these female detectives in Britain during the nineteenth century and the early twentieth century: they exercise surveillance over the culture, including its men, women, public institutions and private domestic spaces. Even though this surveillance existed in an empowering symbolic practise and not in actuality, the idea of a woman exercising power through her gaze is enormously potent for the time. Narratives involving the female detective thus convey an ideology of female professional appropriation of power.

The literary canon, in its selectivity by supposedly universal standards of value or relevance, may privilege those texts which represent empowered women – or the canon may exclude such texts. Since historically the canon has been formed by males, whether in publishing or in the professoriate, the survival of these texts, their accessibility and their exclusion or inclusion in everything from syllabi to reprintings to 'Ten Best' lists to anthologies are all canonical factors influencing the representation of women in literary history.

In addition to the gaze and narratology, a third factor of key significance in assessing texts about the Victorian female detective is the issue of canon. Two statements by E[verett]. F. Bleiler are important. In his introduction to the Dover edition of H. F. Wood's great railway detection novel of 1888, *The Passenger from Scotland Yard*, Bleiler observes:

> The last third of the nineteenth century is a barren period for the detective novel. Between *The Moonstone* (1866) by Wilkie Collins and *The Hound of the Baskervilles* (1902) by Arthur Conan Doyle there is very little that is worth remembering, even as a statistic in the publishing industry . . . The second decade, 1881-1890, produced two famous longer works, *A Study in Scarlet* (1887) and *The Sign of Four* (1890) by Doyle, but oddly enough these are not true novels, but detective short stories tacked onto historical romances, in the manner of Gaboriau. During the third decade-plus, 1890-1902, a younger generation appeared, but all its creative energy went into short stories, with the result that there

are many good short stories in the 1890s, but almost no novels. Here economics played a role: *The Strand, Pearson's Magazine, The Windsor Magazine* and other variety magazines paid well for short stories. (v, vii)

Bleiler's assessment, coming as it does from a man who devoted much enterprise in the 1970s to making Victorian detective texts once again accessible, deserves some scrutiny.

Many of the texts involving the female detective in the Victorian period originated as a series of short stories in important magazines. Such is demonstrated by Grant Allen's *Miss Cayley's Adventures* and *Hilda Wade* appearing in the *Strand*, Pirkis's *Loveday Brooke* in the *Ludgate Monthly*, Meade/Eustace's *Miss Cusack* in the *Harmsworth Magazine*, or Heron-Maxwell's *Lady Pearl-Broker* also in the *Harmsworth*. On the other hand, some key works, such as those by Merrick or Braddon or Hume, were indeed original novels. Even granting that *Madame Midas* is a less effective novel than *A Study in Scarlet* or *The Sign of Four*, it is difficult to accept Hume's text as indicative of the 'mediocrity' (v) of its author, the category to which Bleiler consigns Hume.

Doyle's two novels about Holmes, which appeared before the detective's short story incarnation in 1891, are intended to be and were published as unserialized novels, despite the fact that the short story was to prove Doyle's stronger medium. The relationship of short story to novel is particularly important to Lowndes's novel *The Lodger*, which originally appeared in January 1911 as a short story in *McClure's Magazine*. As Bleiler claims, however, in his introduction to the anthology *A Treasury of Victorian Detective Stories*, '[Doyle's] *Strand* [short] stories were responsible for the second great explosion [after the 1860s] of detective literature in England' (5). Under the influence of Doyle and undoubtedly lured by the money, writers such as Pirkis, Meade and Heron-Maxwell gravitated to the short story to describe the exploits of their female detectives.

The fact that some of these narratives originated as short stories, however, has important consequences for the canon. To begin with, the short story, especially in England, has often taken second place to the novel as a genre. That so much detective narrative has originated in the short story genre has unquestionably damaged its ability to be considered as 'literature' rather than 'detective literature' or worse 'detective fiction.' Furthermore, short stories are elusive unless published as a collection or diligently excavated by anthologizers. Without the aid of works such as Allen J. Hubin's *The Bibliography of Crime Fiction 1749-1975* (1979) or William Contento and Martin Greenberg's *Index to Crime and Mystery Anthologies* (1991) such short stories might vanish altogether from literary history.

That even the detective canon, let alone the 'literary' canon, has access to some of these stories is due to the perseverance of anthologizers. One might note now-famous collections such as those edited by Dorothy Sayers in *The Omnibus of Crime* series (1929, 1932, 1935); G. K. Chesterton, *A Century of Detective Stories* (1935); Ellery Queen, *101 Years' Entertainment* (1941); Hugh Greene, *The Rivals of Sherlock Holmes* (1970) and *The Further Rivals of Sherlock Holmes* (1973); Alan K. Russell, *The Rivals of Sherlock Holmes I* (1978) and *II* (1979); and Bleiler, *A Treasury of Victorian Detective Stories* (1979). More recently, the anthologies edited for Oxford University Press by Michael Cox, *Victorian Tales of Mystery and Detection* (1992); and by Jack Adrian, *Twelve Tales of Murder* (1998) and *Twelve Mystery Stories* (1998) have kept Victorian detective narratives in print.

An additional factor in the survival of the Victorian detective short story has been the appearance of anthologies of stories from the most famous publication of its kind, the *Strand Magazine*. For Oxford University Press, Jack Adrian has edited *Detective Stories from* The Strand (1991) and *Strange Tales from* The Strand (1992). Several parallel anthologies have been edited by Geraldine Beare for the Folio Society, *Crime Stories from* The Strand (1991) and more general in content *Short Stories from* The Strand (1992) and *Adventure Stories from* The Strand (1995). George Locke's checklist to *Pearson's Weekly* (1990) is an important index to series stories by writers such as Hume and Bodkin. In particular, the collections of stories from the *Strand* save from oblivion work by writers whose contributions to detective fiction are enduring. Such anthologies make accessible stellar examples of the genre of the short story during the Victorian and Edwardian eras. Privileging the short story and detective fiction, these collections destabilize the traditional canon.

While these collections include some Victorian and Edwardian tales about female detectives, several anthologies of stories about detecting women were genuinely pioneering, such as those edited by Queen, *The Great Women Detectives and Criminals* (1943); and by Slung, *Crime on Her Mind* (1977). These have been complemented by Laura Marcus's recent *Twelve Women Detective Stories* (1997). Concentrating on female detectives, these anthologies have balanced if not rectified the legacy of the patriarchal canon. Such anthologies in the twentieth century stress the importance of accessibility as a factor influencing the canon.

Other Victorian texts about female detectives, such as those by Pirkis (edited by Slung for Dover in 1986), by Hume (*Hagar* for Greenhill Books 1985), and by Sims (for Greenhill 1986) have recently been reissued. Such volumes permit scholars to research an entire series of stories beyond selections in anthologies. The *Oxford Popular Fiction* series, now discontinued, allowed readers access to a text like Lowndes's *The Lodger* in a scholarly form. Such availability is particularly key in this instance, since Lowndes's text corrects the male version of history by revealing how a woman would solve a case which has confounded male institutions. Other texts, however, such as those by Forrester, Corbett, Merrick, Bodkin, Heron-Maxwell, Allen and Marsh remain unreprinted. Without reprints, canonical status, even if desired, becomes extremely uncertain and practically impossible, as inaccessibility will lead to the inevitable exclusion from university curricula.

In his introduction to *Three Victorian Detective Novels*, Bleiler notes:

> It is not generally known that Wilkie Collins's first 'detective' was also a woman, Anne Rodway . . . The detection that Anne Rodway accomplished, however, was rudimentary, and Collins was really more interested in social matters and the action of fate than in detection. Collins seldom wrote detective stories in the strictest sense. (x-xi)

While Anne Rodway's detection might indeed in retrospect appear 'rudimentary', Bleiler focuses on another anomaly of the canonical process. Many of the writers of Victorian or Edwardian narratives about female detectives are renowned – but for something else. One need only think of Braddon with *Lady Audley's Secret* or *Aurora Floyd*, Allen with *The Woman Who Did*, Orczy with *The Scarlet Pimpernel*, Hume with *The Mystery of a Hansom Cab* or Collins with *The Moonstone* or *The Woman in White* to demonstrate that the writer famous for one or two books often has other achievements which remain unrecognized by the canon. An anthology of critical essays, such as the volume *Beyond Sensation* (Tromp, ed. 2000) about Braddon, can expand the critical perspective by encompassing works not ordinarily researched, rectifying the assessment of a writer who is canonical, if at all, for only one or two productions.

Lastly, the canonical question appears when one considers the intervention of males in defining that canon. Is there the possibility that narratives about female detectives, involving as they do female empowerment, have been neglected or erased in the evolution of literary history? Not only must detective fiction in general confront these elisions, but in particular detective fiction about female detectives is doubly disadvantaged in the process of canon formation by males. Identified as a profession involving reason, which was construed in the nineteenth century to be the province of men rather than women, the female detective is gender-bending in terms of patriarchal constructions of the feminine, since she is a woman empowered primarily through rationality.

The female sleuth, therefore, is to varying degrees a threat to male empowerment and male-identified institutions such as the courts or the detective police. Even valiant male anthologizers such as Ellery Queen in 1943 could not overcome this prejudice against both the female detective and the genre in which she appeared. In this respect, anthologies are double-edged. On the one hand, they preserve a story or two about the female detective; on the other, they encourage a person to think that this story is representative or 'the best'. Hence, an anthology might either stimulate further inquiry or terminate it.

Without accessible or complete texts about the female detective, the form cannot accomplish the aim of readdressing the complex representation of women in the Victorian period. Female detective narratives often construct women triumphing over cultural restrictions instead of succumbing to them, as is the case with indisputably canonical texts such as Eliot's *The Mill on the Floss* or Hardy's *Tess of the d'Urbervilles*. The reinsertion of a sensation text such as Braddon's *Lady Audley's Secret* into the canon (for example as part of Oxford's *World's Classics* series) demonstrates that narratives of such complexity destabilize the male-constructed canon of valued Victorian texts. The recuperation of Braddon by scholars such as Elaine Showalter in *A Literature of Their Own* (1977) and Winifred Hughes in *The Maniac in the Cellar* (1980) has inspired subsequent researchers to extend the canon of Victorian fiction.

Texts about female detectives represent women in situations demanding rationality, enterprise, daring and empowerment. Their exclusion or inaccessibility distorts the entire issue of the representation of women in Victorian or Edwardian fiction. That the stress on the rationality of women in female detective narratives is still necessary as late as 1912 is indicated by the remarks of an individual even sympathetic to the freedom of women, Edward Carpenter. In *Love's Coming of Age* (1911), Carpenter writes:

> It is commonly received opinion that woman tends more to intuition and man to logic; and certainly the male mind seems better able to deal with abstractions and generalisations, and the female mind with the personal and the detailed and the concrete. And while this difference may be in part attributable to the artificial confinement of women to the domestic sphere, there is probably something more organic in it than that . . . This want of power of generalisation has made it difficult for woman (at any rate up to to-day) to emerge from a small circle of interests, and to look at things from the point of view of public advantage and good. (56-7)

The emphasis in female detective fiction on ratiocinative processes clearly runs counter to such received constructions of the feminine as non-logical in Victorian and Edwardian culture. Female detectives do engage 'public advantage and good' in these texts. Carpenter continues, specifically to note the consequences of this 'deficiency in logic' for women:

> While her sympathies for individuals are keen and quick, abstract and general ideas such as those of Justice, Truth, and the like have been difficult of appreciation to her; and her deficiency in logic has made it almost impossible to act upon her through the brain . . . Man has developed the more active, and Woman the more passive qualities. (57-8)

If someone sympathetic to women's 'liberation' (64), as Carpenter labels it, can yet maintain this position in 1911, then the polemical agenda of female detective fiction is both justified and necessary. In such narratives, women deploy logic and are in pursuit of Justice and Truth, contrary to the contention of Carpenter.

These texts about the female detective span a range of decades during which women gradually acquired greater legal, educational, marital and occupational rights. In an essay published in the *Strand Magazine* in January 1914, several prominent individuals were asked to respond to the issue 'Why Men Do Not Marry' in a 'symposium' article. Both men and women agreed that a great change had occurred by 1914. C. W. Saleeby, a male physician, remarked: 'We shall need to make the conditions of marriage, including divorce, infinitely fairer for women if marriage is to maintain its place in the social structure' (50). Actress Sarah Bernhardt declared:

> In many respects girls enjoy almost equal freedom and liberty as do men . . . I cannot help thinking that the chief reason why the marriage rate is declining lies in the fact that intercourse between men and women to-day is ten thousand times less restricted than was the case in the childhood days of our parents. (51)

Mrs Baillie Reynolds believes that in her generation

> we desire to be more prudent. We desire, especially, to be independent . . . The result of waiting often is that the desire to marry, so strong in youth, dies down in us. We grow more fastidious, more set in our own ways, more timorous, more used to do as we like. The longer we wait the greater seems the risk. (53)

Women recognized that the shift in generations had led to behaviours much in contrast to those of the parents of Edwardians.

In particular, in this same *Strand* symposium, women acknowledged the economic access and consequent freedom permitted women by 1914. Hilda Trevelyan declared that 'woman [has] earned for herself far more liberty and freedom than the laws of society have hitherto permitted her' (54), while actress Irene Vanbrugh observed 'the greater freedom women are now allowed' (54). Mrs C. N. Williamson, the novelist, stressed the new occupational freedom of her generation: 'Young women have a better chance of finding work which is fairly well paid than they had years ago; so they need not marry just for the sake of being married' (54). On the other hand, another *Strand* symposium essay, 'Have Undergraduates Deteriorated?' of January 1912, concentrated exclusively on young males.

Narratives about the female detective from the 1860s to the brink of the outbreak of the Great War are crucial pieces of evidence about societal attitudes and cultural practises. In their empowerment through professional surveillance – their enterprise, independence, resourcefulness and survival – the female detectives symbolized the gradual emergence of the model of the twentieth-century woman. Sherlock's sisters – Loveday Brooke, Miriam Lea, Lady Molly, Dorcas Dene, Hilda Wade, Hagar Stanley, Florence Cusack, Annie Cory, Mollie Delamere, Judith Lee – were not deterred by circumstances or adversity.

If Irene Adler, singer and counter-investigator of *A Scandal in Bohemia* (July 1891), remained for Holmes '*the* woman' (5), then she had a stirring range of predecessors and successors in these female detectives. In fact, she effected a revolution. Watson records about Holmes at the end of that memorable case: 'He used to make merry over the cleverness of women, but I have not heard him do it of late' (29).

Select Bibliography

Adams, W. S. *Edwardian Heritage*. London: Frederick Muller, 1949.

Adams, W. S. *Edwardian Portraits*. London: Secker and Warburg, 1957.

Adey, Robert. *Locked Room Murders*. Minneapolis, MN: Crossover Press,1991.

Adrian, Jack, ed. *Detective Stories from* The Strand. New York: Oxford University Press, 1991.

Adrian, Jack, ed. *Strange Tales from* The Strand. New York: Oxford University Press, 1992.

Adrian, Jack, ed. *Twelve Mystery Stories*. New York: Oxford University Press, 1998.

Adrian, Jack, ed. *Twelve Tales of Murder*. New York: Oxford University Press, 1998.

Alewyn, Richard. 'The Origin of the Detective Novel', in *The Poetics of Murder*, eds. Most and Stowe, (1983), 62-78.

Allen, Grant. 'Are We Englishmen?', *Fortnightly Review* 28 (1880), 472-87.

Allen, Grant. *The Conscientious Burglar. Strand* 3 (June 1892), 586-96.

Allen, Grant. *A Deadly Dilemma. Strand* 1 (January 1891), 14-21.

Allen, Grant. *The Great Ruby Robbery: A Detective Story*, in Russell, ed., (1978), 3-14.

Allen, Grant. *Hilda Wade*. London: Grant Richards, 1900.

Allen, Grant. *Jerry Stokes. Strand* 1 (March 1891), 298-307.

Allen, Grant. *Miss Cayley's Adventures*. London: Putnam's Sons, 1899.

Allen, Grant. *The Reluctant Hangman and Other Stories of Crime*. Boulder: Aspen Press, 1973.

Allen, Grant. *The Woman Who Did* (1895). Intro. Sarah Wintle. New York: Oxford University Press, 1995.

Altick, Richard D. *Victorian Studies in Scarlet*. New York: Norton, 1970.

Armstrong, M. Thornton. 'The Detective Story', *The Editor* (May 1906), 218-9.

Arnstein, Walter. 'Edwardian Britain: Epilogue or New Chapter?', Midwest Victorian Studies Association, April 1998. [unpublished essay]

Aydelotte, William O. 'The Detective Story as a Historical Source', in *The Mystery Writer's Art*, ed. Nevins, (1970), 306-25.

Baker, William, ed. *The Beetle*, by Richard Marsh. Stroud: Alan Sutton, 1994.

Batchelor, John. *The Edwardian Novelists*. London: Duckworth, 1982.

Bauer, Carol, ed. *Free and Ennobled*. New York: Pergamon, 1979.

Beare, Geraldine, ed. *Adventure Stories from* The Strand. London: Folio Society, 1995.

Beare, Geraldine, ed. *Crime Stories from* The Strand. London: Folio Society, 1991.

Beare, Geraldine, ed. *Index to the* Strand Magazine *1891-1950*. London: Greenwood Press, 1982.

Beare, Geraldine, ed. *Short Stories from* The Strand. London: Folio Society, 1992.

Beckett, Jane and Deborah Cherry, eds. *The Edwardian Era*. London: Phaidon, 1987.

Beckson, Karl. *London in the 1890s: A Cultural History*. New York: Norton, 1992.

Bedell, Jeanne F. 'Amateur and Professional Detectives in the Fiction of Mary Elizabeth Braddon', *Clues* 4 (1983), 19-34.

Belsey, Catherine. *Critical Practice*. London: Methuen, 1980.

Berglund, Birgitta. 'Desires and Devices: On Women Detectives in Fiction', in Chernaik, ed., (2000), 138-52.

Betjeman, John. *Victorian and Edwardian London from Old Photographs*. New York: Viking, 1969.

Blain, Virginia, ed. *The Feminist Companion to Literature in English*. New Haven: Yale University Press, 1990.

Blake, Fay M. 'Lady Sleuths and Women Detectives', *Turn of the Century Women* 3 (1986), 29-42.

Bleiler, Everett F. 'Female Detectives, Ghost Books and the Relative Importance of It All', *The Armchair Detective* 8 (May 1975), 202.

Bleiler, Everett F., ed. Introduction, in H. F. Wood, *The Passenger from Scotland Yard*. New York: Dover, 1977.

Bleiler, Everett F., ed. Introduction, in *Three Victorian Detective Novels*. New York: Dover, 1978.

Bleiler, Everett F., ed. *Three Victorian Detective Novels*. New York: Dover, 1978.

Bleiler, Everett F., ed. *A Treasury of Victorian Detective Stories*. New York: Scribner's, 1979.

Bodkin, M. McDonnell. *Dora Myrl, The Lady Detective*. London: Chatto & Windus, 1900.

Booth, Charles. *Life and Labour of the People of London*. London: Macmillan, 1903.

Brabin, Angela. 'The Black Widows of Liverpool', *History Today* 52 (October 2002), 40-6.

Braddon, Mary Elizabeth. *Aurora Floyd* (1863). London: Virago, 1984.

Braddon, Mary Elizabeth. *Lady Audley's Secret* (1862). ed. David Skilton. New York: Oxford University Press, 1987.

Braddon, Mary Elizabeth. *Thou Art the Man*. London: Simpkin, Marshall, Hamilton, Kent & Co, 1894.

Brendon, Piers. *Eminent Edwardians*. Boston, MA: Houghton, 1980.

Brent, Peter. *The Edwardians*. London: Cox & Wyman, 1972.

Bristow, Joseph. *Empire Boys: Adventures in a Man's World*. London: HarperCollins, 1991.

Broomfield, Andrea and Sally Mitchell, eds. *Prose by Victorian Women*. New York: Garland, 1996.

Broughton, Rhoda. *Not Wisely, But Too Well* (1867), ed. Herbert Van Thal. London: Cassell, 1967.

Bush, Julia. *Edwardian Ladies and Imperial Power*. Leicester: Leicester University Press, 2000.

Caird, Mona. 'Marriage' in *The Fin de Siècle*, ed. Ledger, (2000), 77-80.

Carpenter, Edward. *Love's Coming of Age*. New York: Boni and Liveright, 1911.

Carr, John Dickson. 'The Locked-Room Lecture', in *The Art of the Mystery Story*, ed. Haycraft, (1983), 273-86.

Cawelti, John G. *Adventure, Mystery, and Romance*. Chicago: University of Chicago Press, 1976.

Cecil, Robert. *Life in Edwardian England*. London: Batsford, 1969.

Chernaik Warren, ed. *The Art of Detective Fiction*. New York: St Martin's, 2000.

Chesterton, G.K., ed. *A Century of Detective Stories*. London: Hutchinson, 1935.

Cobb, Belton. *The First Detectives*. London: Faber and Faber, 1957.

Collier, Price. *England and the English from an American Point of View*. London: Duckworth, 1910.

Collins, Wilkie. *The Diary of Anne Rodway* (1856), in *Mad Monkton and Other Stories*, ed. Norman Vance. New York: Oxford University Press, 1994.

Collins, Wilkie. *The Moonstone* (1868). Baltimore: Penguin, 1966.

Cominos, Peter T. 'Late Victorian Sexual Respectability and the Social System', *International Review of Social History* 8 (1962), 18-48, 216-50.

Conklin, Groff and Noah D. Fabricant, eds. *Great Detective Stories about Doctors*. New York: Collier Books, 1965.

Conrad, Joseph. *The Secret Agent*. Intro. Roger Tennant. New York: Oxford University Press, 1983.

Contento, William G. and Martin H. Greenberg. *Index to Crime and Mystery Anthologies*. Boston: G. K. Hall, 1991.

'Conversations With a Psychoanalyst: Janet A. Kennedy, M.D.', in *Mystery and Detection Annual* (1972), ed. Donald Adams. Pasadena CA: Castle Press, (1972), 191-7.

Corbett, Elizabeth B. [Mrs George]. *When the Sea Gives Up Its Dead*. London: Tower Publishing, 1894.

Cornwallis-West, George. *Edwardian Hey-Days: A Little About A Lot of Things*. New York: Putnam, 1931.

Cox, Michael, ed. *Victorian Tales of Mystery and Detection*. London: Oxford University Press, 1992.

Cox, Tom. *Damned Englishman*. Hicksville, NY: Exposition Press, 1975.

Craig, Patricia and Mary Cadogan. *The Lady Investigates: Women Detectives and Spies in Fiction*. New York: St Martin's, 1981.

'Crime in Fiction'. *Blackwood's* 148 (August 1890), 172-89.

Crittenden, Charles. 'Fictional Characters and Logical Completeness', *Poetics* 11 (1982), 331-44.

Cruse, Amy. *After the Victorians*. London: Allen & Unwin, 1938.

Cummings, J. C. 'Detective Stories', *The Bookman* 30 (January 1910), 2.

Cummings, J. C. 'Inside Views of Fiction', *The Bookman* 30 (January 1910), 499-500.

Cunningham, Gail. *The New Woman and the Victorian Novel*. New York: Barnes & Noble, 1979.

Delamont, Sara and Lorna Duffin, eds. *The Nineteenth-Century Woman*. London: Croom Helm, 1978.

'Detectives', *The Saturday Review* (5 May 1883), 558-9.

'"Detectiveness" in Fiction', *The Nation* (13 August 1912), 141-2.

Dickens, Charles. *Hunted Down: The Detective Stories of Charles Dickens*, ed. Peter Haining. London: Peter Owen, 1996.

Dixon, Ella Hepworth. 'Why Women are Ceasing to Marry' in Ledger, ed., (2000), 83-8.

Dove, George N. *Suspense in the Formula Story*. Bowling Green, OH: Bowling Green University Popular Press, 1989.

Doyle, Arthur Conan. *The Adventures of Sherlock Holmes*, ed. Richard Lancelyn Green. New York: Oxford University Press, 1993. [Contents: *A Scandal in Bohemia, A Case of Identity, The Red-Headed League, The Boscombe Valley Mystery, The Five Orange Pips, The Man with the Twisted Lip, The Blue Carbuncle, The Speckled Band, The Engineer's Thumb, The Noble Bachelor, The Beryl Coronet, The Copper Beeches*.]

Doyle, Arthur Conan. *His Last Bow*, ed. Owen Dudley Edwards. New York: Oxford University Press, 1993. [Contents: *Preface, Wisteria Lodge, The Bruce-Partington Plans, The Devil's Foot, The Red Circle, The Disappearance of Lady Frances Carfax, The Dying Detective, His Last Bow*.]

Doyle, Arthur Conan. *The Hound of the Baskervilles*, ed. W. W. Robson. New York: Oxford University Press, 1993.

Doyle, Arthur Conan. *The Memoirs of Sherlock Holmes*, ed. Christopher Roden. New York: Oxford University Press, 1993. [*Contents: Silver Blaze*,

The Cardboard Box, The Yellow Face, The Stockbroker's Clerk, The 'Gloria Scott', The Musgrave Ritual, The Reigate Squire, The Crooked Man, The Resident Patient, The Greek Interpreter, The Naval Treaty, The Final Problem.]

Doyle, Arthur Conan. *Memories and Adventures.* London: Greenhill Books, 1988.

Doyle, Arthur Conan. *The Return of Sherlock Holmes,* ed. Richard Lancelyn Green. New York: Oxford University Press, 1993. [Contents: *The Empty House, The Norwood Builder, The Solitary Cyclist, The Dancing Men, The Priory School, Black Peter, Charles Augustus Milverton, The Six Napoleons, The Three Students, The Golden Prince-Nez, The Missing Three-Quarter, The Abbey Grange, The Second Stain.*]

Doyle, Arthur Conan. *The Sign of Four,* ed. Christopher Roden. New York: Oxford University Press, 1993.

Doyle, Arthur Conan. *A Study in Scarlet,* ed. Owen Dudley Edwards. New York: Oxford University Press, 1993.

Doyle, Arthur Conan. *Through the Magic Door.* London: Smith, Elder, 1907.

Doyle, Arthur Conan. *The Valley of Fear,* ed. Owen Dudley Edwards. New York: Oxford University Press, 1993.

Drinkwater, John, ed. *The Eighteen-Sixties.* Cambridge: Cambridge University Press, 1932.

Duyfhuizen, Bernard. 'The Case of Sherlock Holmes and Jane Eyre', *The Baker Street Journal* 43 (September 1993), 135-45.

Eastwood, M. 'The New Woman in Fiction and Fact', in Ledger, ed., (2000), 90-2.

Eco, Umberto and Thomas A. Sebeok, eds. *The Sign of Three.* Bloomington: Indiana University Press, 1983.

Edwardian Reflections. Lister Park Bradford: Cartwright Hall, 1975. (Exhibition catalogue.)

Edwards, W. H. *The Tragedy of Edward VII.* New York: Dodd, Mead, 1928.

Ellmann, Richard, ed. *Edwardians and Late Victorians.* New York: Columbia University Press, 1959.

Ensor, Sir Robert. *England 1870-1914.* London: Oxford University Press, 1936.

Fabb, John. *The Victorian and the Edwardian Army.* London: Batsford, 1975.

Fahnestock, Jeane. 'Bigamy: The Rise and Fall of a Convention', *Nineteenth-Century Fiction* 36 (June 1981), 47-71.

Feuchtwanger, E. J. *Democracy and Empire: England 1868-1914.* New York: Routledge, 1985.

Fido, Martin and Keith Skinner, *The Official Encyclopedia of Scotland Yard.* London: Virgin, 1999.

Flower, Desmond. *A Century of Best Sellers 1830-1930.* London: National Book Council, 1934.

Forbes, Litton. 'Malingering', *Strand* 31 (March 1906), 319-25.

'Foreign Undesirables.' *Blackwood's Magazine*. 169 (February 1901), 279-89.

Forrester, Andrew, Jr. *The Female Detective*. London: Ward and Lock, 1864.

Foucault, Michel. *Discipline and Punish*. New York: Random House, 1977.

Fritz, Kathlyn Ann and Natalie Kaufman Hevener. 'An Unsuitable Job for a Woman: Female Protagonists in the Detective Novel', *International Journal of Women's Studies* 2 (March/April 1979), 105-28.

Fulcher, James. 'Murder Reports: Formulaic Narrative and Cultural Context', *Journal of Popular Culture* 18 (Spring 1985), 31-42.

Fussell, Paul. *The Great War and Modern Memory*. London: Oxford University Press, 1975.

Gamman, Lorraine, ed. *The Female Gaze*. Seattle: Real Comet Press, 1989.

Garforth, John. *A Day in the Life of a Victorian Policeman*. London: Allen Unwin, 1974.

Gilbert, Elliot L. 'The Detective as Metaphor in the Nineteenth Century', in *The Mystery Writer's Art*, ed. Nevins, (1970), 285-94.

Gilbert, Elliot L. *The World of Mystery Fiction*. San Diego, CA: University of California Extension, 1978.

Glover, Dorothy, and Graham Greene, eds. *Victorian Detective Fiction*. London: Bodley Head, 1966.

'Good Looks in Men'. *Strand* 57 (June 1919), 485-90.

Gore, John. *Edwardian Scrapbook*. London: Evans, 1951.

Gorrie, John, director. *Edward the King*. Salt Lake City, UT: BWE Video, 1985.

Gorsky, Susan R. 'Old Maids and New Women', *Journal of Popular Culture* 7 (Summer 1973), 68-85.

Grella, George. 'The Formal Detective Novel', in *Detective Fiction*, ed. Winks, (1988), 84-102.

Grella, George. 'The Hard-Boiled Detective Novel', in *Detective Fiction*, ed. Winks, (1988), 103-20.

Green, Richard Lancelyn, and John Michael Gibson. *A Bibliography of A. Conan Doyle*. Oxford: Clarendon Press, 1983.

Greene, Hugh, ed. *The Further Rivals of Sherlock Holmes*. New York: Penguin, 1974.

Greene, Hugh, ed. *The Rivals of Sherlock Holmes*. London: Bodley Head, 1970.

Greene, Hugh, ed. *Victorian Villainies*. New York: Penguin, 1984.

Haining, Peter, ed. *Hunted Down: The Detective Stories of Charles Dickens*. London: Peter Owen, 1996.

Haining, Peter, ed. *Murder at the Races*. London: Orion, 1995.

Haining, Peter, ed. *Murder on the Railways*. London: Orion, 1996.

Halperin, John. *Eminent Georgians*. New York: St. Martin's Press, 1995.

Harris, Jose. *Private Lives, Public Spirit: Britain 1870-1914*. London: Penguin, 1993.

Hartman, Mary S. *Victorian Murderesses*. New York: Schocken Books, 1976.

'Have Undergraduates Deteriorated?'. *Strand* 43 (January 1912), 44-8.

Haycraft, Howard, ed. *The Art of the Mystery Story*. New York: Carroll & Graf, 1983.

Haycraft, Howard. *Murder for Pleasure*. New York: Carroll & Graf, 1984.

Haycraft, Howard. 'Murder for Pleasure', in *The Art of the Mystery Story*, ed. Haycraft, (1983), 158-77.

Hayward, W. S. *Revelations of a Lady Detective*. London: George Vickers, 1864.

Hearnshaw, F. J. C., ed. *Edwardian England A.D. 1901-1910*. London: Ernest Benn, 1933.

Heath, Stephen. 'Difference', *Screen* 19 (1978), 51-112.

Herbert, Rosemary. *The Oxford Companion to Crime and Mystery Writing*. New York: Oxford University Press, 1999.

Heron-Maxwell, Beatrice. *The Adventures of a Lady Pearl-Broker*. London: Century Press, 1899.

Heron-Maxwell, Beatrice. *How the Minister's Notes Were Recovered: The Story of a Bit of Diplomacy*. *Harmsworth Magazine* 1 (September 1898), 250-7.

Hibbert, Christopher. *Edward: The Uncrowned King*. New York: St Martin's Press, 1972.

Hiley, Nicholas. 'Decoding German Spies', in *Spy Fiction, Spy Films, and Real Intelligence*, ed. Wark, (1991), 55-79.

Hobsbawm, Eric. 'The Criminal as Hero and Myth', *Times Literary Supplement* (23 June 1961), 6.

Hodgson, John A., ed. *Sherlock Holmes: The Major Stories with Contemporary Critical Essays*. Boston: Bedford Books, 1994.

Horstman, Allen. *Victorian Divorce*. London: Croom Helm, 1985.

Howe, Ronald. *The Story of Scotland Yard*. London: Arthur Barker Ltd., 1965.

Hubin, Allen J. *The Bibliography of Crime Fiction 1749-1975*. Del Mar, California: Publishers Inc., 1979.

Hughes, Winifred. *The Maniac in the Cellar: Sensation Novels of the 1860s*. Princeton: Princeton University Press, 1980.

Hühn, Peter. 'The Detective as Reader: Narrativity and Reading Concepts in Detective Fiction', *Modern Fiction Studies* 33 (Autumn 1987), 451-66.

Hume, Fergus. *Hagar of the Pawn-shop* (1898). London: Greenhill, 1985.

Hume, Fergus. *Madame Midas* (1888). Intro. Stephen Knight. London: The Hogarth Press, 1985.

Hume, Fergus. *The Mystery of a Hansom Cab* (1886). Intro. Stephen Knight. London: Hogarth Press, 1985.

Hunter, Jefferson. *Edwardian Fiction*. Cambridge, MA: Harvard University Press, 1982.

Hurley, Kelly. *The Gothic Body*. Cambridge: Cambridge University Press, 1996.

Hutter, Albert D. 'Dreams, Transformations, and Literature: The Implications of Detective Fiction', in *The Poetics of Murder*, eds. Most and Stowe, (1983), 230-51.

Hynes, Samuel. 'A Detective and His God'. *The New Republic.* (6 Feb 1984), 39-42.

Hynes, Samuel. *Edwardian Occasions*. New York: Oxford, 1972.

Hynes, Samuel. *The Edwardian Turn of Mind.* Princeton: Princeton University Press, 1968.

'Is England on the Down Grade?', *Strand* 44 (October 1912), 406-12.

Ivimey, Alan. *Robert of London*. London: Hutchinson, 1939.

James, Henry. 'Mary Elizabeth Braddon', in *Literary Criticism I*, ed. Leon Edel. New York: The Library of America, 1984, 741-6.

Johnson, Heidi H. 'Electra-fying the Female Sleuth: Detecting the Father in *Eleanor's Victory* and *Thou Art the Man*', in Tromp, ed., (2000), 255-75.

Jones, L. E. *An Edwardian Youth*. London: Macmillan, 1956.

Jones, Mary Jane 'The Spinster Detective', *Journal of Communication* 25 (Spring 1975), 106-12.

Jullian, Philippe. *Edward and the Edwardians*. London: Sidgwick and Jackson, 1967.

Kaemmel, Ernst. 'Literature under the Table: the Detective Novel and its Social Mission', in *The Poetics of Murder*, eds. Most and Stowe, (1983), 55-61.

Kaempffert, Waldemar. 'The Latest Methods of Tracking Criminals', *Strand* 48 (September 1914), 343-51.

Kaplan, Carola M. and Anne B. Simpson. *Seeing Double: Revisioning Edwardian and Modern Literature*. New York: St Martin's Press, 1996.

Kaplan, E. Ann. 'Is the Gaze Male?', in *Women and Film: Both Sides of the Camera*. New York: Methuen, 1983, 23-35.

Kayman, Martin A. *From Bow Street to Baker Street*. London: Macmillan, 1992.

Kemp, Sandra, Charlotte Mitchell, David Trotter, eds. *Edwardian Fiction: An Oxford Companion*. New York: Oxford University Press, 1997.

Kestner, Joseph A. *The Edwardian Detective, 1901-1915*. Aldershot: Ashgate Publishing, 2000.

Kestner, Joseph A. *Masculinities in Victorian Painting*. Aldershot: Scolar, 1995.

Kestner, Joseph A. *Mythology and Misogyny*. Madison: University of Wisconsin Press, 1989.

Kestner, Joseph A. 'Real Men: Constructions of Masculinity in the Sherlock Holmes Narratives', *Studies in the Literary Imagination* 29 (Spring 1996), 73-88.

Kestner, Joseph A. *Sherlock's Men: Masculinity, Conan Doyle, and Cultural History*. Aldershot: Ashgate Publishing, 1997.

Klein, Kathleen Gregory. *The Woman Detective: Gender & Genre*. Urbana: University of Ilinnois Press, 1995.

Klein, Kathleen Gregory and Joseph Keller. 'Deductive Detective Fiction: The Self-Destructive Genre', *Genre* 19 (Summer 1986), 155-72.

Knelman, Judith. *Twisting in the Wind: The Murderess and the English Press*. Toronto: University of Toronto Press, 1998.

Knight, Stephen. 'The Case of the Great Detective', in Hodgson, ed., (1994), 368-80.

Knight, Stephen. *Form and Ideology in Crime Fiction*. Bloomington: Indiana University Press, 1980.

Knight, Stephen. *Jack the Ripper: The Final Solution*. Chicago: Academy Chicago, 1986.

Krejci-Graf, Karl. 'Psychoanalysis of Sherlock Holmes and Co.', *The Sherlock Holmes Journal* 11 (1973), 45-54.

Lacan, Jacques. 'Seminar on *The Purloined Letter*', in *The Poetics of Murder*, eds. Most and Stowe, (1983), 21-54.

Lambert, Gavin. *The Dangerous Edge*. New York: Grossman, 1976.

Landrum, Larry N., ed. *Dimensions of Detective Fiction*. Bowling Green: Popular Press, 1976.

Laver, James. *Edwardian Promenade*. Boston, MA: Houghton, 1958.

Laver, James. *Manners and Morals in the Age of Optimism, 1848-1914*. New York: Harper & Row, 1966.

Lawrence, Barbara. 'Female Detectives: The Feminist-Anti-Feminist Debate', *Clues* 3, no.1 (Spring/Summer 1982), 38-48

Ledger, Sally. *The New Woman*. Manchester: Manchester University Press, 1997.

Ledger, Sally and Roger Luckhurst, eds. *The Fin de Siècle: A Reader in Cultural History*. New York: Oxford University Press, 2000.

Ledwon, Lenora, ed. *Law and Literature: Text and Theory*. New York: Garland, 1996.

Lee, Sir Sidney. *King Edward VII*, 2 vols. New York: Macmillan, 1925 and 1927.

Linton, Eliza Lynn. 'The Partisans of the Wild Women', *The Nineteenth Century* 31 (March 1892), 455-64.

Linton, Eliza Lynn. 'The Wild Women as Social Insurgents', *The Nineteenth Century* 30 (October 1891), 596-605.

Lock, Joan. *The British Policewoman: Her Story*. London: Hale, 1979.

Lock, Joan. Scotland Yard Casebook: The Making of the CID 1865-1935. London: Hale, 1993.

Locke, George. *Pearson's Weekly: A Checklist of Fiction 1890-1939*. London: Ferret Fantasy, 1990.

Loesberg, Jonathan. 'The Ideology of Narrative Form in Sensation Fiction', *Representations* 13 (Winter 1986), 115-38.

London and Its Environs. London: Ward, Lock, 1910. (Guidebook.)

London, Bette. 'Mary Shelley, *Frankenstein*, and the Spectacle of Masculinity', *PMLA* 108 (March 1993), 253-66.

'Looking Backward', *The Literary Review* (24 November 1923), 283-4.

Lowe, Charles. 'About German Spies', *Contemporary Review* 97 (January 1910), 42-56.

Lowndes, Marie Belloc. *The Lodger*. Intro. Laura Marcus. New York: Oxford University Press, 1996.

Lowndes, Marie Belloc. 'The Lodger' (short story), in *City Sleuths and Tough Guys*, ed. David McCullough. New York: Houghton Mifflin, (1989), 70-96.

MacDonald, Ross. 'The Writer as Detective Hero', in *The Mystery Writer's Art*, ed. Nevins, (1970), 295-305.

Magnus, Phillip. *King Edward the Seventh*. New York: Dutton, 1964.

Maio, Kathleen L. 'A Strange and Fierce Delight: The Early Days of Women's Mystery Fiction', *Chrysalis* 10 (n.d), 93-105.

Mandel, Ernest. *Delightful Murder*. London: Pluto Press, 1984.

Mangan, J. A. and James Walvin, eds. *Manliness and Morality*. Manchester: Manchester University Press, 1987.

Mann, Jessica. *Deadlier than the Male*. New York: Macmillan, 1981.

Marcus, Laura. 'Oedipus Express: Trains, Trauma and Detective Fiction', in Chernaik, ed., (2000), 201-21.

Marcus, Laura, ed. *Twelve Women Detective Stories*. New York: Oxford University Press, 1997.

Marcus, Steven. 'Introduction', in *The Adventures of Sherlock Holmes* by Arthur Conan Doyle. New York: Schocken Books, 1976.

Marsh, Richard. *The Beetle* (1897). Intro. William Baker. Stroud: Alan Sutton, 1994.

Marsh, Richard. *Judith Lee, Some Pages from Her Life*. London: Methuen, 1912.

Masterman, C. F. G. *The Condition of England*. London: Methuen, 1909.

Masterman, C. F. G. *The Heart of the Empire*. London: Unwin, 1901.

Maurice, Arthur Bartlett. 'The Detective in Fiction', *The Bookman* 15 (May 1902), 231-6.

Maurois, André. *The Edwardian Era*. New York: Appleton, 1933.

McDonnell, Frank D. 'Detecting Order mid Disorder', *Wilson Quarterly* 11 (1987), 173-83.

McKellar, Ian B. *The Edwardian Age*. Glasgow: Blackie, 1980.

McLevy, James. *The Casebook of a Victorian Detective*. Edinburgh: Canongate, 1975.

Meade, L. T. and Robert Eustace. *The Detections of Miss Cusack* (1899-1900). Ed. Jack Adrian. Shelburne, Ontario: Battered Silicon Dispatch Box, 1998.

Melchiori, Barbara Arnett. *Terrorism in the Late Victorian Novel*. London: Croom Helm, 1985.

Merrick, Leonard. *Mr Bazalgette's Agent*. London: Routledge, 1888.

Middlemas, Keith. *The Life and Times of Edward VII*. New York: Doubleday, 1972.

Miller, D. A. *The Novel and the Police*. Berkeley: University of California Press, 1988.

Minney, R. J. *The Edwardian Age*. Boston, MA: Little, Brown, 1964.

Mitchell, Sally, ed. *Victorian Britain*. New York: Garland, 1988.

'Modern Man-Haters', *The Saturday Review* (29 April 1871), 528-9.

Morris, Virginia B. *Double Jeopardy: Women Who Kill in Victorian Fiction*. Lexington: University Press of Kentucky, 1990.

Most, Glenn W. and William W. Stowe, eds. *The Poetics of Murder*. New York: Harcourt, 1983.

Mulvey, Laura. 'Visual Pleasure and Narrative Cinema', in *Film Theory and Criticism*, ed. Gerald Mast. New York: Oxford University Press, (1985), 803-16.

Murch, A. E. *The Development of the Detective Novel*. New York: Greenwood, 1958.

Murray, Janet, ed. *Strong-Minded Women*. New York: Pantheon, 1982.

Neale, Steve. 'Masculinity as Spectacle', in *Screening the Male*, eds. Steven Cohan and Ina Rae Hark. London: Routledge, (1993), 9-20.

Nevins, Jr., Francis M., ed. *The Mystery Writer's Art*. Bowling Green: Bowling Green University Popular Press, 1970.

Newman, Beth. '"The Situation of the Looker-On": Gender, Narration and Gaze in *Wuthering Heights*', *PMLA* 105 (October 1990), 1029-41.

Nicolson, Harold. *King George V: His Life and Reign*. London: Constable, 1952.

Nowell-Smith, Simon, ed. *Edwardian England 1901-1914*. London: Oxford University Press, 1964.

Orczy, Emmuska. *Lady Molly of Scotland Yard* (1910). London, Cassell, 1912.

Orczy, Emmuska. *The Man in the Corner*. New York: Norton, 1966.

Orczy, Emmuska. *The Old Man in the Corner: Twelve Mysteries*. Intro. E. F. Bleiler. New York: Dover, 1980.

Orel, Harold, ed. *Sir Arthur Conan Doyle: Interviews and Recollections*. New York: St Martin's Press, 1991.

Ousby, Ian. *Bloodhounds of Heaven*. Cambridge: Harvard University Press, 1976.

Owings, Chloe. *Women Police*. Montclair, New Jersey: Patterson Smith, 1969.

Parkenham, Valerie. *Out in the Noonday Sun: Edwardians in the Tropics*. New York: Random House, 1985.

Pearson, John. *Edward the Rake*. New York: Harcourt Brace, 1975.

Pederson-Krag, Geraldine. 'Detective Stories and the Primal Scene', *The Psychoanalytic Quarterly* 18 (1949), 207-14.

Penzler, Otto. *Encyclopedia of Mystery and Detection*. New York: McGraw-Hill, 1976.

Peterson, Audrey. *Victorian Masters of Mystery*. New York: Ungar, 1984.

Petrie, Charles. *Scenes of Edwardian Life*. London: Eyre & Spottiswoode, 1965.

Pike, E. Royston. *Human Documents of the Age of the Forsythes*. London: Allen & Unwin, 1969.

Pike, E. Royston. *Human Documents of the Lloyd George Era*. London: Allen & Unwin, 1972.

Pirkis, Caterine Louisa. *The Experiences of Loveday Brooke, Lady Detective* (1894). Intro. Michelle Slung. New York: Dover, 1986.

Poe, Edgar Allan. *Thou Art the Man* (1844), in *Selected Tales*, ed. Julian Symonds. New York: Oxford University Press, (1980), 234-47.

Porter, Dennis. *The Pursuit of Crime*. New Haven: Yale University Press, 1981.

Potter, John Deane. *Scotland Yard*. London: Burke Books, 1972.

Pound, Reginald. 'A Maypole in the Strand', in *Sir Arthur Conan Doyle Interviews and Recollections*, ed. Orel, (1991), 166-8.

Pound, Reginald. *The Strand Magazine 1891-1950*. London: Heinemann, 1966.

Priestley, J. B. *The Edwardians*. New York: Harper, 1970.

Priestman, Martin. *Detective Fiction and Literature*. London: Macmillan, 1990.

Priestman, Martin. 'Sherlock's Children: The Birth of the Series', in Chernaik, ed., (2000), 50-9.

Putney, Charles R. *Sherlock Holmes: Victorian Sleuth to Modern Hero*. London: Scarecrow, 1996.

Queen, Ellery. *101 Years' Entertainment: The Great Detective Stories 1841-1941*. Boston: Little, Brown, 1941.

Queen, Ellery. *The Detective Short Story: A Bibliography*. New York: Bible & Tannen, 1969.

Queen, Ellery, ed. *The Great Women Detectives and Criminals: The Female of the Species*. Garden City, NY: Blue Ribbon Books, 1943.

Queen, Ellery. *Queen's Quorum*, in *Twentieth Century Detective Stories*. New York: World Publishing Company, 1948.

Randall, Alfred E. 'A Plea for the Medical Assessment of Crime', *The New Age* (25 April 1912), 610-11.

Randall, David A. *The First Hundred Years of Detective Fiction, 1841-1941*. Bloomington: Lilly Library, Indiana University, 1973. (Exhibition catalogue.)

Rawlings, William. *A Case for the Yard*. London: John Long, 1961.

Read, Donald. *The Age of Urban Democracy: England 1868-1914*. White Plains, New York: Longman, 1994.

Read, Donald, ed. *Documents from Edwardian England*. London: Harrap, 1973.

Read, Donald. *Edwardian England*. London: Harrap, 1972.

Romanes, George J. 'Mental Differences between Men and Women', *The Nineteenth Century* 21 (May 1887), 654-72.

Rook, Clarence Henry. *The Stir Outside the Café Royal*, in Russell, ed., (1978), 223-6.

Roper, Michael. 'Introduction: Recent Books on Masculinity', *History Workshop* 29 (Spring 1990), 184-7.

Roper, Michael and John Tosh, eds. *Manful Assertions: Masculinities in Britain Since 1800*. London: Routledge, 1991.

Rose, Jonathan. *The Edwardian Temperament*. Athens: Ohio University Press, 1986.

Rose, Kenneth. *King George V*. New York: Knopf, 1984.

Rosenthal, Michael. *The Character Factory: Baden-Powell and the Origins of the Boy Scout Movement*. New York: Pantheon, 1986.

Rosenthal, Michael. 'Recruiting for the Empire: Baden-Powell's Scout Law', *Raritan* 4 (1) (Summer 1984), 27-47.

Routley, Erik. *The Puritan Pleasures of the Detective Story*. London: Gollancz, 1972.

Rowntree, Seebohm. *Poverty, a Study of Town Life*. London: Macmillan, 1901.

Russell, Alan K., ed. *Rivals of Sherlock Holmes*. Secaucus, NJ: Castle Books, 1978.

Russell, Alan K., ed. *Rivals of Sherlock Holmes 2*. Secaucus, NJ: Castle Books, 1979.

Rycroft, Charles. 'A Detective Story: Psychoanalytic Observations', *The Psychoanalytic Quarterly* 26 (1957), 229-45.

Salmon, G. 'What Boys Read', *Fortnightly Review* 45 (1886), 248-59.

Sayers, Dorothy L. 'Aristotle on Detective Fiction', in *Detective Fiction*, ed. Winks, (1988), 25-34.

Sayers, Dorothy L. 'Introduction', in *Trent's Last Case*. New York: Harper, (1978), x-xiii.

Sayers, Dorothy L. ed. *The Omnibus of Crime*. New York: Harcourt, Brace, 1929.

Sayers, Dorothy L. ed. *The Second Omnibus of Crime*. New York: Coward-McCann, 1932.

Sayers, Dorothy L. ed. *The Third Omnibus of Crime*. New York: Coward-McCann, 1935.

Scheglov, Yuri K. 'Towards a Description of Detective Story Structure', *Russian Poetics in Translation* (1975), 51-77.

Schivelbusch, Wolfgang. *The Railway Journey*. Berkeley: University of California Press, 1986.

Selections from the Strand Magazine, Vol. 1 (1891), London: Vernon & Yates, 1966.

Shannon, Richard. *The Crisis of Imperialism, 1865-1914*. New York, Oxford University Press, 1978.

Shattock, Joanne. *The Oxford Guide to British Women Writers*. New York: Oxford University Press, 1993.

Showalter, Elaine. 'Family Secrets and Domestic Subversion: Rebellion in the Novels of the 1860s, in *The Victorian Family*, ed. A. S. Wohl. London: Croom Helm, (1978), 101-16.

Showalter, Elaine. *A Literature of Their Own*. Princeton: Princeton University Press, 1977.

Showalter, Elaine. *Sexual Anarchy*. New York: Penguin Books, 1990.

Silverman, Kaja. *Male Subjectivity at the Margins*. London: Routledge, 1992.

Sims, George R. *Dorcas Dene, Detective* (1897). London: Greenhill, 1986.

Slung, Michele B., ed. *Crime on Her Mind*. Harmondsworth: Penguin Books, 1977.

Slung, Michele B. 'Introduction', in *The Experiences of Loveday Brooke, Lady Detective* [Pirkis]. New York: Dover, (1986), vii-xiii.

Sparrow, Gerald. *Vintage Victorian Murder*. New York: Hart, 1971.

Stafford, David. 'Spies and Gentlemen: The Birth of the British Spy Novel, 1893-1914', *Victorian Studies* 24 (Summer 1981), 489-528.

Steele, Timothy. 'Matter and Mystery', *Modern Fiction Studies* 29 (Autumn 1983), 435-50.

Steele, Timothy. 'The Structure of the Detective Story: Classical or Modern?', *Modern Fiction Studies* 27 (Winter 1981-2), 555-70.

Steinbrunner, Chris and Otto Penzler, eds. *Encyclopedia of Mystery and Detection*. New York: McGraw-Hill, 1976.

Stephen, James Fitzjames. 'The Criminal Law and the Detection of Crime', *Cornhill Magazine* 2 (1860), 697-708.

Stephen, James Fitzjames. 'The Decay of Murder'. *Cornhill Magazine* 20 (1869), 722-33.

Stephen, James Fitzjames. 'Detectives in Fiction and Real Life', *Saturday Review* 17 (1864), 712-13.

Sterett, Susan. 'Daydreaming a Woman's Life', *Studies in Law, Politics, and Society* 14 (1994), 69-88.

Stevens, Maryanne, ed. *The Edwardians and After.* London: Royal Academy of Arts, 1988.

Stevenson, Robert Louis. *Dr Jekyll and Mr Hyde* (1886). New York: Oxford University Press, 1992.

Stowe, William W. 'From Semiotics to Hermeneutics: Modes of Detection in Doyle and Chandler', in *The Poetics of Murder*, eds. Most and Stowe, (1983), 366-84.

Sutherland, John. *The Longman Companion to Victorian Fiction.* Essex: Longman, 1988.

Sweeney, S. E. 'Locked Rooms: Detective Fiction, Narrative Theory, and Self-Reflexivity', in *The Cunning Craft*, ed. Walker, (1990), 1-14.

Swinnerton, Frank. *The Georgian Literary Scene.* London: Hutchinson, 1950.

Symons, Julian, ed. *Detective Stories from the* Strand Magazine. London: Oxford University Press, 1991.

Symons, Julian. *The Detective Story in Britain.* London: F. Mildner & Sons, 1962.

Symons, Julian, ed. *Strange Tales from the* Strand Magazine. London: Oxford University Press, 1992.

Terry, R. C. *Victorian Popular Fiction, 1860-80.* Atlantic Highlands: Humanities Press, 1983.

Thomas, Ronald R. *Detective Fiction and the Rise of Forensic Science.* Cambridge: Cambridge University Press, 1999.

Thomas, Ronald R. 'The Fingerprint of the Foreigner: Colonizing the Criminal in 1890s Detective Fiction and Criminal Anthropology', *ELH* 61 (Fall 1994), 653-81.

Thomas, Ronald R. 'Minding the Body Politic: The Romance of Science and the Revision of History in Victorian Detective Fiction', *Victorian Literature and Culture* 19 (1991), 233-53.

Thomas, Ronald R. 'Victorian Detective Fiction and Legitimate Literature: Recent Directions in Criticism', *Victorian Literature and Culture* 24 (1996), 367-79.

Thompson, Paul. *The Edwardians.* Bloomington IN: Indiana University Press, 1975.

Thoms, Peter. *Detection and Its Designs.* Athens: Ohio University Press, 1998.

Thomson, H. Douglas. *Masters of Mystery.* New York: Dover, 1978.

Thomson, Patricia. *The Victorian Heroine.* New York: Oxford University Press, 1956.

Thou Art the Man. (review), *Athenaeum* (30 June 1894), 833-4.

Thou Art the Man. (review), *Spectator* (28 July 1894), 118.

Tillotson, Kathleen. 'The Lighter Reading of the Eighteen-Sixties', Introduction to Wilkie Collins, *The Woman in White*. Boston: Houghton Mifflin, (1969), ix-xxvi.

Trodd, Anthea. *Domestic Crime in the Victorian Novel*. London: Macmillan, 1989.

Trodd, Anthea. *A Reader's Guide to Edwardian Literature*. Calgary, Canada, University of Calgary Press, 1991.

Tromp, Marlene, ed. *Beyond Sensation: Mary Elizabeth Braddon in Context*. Albany: State University of New York Press, 2000.

Trotter, David. 'The Politics of Adventure in the Early British Spy Novel', in *Spy Fiction, Spy Films and Real Intelligence*, ed. Wark, (1991), 30-54.

Usborne, Richard. *Clubland Heroes*. London: Constable Publishers, 1953.

Vance, Norman. 'The Ideal of Manliness', in *The Victorian Public School*, eds. Brian Simon and Ian Bradley. Dublin: Gill and Macmillan, (1975), 115-28.

Vance, Norman. *The Sinews of the Spirit*. Cambridge: Cambridge University Press, 1985.

Vicinus, Martha. '"Helpless and Unfriended": Nineteenth-Century Domestic Melodrama', *New Literary History* 13 (1981), 127-43.

Walker, Roanld G. ed. *The Cunning Craft*. Macomb, Illinois: Yeast Printing, 1990.

Walkowitz, Judith R. *City of Dreadful Delight*. Chicago: University of Chicago Press, 1992.

Ward, Ian. *Law and Literature*. Cambridge: University Press, 1995.

Warden, Florence. *The House by the Vaults*. Strand 29 (June 1905), 639-50.

Wark, Wesley K., ed. *Spy Fiction, Spy Films and Real Intelligence*. London: Cass, 1991.

Welsh, Alexander. *Strong Representations*. Baltimore: Johns Hopkins University Press, 1992.

White, S. P. 'Modern Mannish Maidens', *Blackwood's* 147 (February 1890), 252-64.

Whitt, J. F. *The* Strand Magazine *1891-1950, A Selective Checklist*. London: J. F. Whitt, 1979.

'Why Men Do Not Marry.' *Strand* (January 1914), 50-4.

Wiener, Martin J. *Reconstructing the Criminal*. Cambridge: Cambridge University Press, 1990.

Willson, Beckles. 'Inches and Eminence', *The Strand* 28 (August 1904), 209-16.

Winks, Robin W. ed. *Detective Fiction*. Woodstock, Vermont: Countryman Press, 1988.

Winks, Robin W. 'Introduction', in *Detective Fiction*, ed. Winks, (1988), 1-14.

Wolff, Robert Lee. *Sensational Victorian: The Life and Fiction of Mary Elizabeth Braddon*. London: Garland, 1979.

Woods, Robin. '"His Appearance is Against Him": The Emergence of the Detective', in *The Cunning Craft*, ed. Walker, (1990), (1990), 15-24.

Worsick, Clark. *An Edwardian Observer: The Photographs of Leslie Hamilton Wilson*. New York: Crown, 1978.

Wright, Willard Huntington, ed. *The Great Detective Stories*. New York: Scribner's, 1928.

Wright, Willard Huntington. 'The Great Detective Stories', in *The Art of the Mystery Story*, ed. Haycraft, (1983), 33-70.

Wrong, E. M. 'Crime and Detection', in *The Art of the Mystery Story*, ed. Haycraft, (1983),18-32.

Wyles, Lilian. *A Woman at Scotland Yard*. London: Faber and Faber, 1952.

Yates, Donald A. 'An Essay on Locked Rooms' in *The Mystery Writer's Art*, ed. Nevins, (1970), 272-84.

Zedner, Lucia. *Women, Crime and Custody in Victorian England*. New York: Oxford University Press, 1991.

Index

(The definite and indefinite articles are disregarded in titles but not inverted. Fictional characters are denoted by (fic))

#0011 - 090914 - C0 - 234/156/18 [20] - CB